ANATOMY OF A BEAST

The publisher gratefully acknowledges the generous support of the General Endowment Fund of the University of California Press Foundation.

ANATOMY OF A BEAST

OBSESSION AND MYTH
ON THE TRAIL OF BIGFOOT

MICHAEL McLEOD

UNIVERSITY OF CALIFORNIA PRESS

Berkeley   Los Angeles   London

University of California Press, one of the most distinguished
university presses in the United States, enriches lives around the
world by advancing scholarship in the humanities, social sciences,
and natural sciences. Its activities are supported by the UC Press
Foundation and by philanthropic contributions from individuals
and institutions. For more information, visit www.ucpress.edu.

University of California Press
Berkeley and Los Angeles, California

University of California Press, Ltd.
London, England

Library of Congress Cataloging-in-Publication Data
McLeod, Michael.
    Anatomy of a beast : obsession and myth on the trail of Bigfoot /
Michael McLeod.
        p.   cm.
    Includes bibliographical references and index.
    ISBN 978-0-520-25571-5 (cloth : alk. paper)
    1. Sasquatch.   I. Title.
QL89.2.S2M38   2009
001.944—dc22   2008025292

Manufactured in the United States of America
18   17   16   15   14   13   12   11   10   09
10   9   8   7   6   5   4   3   2   1

For Catherine, for her enduring patience

CONTENTS

Introduction

1

PART I / THE ESSENTIAL BIGFOOT

1. Harrison

9

2. The Missing Link

20

3. Bluff Creek

45

4. The Backup Man

58

5. The Klamath Knot

65

PART II / OBSESSION

6. Mountain Devils

87

7. Show Time

107

8. Bigfoot Daze

123

9. Cryptid Wars

130

PART III / REASON AND TRUTH

10. The Goblin Universe

145

11. Reason and Truth

158

12. Bigfoot's Kitchen

172

Notes

187

Select Bibliography

205

Index

209

Illustrations follow p. 122.

INTRODUCTION

Much of my career has been spent making documentaries, an avocation that has exposed me to subjects ranging from the odd and the bizarre to the genuinely mysterious. Gathering people's thoughts and opinions for a living has shown me time and again that everyone has their own special relationship with the truth, and it is not unusual for that relationship to be fuzzy. No experience has ever brought this home to me more vividly than my quest for the story behind the reclusive giant hominid known as Bigfoot.

I grew up in Oregon's lush Willamette Valley, surrounded by forests and mountains and whitewater rivers. Being native to such an environment does not necessarily qualify anyone as a Bigfoot expert, but evocative landscapes have a way of molding one's perceptions of the world, so it is not surprising that I developed a fascination with the mysteries of nature.

Bigfoot hit the news in the late 1950s, when I was in grade school. The first reports of the animal came from California, but sightings were soon reported in the Cascade Mountains of central Oregon, close to where our family often camped. I remember my dad talking about a neighbor, Ben

Trippett, who investigated reports of such a creature even before the media gave it its distinctive name.

A decade later, I saw a magazine article about a guy named Roger Patterson, who claimed to have filmed a Bigfoot. A blowup of one of the frames from his film showed a hairy, two-legged figure walking in the trees. It looked exactly the way I imagined the animal would look.

In 1969, the year after Patterson's film appeared, an outbreak of Bigfoot sightings along the Columbia River led to one of my first assignments as a television news cameraman: to travel to Skamania County in Washington State, where the sightings had been reported, and interview eyewitnesses. The experience struck me as odd enough at the time that I took still photographs for my scrapbook. One shows a plaster cast of a huge footprint propped on a chair in a sheriff's office; another a view of a towering monolith called Beacon Rock, rising out of the Columbia, near where a fisherman told me a Bigfoot had bounded across the road in front of his car.

The visit to Skamania County was a curious experience. The sightings described to us by several seemingly rational people—including one extremely close-up encounter—sounded absolutely convincing. My ultimate conclusion was that someone in an ape suit had gone berserk and that the sense of mystery that oozes from every old snag and deep shadow in that verdant landscape had spooked witnesses into believing the unbelievable. Still, there was an eeriness about the experience that stayed with me.

Two decades passed, during which Bigfoot became a fixture in the tabloid media. As I was involved with more conventional fare, the beast never appeared on my radar. Then, one afternoon a few years ago, as I was flying home to Oregon, Bigfoot reentered my life. Watching Mount Shasta pass below as the plane neared the California-Oregon border, I realized that the swath of wilderness lying between that magnificent snow-clad peak and the Pacific, a hazy blue line on the horizon, was the place where Roger Patterson had shot his famous film. I had recently seen the clip on television again and was reminded of how real it seemed: if I were to fake such a film, I would shoot it exactly the same way.

I never heard that anyone had ever identified the person who wore the ape suit, or otherwise revealed the story behind what I always assumed was a hoax. Looking down on that vast wilderness, I felt inexorably drawn to visit it and discover how Patterson—far from the Hollywood mainstream—had managed to make an imaginary character come so fully alive. By the time we touched down in Portland, I had made a decision to pursue Roger Patterson's story wherever it led.

. . .

Bigfoot, also known as Sasquatch, entered the public consciousness at the height of the TV Western's popularity. This juxtaposition may help explain why the wily beast became instantly popular: it represented a powerful, self-reliant symbol of the frontier that had nourished the American dream. By the mid-1960s, television Westerns were in decline and the cowboy mystique faltering. Less than two years after *Gunsmoke* ended its run in 1975, *Star Wars* ushered in the age of galactic battles and hyperspace, and the simple, rugged life of the Wild West lost its popular appeal—and, in many ways, its innocence. When people talk of a "simpler time," it ended about then.

With the bloom taken off the Western mystique, one might assume Bigfoot would have drifted into obscurity, but it didn't happen. The beleaguered creature became a national symbol of sorts. It has spawned Bigfoot truck competitions, auto body shops, Internet sites, software enterprises, and manufacturing enterprises. Books, films, and TV programs about Bigfoot have become a small but hardy industry.

The beast's enduring popularity may be due, in part, to the word itself. *Bigfoot* is visually graceless, and coarse as it rolls off the tongue—an anomaly in the realm of mythology, where literary elegance helps an idea transcend the ages. In a word: crude. Exactly the kind of creature America can embrace: big and strong and afraid of no one.

Across the country, devotees pay dues to Bigfoot organizations and attend conventions to commune with other believers. Bigfoot "researchers" comb America's backcountry looking for signs. Ironically, although the faith of die-hard Bigfooters is unassailable, so is the futility of their cause. Even more puzzling is the fact that they seem to be keenly aware of it.

Bigfooters themselves use the term *Bigfoot phenomenon* to describe the brain freeze that seizes them when trying to reconcile the irreconcilable. "How does one explain all the sightings over the years?" they earnestly exclaim. "And the thousands of footprints? If even one report or footprint is real, then *something* is out there!" Considering that not a single piece of genuine physical evidence has been found to support Bigfoot's existence, it is a whale of a conundrum.

. . .

Bigfoot is more than just a silly slice of history. The beast's appearance on the national scene marked an important milestone: the first widely popularized example of pseudoscience in American culture. The debate over its legitimacy reached a zenith in the 1970s, with a slew of high-profile magazine stories and TV specials that gave prominent coverage to theories supporting the creature's existence, concocted by self-styled Bigfoot "experts" spouting factoids cherry-picked from bona fide scientific research. The controversy led anthropologists and other scientists to run for cover to avoid being tarred by association with such specious ideas. As a result, the "evidence" in Bigfoot's favor was presented essentially unchallenged, effectively legitimizing the pseudoscientific claims. Because the existence of the beast could not be disproved, many readers and viewers were left feeling that its existence was quite probable. By absenting themselves from the debate, the scientific community appeared out of touch and elitist. In the three intervening decades, the increasingly common use of pseudoscience—junk science, voodoo science, pathological science, or whatever you choose to call it—has transformed public debate, as reflected in the anti-intellectualism now sweeping the country. This book makes the case that it all began with Bigfoot.

My purpose in writing the book was not to refute Bigfoot, recount a mystery, or craft a paean to nature. Books that do so abound in libraries and bookstores. My interest lay in the people behind the legend, those who perpetuate it, and the reasons why they do so. This is an important question, for if people can delude themselves into believing in the existence of an eight-foot-tall ape-man, what on earth might they be thinking about truly important matters? I was also curious to know if such thinking was contagious, for I had a suspicion it might be.

I am indebted to David Rains Wallace and to his insightful book *The Klamath Knot,* which helped me formulate my thoughts about man and the wilderness. The Klamath Knot can't be found on any map. Wallace coined the term to describe the ecosystem of the Bluff Creek watershed where Bigfoot was first "discovered" and where Roger Patterson shot his infamous film: a craggy, beguiling wonderland of exotic plants and animals that puzzles scientists and conjures in visitors a sense of the mysterious. I never lost sight of Wallace's premise that "myths began as imaginative projections of human consciousness onto nature," or of his central character, a shadowy figure whom he calls the "giant."

PART I
THE ESSENTIAL BIGFOOT

1

HARRISON

Every man, wherever he goes, is encompassed by a cloud of comforting convictions, which move with him like flies on a summer day.

—Bertrand Russell, *Skeptical Essays*

Old Jim and I stood on the shore of Harrison Lake drinking in the sunshine, gazing out on thirty-five miles of frigid Canadian water, two tiny specks on the edge of a wilderness larger than any in the continental United States. The sound of bagpipes cut the morning air, and we turned to see a parade of bagpipers trailed by a small figure dressed in an ape costume, wearing a banner that said "Ms. Sasquatch." We returned her perky wave, and I skimmed a schedule of the day's events: a round of Sasquatch Golf, a Sasquatch Raffle, the Spring Box Party, and on the main program, the Sasquatch Forum, parts 1 and 2.

Just across the street stood the Harrison Hot Springs Hotel, a dowdy, British-looking structure with a picture of the queen behind the reception desk and tables in the lobby permanently set for afternoon tea. It seemed an absurdly formal venue for a Bigfoot meeting—but then again, why not?

The audience headed for the Coronet Room was predominantly male. Many wore shirts with nature themes: pictures of wolves and grizzly bears, and eagles attacking with outstretched claws. The attendees appeared earnest and eager for information. Vendors in the corridor offered books about Bigfoot and the Loch Ness Monster as well as more obscure creatures like the Orang Pendek and the Ogopogo. There were T-shirts bearing ape-man likenesses and audiotapes with titles like *Bigfoot: The*

Ultimate Adventure. One bookseller was offering memberships in the Cryptozoology Society, an international organization devoted to the investigation of undiscovered animals. Tables near the door were covered with pamphlets and business cards offering "Sasquatch Research" and "Big Foot Investigations."

Somewhere in the crowd was John Green, the man who had lured me to the conference. After reading his book *On the Track of the Sasquatch,* I had phoned him at his home in Harrison and introduced myself as a journalist interested in learning more about Bigfoot, hoping he could answer some questions. In particular, I wanted to know about Roger Patterson and Bob Gimlin, the men who shot the film of the beast in the late 1960s. Were they alive? And had the film ever been disproved?

Green told me on the phone that Patterson had died a few years after the filming. Gimlin lived in Yakima but generally refused interviews. As for the film, my timing was remarkable. In a few weeks an event called the Sasquatch Forum was convening in Harrison Hot Springs, and he suggested that I might want to attend one of the sessions, titled "The Patterson Film on Trial." When I expressed surprise that there were enough enthusiasts to warrant a conference, he noted this was the third annual event, "and interest is growing."[1]

My home base in Portland being a hotspot for Bigfooters, Green put me in contact with a longtime local devotee named Jim Hewkin, who was also attending, and I hitched a ride with him to British Columbia. Old Jim was a wealth of Bigfoot arcana. A field biologist for forty years, he had no doubt the beast was out there. It didn't bother him that he'd never seen one. Quite the contrary. "That's the reason it's got half a chance," he said. "The thing about wild animals—they're solitary. And Bigfoot is *the* most solitary of all." He attributed its elusiveness to an ability to hide out in vast stretches of wilderness. "There's a lot of country up and down the coast here no one ever visits," he said. "Sixty-some planes have gone down in this area since the war that have never been found."

He believed Bigfoot ate carrion, which would explain its widely reported odor. He had studied several cases in which dead farm animals had been moved by a very powerful creature and eaten over a period of time. Only a Bigfoot could do that, he said. His favorite story involved a logger who had watched a Bigfoot family dig a pit in a rocky hillside to reach a nest of hibernating ground squirrels, which they snatched up and ate like bananas. I quizzed him about the Patterson film and got the impression it was the single reason many of the Bigfooter community believed in the creature—though most, he said, would deny that reasoning.

The forum's lead-off session featured Henner Fahrenbach, a short, trim man with a cordial demeanor and a soft German accent. Fahrenbach was a microbiologist at a primate research center who exuded competence from every pore. He had analyzed the beast's physical characteristics and knit them into a slide show. "Forget all this chit-chat about missing-links," he began. "That word should be purged. By whatever name you choose to call this creature, it's at the top of the food chain. You have a very small population with a low reproductive rate but a very high probability of survival."[2]

The lights dimmed, and a fuzzy photograph of Bigfoot appeared on the screen beside him. "Height," he intoned, tapping the image with a pointer. "Right below eleven feet seems to be the tallest reliable report. The shortest we have seen documented in the literature is . . . four foot seven." Weight: he couldn't talk about weight, as no reliable means had been developed to gauge it. Smell: like "they roll in carrion or something of this nature." Hair color: "People have reported everything from black, brown, cinnamon, grayish white to a near white." He remarked that people mail him bits from time to time, and he launched into a description of hair follicles accompanied by photographs taken with an electron microscope, which rendered them on the screen like giant fir trees.

Fahrenbach's expertise seemed infinite. He had even deduced the beast's average brain size: 800 cubic centimeters, much larger than that of the gorilla, whose average brain size is a mere 550 cc. "The eyes generally seem to have an animal look about them," he said. "Contrary to many reports, [the arms] probably do not hang way down. The Sasquatch walks with bent knees and has reasonably long arms, and walks stooped over so that brings the arms somewhat lower. . . . They don't shuffle, they stride. . . . Concerning the hands: the thumb is short and stubby . . . the fingers are surprisingly pointed. . . . [They have] an opposable thumb, there's no question about it . . . it's the hallmark of primates. . . . The chest . . . has a circumference of something like sixty-five to seventy inches, which probably accounts for the aerobic reserves they have." The teeth are described as similar to ours. There's "not too much in the way of fang reports other than sensationalists who want to impress you how brave they were chasing a monster that had fangs."

Fahrenbach's presentation was so precise that I had a hard time believing zoos didn't have these things behind bars. After my lifetime of assuming Bigfoot didn't exist, here, apparently, was evidence not only that it was real but that its body parts had been thoroughly studied and analyzed. "On the subject of breasts," he deadpanned. "One report I have, the observer described a young female . . . as having pert breasts. Presumably, he was a connoisseur."

At the break, Jim introduced me to John Green, a tall, slender man who looked to be in his seventies, with a shock of white hair. He invited Jim, Fahrenbach, and me to join him for lunch. A short walk through the village brought us to Green's home, where he laid out half a dozen plaster footprints for our inspection. They differed widely in size and shape and showed varying degrees of detail, but they were all much larger than the average human foot. To me they looked like clown feet squared off at the toes, with no arch. A few had vegetation stuck in the plaster.

Green's intelligence and collegial manner lent a powerful air of authenticity to the casts lying before us. I asked him what one would find in a primer about Bigfoot. "Lobbing rocks is a purposeful activity the apes have been known to do," he said patiently. "And they have a real connection to water." Fahrenbach quizzed Green about the history of the casts, and I took photographs. Green had me take a shot of him holding the largest specimen against Fahrenbach's forearm—elbow to end of hand—to illustrate its size.

Over lunch Green recounted how the Sasquatch business began: In

1956, René Dahinden, a recent immigrant to Canada from Switzerland, appeared at Green's newspaper office in Agassiz, not far from Harrison, with the idea that he was going to hunt for Sasquatch. Green told him it was just a tall story, but Dahinden couldn't be dissuaded. After a few days Dahinden went home. Green wrote a story about him for the paper and thought no more of the matter. The next year, the Agassiz village council asked for a grant from the British Columbia Centennial Committee to finance a Sasquatch hunt to commemorate the hundredth anniversary of the province, and Dahinden returned to lead it. This unabashed publicity stunt was picked up and reported by news outlets worldwide. Soon thereafter, several seemingly credible reports surfaced of Sasquatch sightings in the province.

Dahinden and Green teamed up to investigate. A hiker told them he'd observed a six-foot-tall female Sasquatch, weighing in the neighborhood of three hundred pounds, nibbling leaves from a bush in a mountain clearing. A logger claimed that while on holiday exploring for gold, he was kidnapped and held for several days by a Sasquatch family before escaping. Green had several interviewees swear to the truth of their accounts before a magistrate. He researched government archives and found reports of ape-man-type creatures in British Columbia going back to the 1880s. After these Sasquatch reports came the reports of ape-man activities in California: footprints that appeared at Bluff Creek in Northern California in 1958, and Patterson's film in the same area nine years later, all of which Green wrote about in *On the Track of the Sasquatch*. Since then, he has spent innumerable hours compiling reports.

After lunch Green booted up a computer in his office and showed us reports he'd entered into a database. There were 1,331 incidents (tracks and sightings) that met his standards for plausibility, rated on a ten-point scale. The walls were covered with huge maps that showed every water course and elevation in Canada and the western United States; they were plastered with stickers, each representing a report.

I asked him what he thought of the fact that some people think you must be a nut to believe in Sasquatch, and he answered me calmly, as a benevolent professor might recite ground rules to a freshman. Early on, he said, when he was young and new in this area, he hadn't given the idea much credence. But when he got to talking to people, he kept hearing things that couldn't be neatly explained away. He was now absolutely certain such an animal existed, although, contrary to what some people think, he believed "it is not near-human but [lives] a life similar to that of a bear." Also contrary to popular belief, it was in no danger of extinction, being one of the most widespread species on Earth. On the Northwest coast alone, he said, the creatures had 90 percent of the area to themselves.

Asked about recent sightings, he pointed to a small red triangle on the map, on the coast of northern California south of Eureka, where tracks had been reported just a few months before by the local newspaper, the *Southern Humboldt Life and Times*. I asked if he always believed news reports.

"There are certain things to look for in reports," he replied. "That the primates don't have claws. That the stories aren't too remarkable. Or a person who sees too much. There's a lot of that." He swept his hand across the maps. "You plot sightings on a map and you'll find where people are searching the most. The more people look, the more reports that turn up. It's always been that way."

After lunch, the forum resumed with presentations by two investigators from northern Canada, who played videotape interviews with people who said they'd observed the creature. A woman described seeing the animal two hundred yards away, striding rapidly past a herd of horses. The next presenter—a weightlifter, judging by the size of his biceps—offered a biomechanical analysis of the animal's stride, using the Patterson film as an illustration. Seeing the clip on a large screen, I was reminded how convincing it is if one is not predisposed to reject Bigfoot out of hand.

The existence of the animal can't be disproved just by studying the celluloid image. The figure looks small and very dark in the frame, and it is constantly moving. The clip is roughly forty seconds long. The most arresting moment of the sequence occurs about midway, when—without breaking stride—the figure (a female, judging by its sizeable breasts) turns its upper body and looks at the camera. It is a powerful, almost chilling moment that lasts only for a beat. Then, as if simply deciding in that fraction of a second that the cameraman was not a danger, it turns away and continues its methodical retreat.

An overflow crowd pushed into the Coronet Room for the keynote presentation, "The Patterson Film on Trial," presented by Danny Perez, listed in the program as the Center for Bigfoot Studies. Hollywood couldn't have created a stranger character to address a crowd of mountain men than Perez, a short, slender man in his mid-thirties, with a deep coppery complexion, coal black eyes, pomaded, wavy black hair, and an ultrathin mustache.

Standing onstage in a loud checked sport coat over a black shirt, accented by a red tie inflamed with white polka dots, Perez scanned the crowd intensely, then thrust his arms in the air and shouted: "The Patterson film on trial! Is this famous film the best tangible evidence we have to prove the existence of Sasquatch? Or is it . . . a *fraud?*"[3]

He paused a moment for dramatic effect. "We're trying to believe Roger Patterson," he said. "We want to believe him—but!" He turned to an easel and wrote: "1. NO CAMERA EVER RETRIEVED." "No camera was ever retrieved. They never found OJ's knife, and they never found Roger Patterson's camera."

From the back of the room came a strained voice: "Oh, shit, come on, Danny!" Perez ignored the comment. "Another important piece of information about the film," he proclaimed: "Roger Patterson filmed his partner walking along the Bigfoot tracks . . . and the film *disappeared!*"

"Hold it a second!" came the voice from the back again. I turned to see a short, angry, elderly man with close-cropped gray hair, on his feet, shouting with an accent that sounded vaguely Germanic: "You're giving a speech on one side, I want to be on the other!" Perez began to protest, but the man shouted him down: "Why don't we do it right now! You make a statement, and I rebut. We can cut the bullshit and stop wasting time."

Jim leaned over to me with a grin and said, "That's René."

A ripple of laughter ran through the crowd. Perez replied with an emphatic "No," and René Dahinden angrily snatched up a video camera on a tripod. "End of discussion. I'm not going to put up with this crap!" he muttered and stomped from the room.

Perez continued as if nothing had happened. Using slides and an easel to illustrate his points, his list of problems with the Patterson film grew. Finally he came to a picture of an old man sitting with his feet stuck out toward the camera, wearing two huge ducklike feet that loomed large in the frame. "This picture," intoned Perez, "is from Louisiana. This man, Tony Signorini, fooled a whole goddamn town for thirty years. A world-famous zoologist wrote a very long, extensive paper on these tracks, saying it was apparently a large, unclassified penguin. He went out to look at the tracks and he said, 'Wow, I see toe movement, I see this, I see that.' But he was wrong. And that guy was—? Ivan T. Sanderson— the late Ivan T. Sanderson—the very distinguished Ivan T. Sanderson. A TV personality. Ivan saw these tracks and bought everything—hook, line and sinker. And fell right on his ass!"

That evening the audience filed once again into the Coronet Room. René Dahinden sat by himself behind a table on the stage, a small figure wearing a plaid flannel shirt. In a rambling speech—part plea, part proclamation—delivered in a mesmerizing sing-song accent, cursing freely, he described how, not long after Patterson brought his film out of the woods, he took it upon himself to personally investigate the circumstances behind it.

"I didn't like Patterson particularly," he said. "I didn't dislike him. What I was trying to determine was: was it a man in a fur suit?" He diagramed on an easel the measurements he had made at the site where Patterson shot his movie and sought to explain his deductions. But the lines and figures and trajectories he scribbled were overwhelming; they soon clouded his presentation, and he grew anxious. "I spent since 1968 to today," he pleaded, looking out at the audience. "Twenty-eight damn years. You name it, I did it. I went to Los Angeles. I went to pawn shops. I went to film labs. Seven trips to the film site. And I measured the creature's walk. And what I'm saying to you," he declared, jabbing the air for emphasis, "is that a man, even without the fur suit and fake feet, couldn't cover this distance in the same time."

It was an odd scene: Dahinden trying desperately to drive his point home when, judging from the faces in the room, the audience was already on his side. All I could figure was that I was watching years of frustration boiling to the surface. Indeed, he appeared to be addressing an audience far beyond the people gathered around me.

He held out his hands in supplication. "All our doubts. We argue, we doubt and really get blue about it and say, 'Jesus Christ, what the hell are we doing, we're wasting our time.' But we always come back to this damn film and say: 'What about the film?'"

The next morning Jim and I ate breakfast with John Green in a waterfront cafe, at a table crowded with Bigfooters. They passed gossip back and forth over pancakes and eggs like stockbrokers analyzing the markets. Talk turned to a theory that the creatures were spirits from another dimension, which the table did not generally favor, followed by discussion of an underground city of the creatures, which was likewise pooh-poohed. The conversation then shifted to Indians, which elicited some shared frustrations about the tribes being less than helpful. "You can't believe the Indian stories," Green said with an air of exasperation. "They don't separate spirituality from reality."

Mention of the name Peter Byrne produced much shaking of heads and a few expletives. Apparently Byrne had received a grant to hunt Bigfoot (nearly half a million dollars was the rumor) from a shadowy East Coast group called the Academy of Applied Sciences. "More or less a post office box," Green said acidly, a response strangely at odds with his otherwise serene demeanor. The general consensus pegged Byrne as a relentless self-promoter who had pissed off the Bigfoot mainstream by refusing to share information. Worse yet, he'd succeeded in parlaying old-money connections into a handsome living investigating Bigfoot while receiving copious national publicity. And now he had a hotline: 1-800-BIG-FOOT.

The forum didn't make me a believer, but a lot of people apparently were. From what I'd learned, tracks and sightings were not uncommon; there were Bigfoot organizations around the country; and the hunt even had its own pseudoscientific underpinnings.

On the way home I peppered Jim with questions, starting with Dahinden. Over the years, he said, René had developed a reputation as kind of a rabid dog. His estrangement with Green was long-standing and bitter (Jim had no idea what it was about). He sniped (as I'd seen) at anyone who professed to be a Bigfoot expert. He had even sued Patterson's widow for rights to the film clip—and won. As for Gimlin, Patterson's filming partner, Jim said he'd never met him, but people who had said he was a straight shooter who claimed he saw a real animal.

As a filmmaker, I appreciated Patterson's creativity: the semibelievable ape suit, the choice of location, the jiggly camera, the film running out just as the beast disappeared into the shadows. Only a craftsman with a flair for the dramatic, and guts enough to go for it, could have pulled off such a feat. And he capped it, apparently, by sticking to his claim even as he lay dying of cancer. This was the kind of story that could take on a mythological quality of its own. What intrigued me most—baffled me, actually, as I found my mind going in circles trying to reconcile the thought—was that Patterson apparently believed in Bigfoot enough to go to his grave espousing the idea, yet he faked the film. On the one hand, that mental dissonance didn't seem incompatible at all; on the other, it seemed absolutely weird.

. . .

Mythology comes from the Greek word *mythos,* meaning "story" or "word," which today's dictionaries define as being associated with deities and demigods, invented ideas, unproved beliefs, and imaginary things or people. This definition strikes me as outdated, for I've seen mythologies created instantly from the real world.

Take the plains of central Texas outside Waco, where, only weeks before, my camera crew and I had been shooting a documentary. A hot wind picked at the photographs of seventy-six people staked beneath seventy-six flowering quince trees in a field where the children of a religious order called the Branch Davidians used to run their go-karts. All that remained of the home they once called Mount Carmel was a crumbled foundation, surrounded by solidified piles of dirt infused with bric-a-brac and household items like barrettes and detergent bottles—just about the only things that hadn't been ripped off by sightseers who showed up at all hours of the day and night to vicariously relive the gunfight and ensuing standoff with the FBI.

My cameraman swung around for a shot as a carload of tourists turned off the road into the site. The occupants spilled out looking puzzled, trying to reconcile the emptiness before them with the scenes they'd witnessed on TV. Any way you cut it, Waco was a tragedy, and the mythologizing of it was well underway. But that myth had its genesis, more or less, in fact. Bigfoot's story is less clear-cut.

2

THE MISSING LINK

Neither in body nor in mind do we inhabit the world of those hunting
races of the Paleolithic millennia, to whose lives and life ways we nevertheless owe the very forms of our bodies and structures of our minds.
Memories of their animal envoys still must sleep, somehow, within us;
for they wake a little and stir when we venture into the wilderness.

—Joseph Campbell, *The Way of the Animal Powers*

After meeting the Bigfooters in Canada, I spent a considerable amount
of time reading and talking with people about Bigfoot, but I discovered little about the circumstances surrounding Roger Patterson and
his film. John Green, René Dahinden, and Peter Byrne, who hunted the
beast longer than anyone, all wrote books about their experiences and
talked extensively about the film, but they said surprisingly little about
Patterson.

Frustrated, I called Patterson's widow, explained what I was up to, and
asked if I could see her. She agreed—within limits. An awful lot of bad
feelings had come down over the years, she said, and she just didn't want
any more publicity. We visited one morning at her home in the rolling
hills outside Yakima, Washington. Our conversation was pleasant, but
years of bother by the media and protracted legal battles over the film
had made her wary of even the most casual question.

The subject of Roger's cancer arose. I was surprised to learn that not
only was he was in remission when he shot the film, but he'd lived with
the disease for nearly a decade. The depressing cycle of cobalt treatments,
doctors' visits, and home injections had worn her down.

She talked about his love for horses, in particular a wild cayuse named Buggylight on which he used to practice bronc riding in a place called Cottonwood Canyon. He always rode horses when he scouted for Bigfoot, she said. One of his favorite places to look was around Mount St. Helens, about seventy miles due west of her kitchen table.

Roger wrote a book, *Do Abominable Snowmen of America Really Exist?* When I told her I'd been unable to find a copy, she dug one out of a closet and gave it to me. She recalled him sitting at his desk writing the introduction. She opened the cover and slid it toward me, pointing to a picture of Roger wearing a cowboy hat. Underneath it said:

> He who seeketh long enough and hard enough will find the truth, whatever that truth may be.
> —Roger Patterson, Author

After the interview I drove into the Yakima hills and stopped on a ridge, with a view of Mount St. Helens shimmering on the horizon. Mrs. Patterson's description of Roger and his preoccupation with Bigfoot contained an undercurrent of sadness. I couldn't shake the feeling that there had been a disconnect between them and that she really didn't know much about his business. Or maybe the intervening years had loaded her up with so much misery that she'd just blanked. Then again, with my being a journalist, she probably assumed the less said, the better. I'd learned just enough about Bigfoot history at that point to know that Roger's film had engendered a firestorm of publicity and speculation and a quagmire of disingenuousness among all parties involved. I felt lucky she'd even talked with me.

Do Abominable Snowmen of America Really Exist? is a slim, homemade affair with a close-up sketch of Bigfoot on the cover, drawn by Patterson himself. The book is mostly a collection of newspaper and magazine articles, combined with a short narrative describing his search for the beast, a few photographs and maps, and sixteen more of Patterson's drawings depicting Bigfoot in various encounters with humans and other animals. Three of the articles originally appeared in *True Magazine* under the byline of Ivan Sanderson. "Without his effort," Patterson wrote in the ac-knowledgments, "this book would not have been written."

Indeed, if it hadn't been for Sanderson, Patterson might never have known about Bigfoot at all. "It all started (for me, anyway)," Patterson wrote, "in December, 1959, when *True Magazine* first startled America with a story about the unbelievable 'Bigfoot' of the vast wilderness of Humboldt County in Northern California." Sanderson's article follows in its entirety. As it originally appeared in *True,* it features a photograph of Sanderson that shows a slender, middle-aged man with an intelligent, alert face, dark hair slicked back, a pencil-thin mustache, and a safari shirt rolled to the elbows. The caption reads: "One of the world's fore-most zoologists, Sanderson is also a widely-traveled explorer, a veteran animal collector (of both known and previously unknown animals) and a highly respected research scientist."[1]

Sanderson's credentials were genuine, his rise to prominence in the publishing world testimony to a unique talent for synthesizing the known and the unknown. For forty-five years he enjoyed unparalleled success writing and talking about nature, plowing the ground between science, journalism and fiction. A self-appointed expert on undiscovered natural phenomena, he often declared that the establishment were fools for ignoring evidence laid before them and denying the honest reports of ordinary citizens. In the article for *True* that caught Patterson's eye, he challenged the scientific establishment by making a bold case for the existence of Bigfoot in North America: "We now know there were men on this continent before the last ice-advance. And during the last million years, during which man evolved, many large and less competent mam-mals crossed back and forth between the Old and New Worlds in the northern hemisphere—the elk, mammoth, moose, brown or dish-faced bears, and lesser folk like the beaver, marmot, mink and others. Why should not have Sub-men or Ape-men that were resident in what is now northern China, have done so too?"[2]

Ivan Terence Sanderson inherited a taste for adventure. He was born in Edinburgh, Scotland, in 1911, the son of the whisky manufacturer

Arthur Sanderson, who founded the first game reserve in East Africa. When Ivan was five, the family moved to Provence in the south of France, where the boy chased butterflies in a yard overlooking the Mediterranean.[3] An uncle who lived in the tropics gave him a book called *The Malay Archipelago,* filled with pictures of exotic animals, and a nanny taught him to shout out the names of the beasts as she turned the pages. The Sanderson clan were vagabonds, and much of Ivan's childhood was spent sailing in the North Atlantic and the Mediterranean. After the "grey and cold and damp [of Edinburgh], I craved the sun from pure cussedness," he wrote in his first book, *Animal Treasure.* "Somehow the ideas of sunlight, beasts, and palm trees got all mixed up in my childish fancies like a hybrid seed planted in a fertile soil."[4]

He recalled another deeply formative moment: himself as a small boy standing in the map room of the Royal Geographical Society in London, transfixed by ancient globes and maps, gazing wide-eyed at the portraits of the explorers of the British Empire lining the paneled walls, many of whom were Scots. They included men like David Livingstone, also from Edinburgh, "discovered" in the African jungle in 1871 by the journalist Henry Stanley, who uttered the famous greeting "Dr. Livingstone, I presume?" And Mungo Park, the first Westerner to trace the course of the Niger River, after so many others had died in the attempt: "I saw with infinite pleasure," Park recounted in a narrative published in 1799, "the great object of my mission, the long-sought-for, majestic Niger, glittering in the morning sun, and flowing slowly to the east. I hastened to the brink, and having drunk of the water, lifted up my fervent thanks in prayer to the Great Ruler of all things for having thus far crowned my effort with success."[5]

Sanderson most clearly embraced the sensibilities of Sir Harry Johnston, who made a career in Africa during the reign of Queen Victoria. In his *Book of Great Jungles,* Sanderson devoted several pages to Johnston, whom he viewed as the forerunner of a new guard of explorer: the naturalist. "Johnston went to 'the dark continent' on a shooting trip in 1882," he wrote, "and stayed simply because he wanted to paint pictures and see the country, not explore for new routes or opportunities for trade." Defying a legion of naysayers, Johnston became the first Westerner to prove the existence of the okapi, an odd, horse-sized mammal with a striped rump and legs and a long neck. The reigning scientists in London finally had to acknowledge his success when he presented them a skull and hide from the animal, which they hurriedly named *Okapia johnstoni.* Sir Harry collected animals for the London Zoo and had his own zoological garden at home. Several of his pets accompanied him on his expeditions, and no matter the equatorial weather, he always dressed for dinner.[6]

When Ivan was twelve, his father was killed by a rhinoceros while making a film in Kenya. The boy was returned to England and entered Eton, where he developed a passion for nature studies. On graduation he "bolted from Europe like a shot rabbit," spent his seventeenth birthday atop the great pyramid of Cheops in Egypt, and two months later set off on a voyage (financed by his inheritance) to the equatorial jungles of the East Indies to collect animals.[7] Somewhere along the way he lost his heart to the apes. In his book *Green Silence*—a record of this first adventure—he described an environment ruled by the siamang (one of the lesser apes), "the most magnificent animal to be found in Sumatra": "At dawn and at sundown they make the mountain valleys literally ring with their tremendous, prolonged, barking hoots that, led off by one and taken up by all others within hearing, mount to a deafening crescendo that makes your eardrums ring and reduces every other jungle creature, even the most raucous bird, to abject silence. This uproar usually stops abruptly, and then echoes go rolling away over the canyons until other, distant troupes pick up the call. Then off they all go again."[8]

Sanderson had a problem that represented a real handicap for a budding zoologist. Virtually blind in one eye from birth due to a misshapen eye socket, and with poor vision in the other, he couldn't operate a camera, for he could not see through a viewfinder—a distressing situation for a man set on a life of observation. "I had no means of recording visually most of what I wanted to record of these animals," he wrote, "except by trying to draw them."[9] So that is what he did: holding a dead animal in his left hand, he took to sketching in a notebook what he called the animal's "spare parts," which he later combined into a finely detailed picture of the whole. His drawings cast the animals in an empathetic, vulnerable light that helped several of his books become best sellers.

Roger Patterson did the same thing in his book, sketching nearly all the figure drawings and maps himself. He lacked Sanderson's drawing skills, but what he lacked artistically he compensated for in bravado, drawing a dozen renditions of an animal no one had ever seen, including the close-up of Bigfoot on the cover, offering an interpretation (something about the eyes) that evidenced some deep thinking about the soul of an animal supposedly evolved to a point midway between human and ape. All the claims in Patterson's book are presented fearlessly, without a trace of doubt—a confidence his mentor had in spades.

Returning from Africa and Asia in 1927, still a teenager, Sanderson traveled to the United States, bought a Stutz Blackhawk—the hippest sports car of the day—and drove through thirty-two states, working odd jobs as he went. He returned to England and entered Cambridge, where it became apparent that the thin, unflappable Scot was cut from a different cloth from his classmates. The glacial pace of the scientific process bored him, and he had some strange ideas. Most notably, he envisioned the establishment of an entirely new field of study specializing "in the collection and examination of evidence for the existence of any creatures as yet unknown to and unidentified by zoologists." He invented a word for it: *cryptozoology.*[10]

The fledgling zoologist displayed a pronounced aptitude for communicating the wonders of nature to the general public; many would later call it showmanship. He did his first radio show for the British Broadcasting Corporation in 1930 and was in demand for lecturing while still a student. He once told a friend, "My mother said I was born talking."[11]

His penchant for the exotic was manifest on a school weekend in Switzerland, when he met a very dark, petite woman named Alma, herself a student on holiday from the Sorbonne in Paris. Her mother was Madagascarese, and her father was French. They fell in love, married on his graduation, and honeymooned in Morocco. They would spend forty years together.

He graduated with a degree in zoology, geology, and botany and immediately received a plum assignment to head up a collecting expedition to the Assumbo Mountains in West Africa.[12] His account of this trip became *Animal Treasure,* his first book. Illustrated with dozens of his drawings of jungle creatures, it was a Book-of-the-Month Club selection in 1937 and launched his career. In it, he describes an encounter in Nigeria with a gorilla shot by a frightened villager:

> We stood there gazing at this sad old man of the mountains . . . more than a quarter of a ton in weight. . . . The arm-span . . . measured nine feet, two inches. I had always been taught to think of the gorilla as the very essence of savagery and terror, and now there lay this hoary old vegetarian, his immense arms folded over his great pot belly, all the fire gone from his wrinkled black face, his soft brown eyes wide open beneath their long straight lashes and filled with an infinite sorrow. Into his whole demeanor I could not help but read the tragedy of his race.[13]

His fascination with primates never left him.

. . .

Sanderson was a born showman, and it came across in his writing. He never hesitated to blur the line between reality and conjecture if it served the story. He included a scene in *Animal Treasure* so charged with mystery that publications around the world reprinted it for years, including *Popular Science Monthly* in 1959, from where it found its way into Roger Patterson's book:

> A traveler in Africa . . . heard from natives of . . . a bird he took to be a [prehistoric] pterodactyl. Other travelers also heard of the strange flying beast, but only one of them—Ivan T. Sanderson, leader of an expedition into West Africa—ever saw it. Working along a river, he shot a fruit-eating bat and went into the water to recover it. Suddenly his companion shouted: "Look out!"

"And I looked," Sanderson later reported. "Then I let out a shout also and instantly bobbed down under the water, because coming straight at me only a few feet above the water was a black thing the size of an eagle. I had only a glimpse of its face, yet that was quite sufficient, for its lower jaw hung open and bore a semi-circle of pointed white teeth set about their own width apart from each other."[14]

Sanderson's private correspondence reveals that he believed the creature was a rare species of bat. But in the published narrative he refrained from speculation, leaving the reader to fill in the blank; a tried-and-true device of a mystery writer, one he would use again and again. In Sanderson's world, nature was a fascinating, endless subject for speculation. He had little patience for those who shut out the wonder and none for those who thought they knew it all.

As a lecturer at Cambridge in the mid-thirties, he crossed swords with other faculty members and quit his post, disillusioned with traditional science. For the next decade he prowled the jungles of the Caribbean and Central and South America, collecting animals, reporting on regional events for the North American Newspaper Alliance (NANA, a news service feeding papers in South Africa, Canada, Australia, and London), and writing two well-received books.[15] His dissatisfaction with traditional science festered. Technically independent, he still worked at the behest of the museums and universities that financed his expeditions and often found himself at odds with their in-house scientists.

Sanderson's fellow researchers may have been reacting to his burgeoning infatuation with jungle stories, in particular what he called "mystery peoples": real and alleged branches of the human family tree. He reported on creatures like the Dwendis of British Honduras, said to be elflike "wild men"; the Orang Pendek (little man) of Sumatra, an upright-walking creature about five feet tall, covered with black hair; and the legendary Sisemite of Guatemala, "a great hairy creature much larger than human size and more powerful than any animal ever known."

Sanderson thrived on controversy and was driven by an unwavering self-confidence. His books had a patina of science, but not for a moment would one consider them to be *about* science. They were travel books, imbued with mystery and wonder, intended for a popular audience.

. . .

Sometime during this early period of exploration, writing and teaching, Sanderson became a fervent adherent of the writer Charles Fort, who achieved notoriety in the 1920s with the publication of a series of books popularizing what are now called paranormal phenomena. Poltergeists, ghosts, psychics, astronomical mysteries, clairvoyance, astral projection, levitation, psychokinesis, telepathy, UFOs (years before the emergence of the acronym)—anything weird or mysterious that didn't fit with current scientific theories, Fort seized on as grist for his mill.[16]

Written in a frenetic, stream-of-consciousness style that challenges the reader's patience and understanding, Fort's books were the result of twenty-six years holed up in libraries and museums in New York and London poring over old magazines, newspapers, and journals that chronicled improbable yet well-established events.[17] He never questioned his sources or attempted to make sense of the events he described: "Red rain over Blankenbergue on 2nd November, 1819; a rain of mud in Tasmania on 14th November, 1902. Snowflakes as big as saucers at Nashville on 24th January, 1891; a rain of frogs in Birmingham on 30th June, 1892. Meteorites. Balls of fire. Footprints of a fabulous animal in Devonshire. Flying disks. . . . Engines in the sky. Erratic comets. Strange disappearances. Inexplicable catastrophes. Inscriptions on meteorites. Black snow. Blue moons. Green suns. Showers of blood. . . ."[18]

Fort's rise to cult status came from the particular delight he took in criticizing the "priesthood" of science and its practitioners, whom he accused of ignoring anything they couldn't explain—a point of view that resonated deeply with Sanderson, who had seen such behavior demonstrated at first hand. Fort's antiscience philosophy served as a template for Sanderson's evolving counterfactualist view of the world, and his ardent "Fortean" mindset became an anchor as the seas of reason, later in his career, began to swamp his unorthodox beliefs.

. . .

With war looming in Europe, Sanderson was conscripted into espionage by British Naval Intelligence.[19] After training in Britain on the operation of field communications equipment, he returned to the Caribbean in the dual role of animal collector and writer, and, covertly, British agent, roaming the port cities and islands of the Caribbean on the schooner on which he and Alma lived, ferreting out German sympathizers. When America entered the war, he was redirected into antisubmarine warfare with orders to continue sailing the Caribbean waterways, still in the guise of a researcher and writer, but now charged with watching for Nazi submarines, which used the islands to lay up for repairs and provisioning.[20]

In *Uninvited Visitors: A Biologist Looks at UFO's,* written years later, he recounted an experience sailing off the coast of Nicaragua:

> It was such a night as one can witness only in the tropics, without moon but with stars so bright you could almost read. We had a fair breeze from the north and had winged our main and foresails and were scudding silently along like a square-rigger. . . . I lay on my back just looking at the stars awhile the spume hissed along the hull. . . .
>
> I had been watching a particularly bright star. . . . While I watched the star it got bigger. What is more, it continued to do so at an ever-increasing rate. In no time at all it was the size of a quarter, then of a soup plate and seemed to light up the entire world.
>
> Then it "exploded" and more than a minute passed before [I] could even see the binnacle light. I say exploded, but there was no sound. Before it became terrifying, it was the most beautiful object I have ever seen, perfectly spherical, and shaded to show its sphericity from intense green to deep peacock blue all around its edge. I reported this one.[21]

Of all the offbeat subjects Sanderson grappled with in the years to come, UFOs (he preferred Charles Fort's term *OSF*—objects seen floating) became his consuming passion.

In 1943, Sanderson was transferred to the British Foreign Office in London, where his literary skills were turned to the task of writing propaganda. Shortly thereafter he was moved to an office in New York City and given the title of press analyst for the British government, a civilian cover for his real job, putting out slanted information about the progress of the war for release to the American public. He recalled being told how to put a good face on difficult situations faced by the Allies abroad: "'Colossal advance by the Allies' meant we were holding. 'Allies are holding,' [meant] we were retreating. A 'slight withdrawal' meant a rout."[22]

At the war's end, Sanderson decided to stay in New York. Postwar Manhattan was the perfect milieu for a person of his proclivities. The genres of science fiction and the supernatural had become lucrative in the publishing business. Pulp magazines like *Amazing Stories* and *Astounding* had huge fan bases: especially popular were tales of disc-shaped flying machines and encounters with bug-eyed monsters, illustrations of which appeared frequently on their covers. The Fortean Society, formed by Charles Fort's acolytes, was promoting the claim that the planet was under surveillance by aliens and the government was concealing the truth. As if on cue, in 1947, the very year Sanderson resigned his British navy commission and established permanent residence in the United States, a pilot named Kenneth Arnold sighted a formation of saucer-shaped discs flying near Mount Rainier in Washington State. Two weeks later, a story broke on the news wire about the crash of an alien spaceship near Roswell, New Mexico. The ensuing UFO panic unleashed reports around the world of strange aerial and terrestrial phenomena, including a widespread number of people claiming to have been abducted by aliens.

Sanderson was soon in the thick of it. Still continuing his reporting for NANA, he was also in high demand for lecturing and reviewing books. He hosted a popular five-days-a-week radio show on WNBT devoted to animals and nature and wrote high-profile features for the *Saturday Evening Post*.[23] One of his first articles for the magazine was titled "There Could Be Dinosaurs."[24]

Sanderson's eagerness to explore the outer limits of the natural world in the guise of a bona fide scientist was in perfect sync with the public's appetite for the fantastic. Where science-fiction writers had to invent science, Sanderson displayed a genius for dreaming up new ways of looking at existing science. If fringe science had a founding father, it might well have been Ivan Sanderson:

> If tortoises, tuatara and crocodiles have managed to survive from the age of reptiles, there is no reason why members of much less primitive [strains]—including those we may choose to call dinosaurs—should not also have survived. The majority of these reptiles disappeared at the end of what is called the Cretaceous period, after which the more active and clever mammals took over. But there is no reason why some might not have lingered on until today in the vast and isolated swamps of Africa—the one part of the world that has remained tropical and comparatively stable since the Cretaceous period and which was almost entirely unaffected by the great ice ages and the mountain-building disturbances of intervening times.[25]

Positing the unknowable became Sanderson's credo. "The pursuit of knowledge," he often said, "starts with imagination."[26]

His output was prodigious: innumerable magazine articles and a book a year; fiction, nonfiction, and children's books.[27] The bulk of his work at this point was straight nature writing, but he also churned out pieces for small magazines, like *Fantastic Universe* and *Fate,* that specialized in "true accounts of the strange and unknown." *Fate* was published by Curtis and Mary Fuller, with whom Sanderson began collaborating in the mid-1950s, writing twenty-five stories for the magazine over a twenty-year period. After Sanderson's death the Fullers recalled their long and fruitful collaboration and their shared, "consuming interest in Fortean phenomena."[28]

. . .

Sanderson's interest in hominids led him to visit the American Museum of Natural History and the laboratory of the anatomist Franz Weidenreich, who had established his reputation with an analysis of Peking Man, considered one of the most important fossil finds in history. At the time, Weidenreich was working with the Dutch paleoanthropologist Ralph von Koenigswald to evaluate a collection of ancient bones, including three gigantic teeth Von Koenigswald had discovered in China.

Von Koenigswald believed the teeth came from an apelike creature twice the size of a gorilla, which he named *Gigantopithecus,* or "gigantic ape." He had made plaster copies of the teeth in his lab in Java and sent them to Weidenreich in New York. Shortly thereafter, at the outbreak of World War II, he was captured by the Japanese.

Meanwhile, in New York, Weidenreich examined the plaster teeth and formed the opinion that the creature was more human than ape. In an act of paleoanthropological bravado, he gave a series of lectures promoting the idea that *Gigantopithecus* might be the Missing Link, and published his talks in book form as *Apes, Giants, and Man.*

Von Koenigswald survived the war in a prison camp. After his release, he dug up the bones, which he'd hidden from the Japanese army, and joined Weidenreich to analyze the artifacts. During Sanderson's visit, Von Koenigswald handed him a *Gigantopithecus* tooth. Sanderson said that, compared to a human tooth, it was "like holding a tennis ball next to a golf ball."[29]

Giganto sent Sanderson's imagination spinning, for here was proof that at least one giant hominid had walked the earth. Sanderson understood that von Koenigswald and Weidenreich held opposing views of the beast: one claimed it was an ape, the other human. But they did agree it was at least related to humans.[30] A lover of lists, Sanderson posited five stages of hominid development: Ape to Man-Ape, to Ape-Man, to Sub-Man, and finally true Man.[31] He considered the "Ape-Man" creature to be the Missing Link and drew a picture of it in his book *The Monkey Kingdom.* Seen in profile, his creation looks nearly human: lithe and naked, covered with short, bristly hair. Its ear is absolutely human in scale and position. The brow projects in simian fashion but sits high on the forehead, not low and brooding. The eye and nose are also distinctly human; the mouth is more apelike, resembling the masks used in *Planet of the Apes.* It squats, feet flat on the ground, bent at the knee like a contortionist. The thigh is slender and exceptionally long, so that the creature's rump rests on the ground behind its heels. An arm, rather thin but with well-defined musculature, is outstretched, and the humanlike hand has long, straight fingers that are fully extended, palm up, holding a small ball as if making an offering, but to whom we will never know.

. . .

After the publication of his dinosaur article, Sanderson received a letter from a Paris-based writer of Belgian extraction named Bernard Heuvelmans, who had been deeply affected by the piece. A zoologist by education (his doctoral thesis focused on the classification of aardvark teeth), Heuvelmans, too, was disillusioned with the staid mindset of traditional science and had been seeking a niche in which to apply his diverse talents. He had worked as a comedian and a jazz musician, written several books, and translated scientific texts, but his real passion was zoologic anomalies, or what he called "hidden" animals, a subject even Charles Fort hadn't plumbed. As Heuvelmans saw it, the sale of an article about twentieth-century dinosaurs to a magazine as important as the *Post* was evidence of a market for nature writing that challenged the scientific status quo. When Sanderson learned that Heuvelmans had informants who provided him with news of strange natural phenomena, he embraced him as a kindred spirit.[32]

The two didn't actually meet for many years, but they became close friends through letters, swapping information about everything from proto-men to sea serpents, gleaned from contacts from Mongolia to Tierra del Fuego. At the start, however, it was Sanderson's influence as a mentor, in much the same way he later influenced Roger Patterson, that induced Heuvelmans to take up the challenge to become an expert in the new field Sanderson had envisioned years before, cryptozoology.

In addition to writing and lecturing, Sanderson established a pioneering career in television.[33] In 1951, he hosted the first series broadcast in color, *The World Is Yours,* for CBS, in which he displayed animals (generally small and very rare) and artifacts he'd gathered on his travels.[34] The program was short-lived, but Sanderson parlayed his exotic-animal show-and-tell act into a twenty-six-week series for ABC called *The Big*

Game Hunt and forged a regular role for himself as the "animal man" on the *Garry Moore Show* on CBS. There he appeared for more than half a decade, becoming a national celebrity.

The constant need for new species to exhibit got him into the exotic-animal collection business. The problems of housing a growing collection of wild animals (including a baboon and a cheetah) in a New York apartment soon precipitated a move to rural acreage near the Delaware River in New Jersey, where he installed his menagerie in a private zoo. Locals remember the eccentric Scotsman as a tall, lean figure, always with a cigarette in hand. "Egotistical and a bit arrogant," one acquaintance recalled. "Generous. Religious in his own way. Funny at times. Most of all curious. The world was an exciting and mysterious place to him, whether in a jungle somewhere or on the porch of his farmhouse."[35]

Shortly after the move, a fire destroyed an outbuilding on the property, incinerating ninety rare animals. He replaced the animals, only to see the zoo destroyed the next year in a flood. "Sixty feet of water came over my zoo down here, and all my animals were washed out," he recalled. "A hundred and seventy thousand dollars cash property went down the river in half an hour."[36] The insurance company refused to pay for the loss. Devastated, Sanderson gave the animal business over to his assistant, Ed Schoenenberger, and turned full-time to television, writing and criss-crossing the country on the lecture circuit.[37]

I contacted Schoenenberger in New Jersey, and we talked about his old boss. He said he met Ivan in 1951 at a National Speleological Society meeting at the American Museum of Natural History (both were ardent cavers).[38] Ivan was already a media personality by virtue of his radio show and his magazine articles. CBS had just given him an experimental TV series to produce (*The World Is Yours*), and he needed help. Schoenenberger went to work for him as an animal wrangler two months later.

They originally borrowed their animals from the Staten Island and Bronx zoos, but when Ivan began appearing on the *Garry Moore Show*, the constant need for new species to exhibit forced them to begin importing animals directly. Their new venture, Animodels, quickly expanded beyond television appearances to include renting their creatures out for film shoots and exhibitions.

Schoenenberger recalled it as a heady time. "We went to dinner every night. There was always a party." And Sanderson loved to talk. Around a crowded dinner table, he commonly monopolized the conversation. Alma was occasionally heard to remind him that he might want to give someone else an opportunity to speak.

New York being the center of the action, Sanderson always maintained an apartment in the Whitby, close to Times Square and the television studios. "Ivan met a lot of people," Schoenenberger said. "And a lot of people he went to school with at Cambridge had become famous." It wasn't unusual to walk into Ivan's apartment and meet someone like Edmund Hillary.

While lecturing in Texas, Sanderson met an oilman and entrepreneur named Tom Slick, who shared his fascination with the idea that "mystery peoples" still roamed the earth. One of Slick's many ventures was an air-freight operation called Slick Airways, which operated out of a metal shack at the old Newark Airport. Sanderson and Schoenenberger soon began using Slick's planes to transport their newly acquired animals into the country, and the Sanderson-Slick connection soon led to adventures far beyond New York.

Sanderson received a "tremendous amount" of mail, Schoenenberger said, much of it about strange phenomena. By the time they met, Sanderson had already investigated several peculiar incidents, including reports of giant tracks discovered on a beach in Florida in 1948.[39]

The first time Schoenenberger himself got sucked into "one of [Ivan's] things" was their investigation of the Bayhead Monster in New Jersey, a creature that left three-toed footprints. "Two years later," Schoenenberger said dryly, "it turned out it was all a hoax by Rutgers students." He also remembered the tremendous press coverage surrounding their investigation of the Flatwood Monster in West Virginia: a huge creature with a bright red face, bright green clothing, and a head that resembled the ace of spades.

As for Bernard Heuvelmans, he was "a lot like Ivan," Schoenenberger said. "He loved to talk." And he knew a lot of facts. "Bernard's arrival on the scene gave Ivan a new passion."[40] It was a true meeting of the minds. Had Sanderson and Heuvelmans never forged a relationship, Bigfoot would be just another character in the mythological bestiary. But by applying the veneer of science to stimulating but implausible notions, the two disaffected "scientists" created a popular—and lucrative—market for some very old ideas.

．．．

The first real inkling of human origins came to light in 1856 with the discovery of bones in Germany's Neander Valley of what appeared to be an upright-walking creature. Neanderthal Man—as the famous cranium with the protruding brow came to be known—looked remarkably similar to modern humans but, as far as researchers could infer, had only the rudiments of culture and speech. Fossils were a contentious issue in the scientific community (the word *science* itself had been coined only a few years earlier), as they threatened the prevailing belief that humans, plants, and animals had not changed since the biblical creation. Debate raged over whether Neanderthal was evidence of a primitive race that begat modern man or simply the bones of a deformed human.[41]

Into the fray stepped Charles Darwin, with his 1859 book *On the Origin of Species* proposing the theory of evolution, and, twelve years later, another book putting forth the even more revolutionary idea that humans had evolved from the apes. An early—and influential—supporter of Darwin, the German anatomist Ernst Haeckel, actually beat Darwin to the mark in applying the evolutionary theory to humans by proposing in 1868 that humankind had developed in phases, one of them being a step halfway between apes and humans that he called the Missing Link.[42] He dubbed his theoretical creation *Pithecanthropus alalus,* "speechless ape-man," eliciting scathing criticism from his contemporaries for bestowing a scientific name on a creature that existed only in the abstract (he was one of the first but by no means the last to do so, and nearly all the many concepts he postulated turned out to be wrong—including a number of hypothetical microorganisms that have never been found to exist). Nevertheless, the name caught on, and Haeckel's brainstorm became one of the great scientific preoccupations of the day.

The Dutch anatomist Eugene Dubois became obsessed with the idea of this in-between creature and journeyed to the Dutch colony of Java to find it. In 1891 his diggers turned up the bones of a long-legged animal perfectly adapted for walking upright. Believing he'd found the Missing Link, Dubois named his discovery *Pithecanthropus erectus,* "the ape-man who walks erect."

Dubois's "Java Man"—the first specimen of a species anthropologists now call *Homo erectus*—electrified the paleontology world. But his audacious claim to have found the Missing Link and the manner in which he announced it (publishing only the field notes written immediately after his discovery, and not updating them for three decades), coupled with his personality—described variously as prickly, contrary, impatient, defensive, and obstinate—worked against him. He made enemies of anyone who disagreed with his interpretations of the fossils and hid the bones under his dining-room floor. Colleagues were perplexed and suspicious. The antievolutionary crowd excoriated him.

By the turn of the century, a wave of fossil discoveries in Europe and Asia were making headlines, and the origins of the human race had become a hot subject in publishing, spilling over even into fiction. Jack London set his story *Before Adam* in "a past so remote as to be contemporaneous with the raw beginnings of mankind" and created a protagonist whose father was "half man, and half ape, and yet not ape, and not yet man."[43]

The inevitable soon followed. Beginning in 1911, several pieces of a cranium and part of a lower jaw turned up in a gravel pit in southern England.[44] Whereas Java Man and Neanderthal Man clearly had humanlike teeth and ape-sized brains, the Piltdown Man had the brain of a modern human and the face and teeth of an ape.[45] A fish paleontologist at the British Museum proclaimed it a new and very primitive form of human. The extraordinary combination of apelike jaw and a cranium with a human-shaped forehead raised questions about whether the two artifacts belonged together. The jaw joint that would have answered that question was missing. The British anthropological establishment overrode criticism from scientists in Europe and North America in concluding that the jaw and cranium belonged together and pronouncing the fossil an ancient form of humanity, on the order of two million years old.[46]

In fact, Piltdown Man was a hoax. Forty years later, investigations at Oxford and the British Museum determined that the fossils were an assemblage of fragments from a relatively modern human cranium put together with an orangutan's jaw: the bones had been artfully tinted to conceal their age and the teeth filed to alter their shape.

The search for the Missing Link begat a fierce competition between Western museums and universities to discover the world's biological treasures. From central Africa came the mountain gorilla, the okapi, and the pygmy hippo; from Southeast Asia, the white rhinoceros and the Komodo dragon; from China, the giant panda.

Newspaper accounts of the expeditions that produced such finds, and tales of mountaineers and their heroic attempts to conquer Mount Everest, became wildly popular after the First World War. Britain's Royal Geographical Society sponsored the first Everest expedition in 1921, and the press trumpeted the news: "Where White Man Has Never Trod!"

The amateurish expedition failed to summit the mountain, but its dispatches captivated readers, especially a report by the expedition leader, Lieutenant Colonel Charles Howard-Bury, who reported that, on the way from Kharta to the pass at Lhapka-la, somewhere above twenty thousand feet, he and his companions saw dark figures moving over the snow at a distance. On reaching the spot, they found footprints three times larger than a human's. The colonel thought they'd been made by wolves. The Tibetan porters told him they belonged to the *metoh kangmi,* or yeti.

Intrigued by what he considered local folklore, the colonel mentioned the creature in a report he sent to Kathmandu to be telegraphed to India. In so doing, he miswrote the name given by his porters, and a British translator, unfamiliar with the Nepalese languages, translated the name as "Abominable Snowman." A legend was born.[47]

Howard-Bury's report might have been a delicious sidenote if it hadn't been so essential to the success of later expeditions. As successive summit attempts failed, expedition organizers increased the scope of their efforts, climbing budgets soared, and sale of the expeditions' stories (often serialized) to newspapers became a crucial source of income. Publishers, in turn, knew what sold papers, and the search for the Abominable Snowman quickly became a regular feature of all Himalayan expedition reports.

In an ancient Tibetan dialect, *yeti* means "snow bear," a fact that, to the discerning reader, suggests something about the true nature of the beast. But the search for the yeti transcended facts. In Tibet, a desperately poor country with a burgeoning new source of income in servicing the mountaineers, the locals quickly learned how to play the game. When General Charles Bruce, the leader of the second British Everest expedition, asked the lama at the Rongbuk Valley monastery about the "beasts" that had been reported in the vicinity the previous year, the lama replied with a straight face that there were five yetis living in the upper reaches of the valley. Other monks concurred. The yetis were fearsome creatures, they said, who looked somewhat like men covered in long hair. It was commonly known that they raided villages, killed men, carried off women, and drank yak's blood.

During a 1935 British assault on the mountain, the climbing leader, Eric Shipton, not only saw what he believed to be yeti footprints on his first summit attempt but teamed up with his climbing partner Frank Smythe to publish a story and photos of the tracks in the *London Illustrated News* and *Paris-Match*. The report created a huge sensation. Decades later, in his book *My Quest for the Yeti: Confronting the Himalayas' Deepest Mystery,* the mountaineer Reinhold Messner reprinted a letter he had received from the German explorer and zoologist Ernst Schafer that added another perspective to Shipton and Smythe's report:

In 1934, General Liu Hsiang, the former warlord of the province of Sichuan, had asked me to uncover the mystery of the Yeti and to bring him a male and female pair of these longhaired "Snowmen" for his zoo. The following year I had the opportunity to set out on such an expedition to the uninhabitable regions of Inner Tibet, the source of the Yangtze River. There I shot a number of Yetis, in the form of the mighty Tibetan bear.

In 1938, after I had uncovered the whole sham in my publications . . . and established the Yeti's real identity with the pictures and pelts of my Tibetan bears, Smythe and Shipton came to me on their knees, begging me not to publish my findings in the English-speaking press. The secret had to be kept at all costs—"Or else the press won't give us the money we need for our next Everest expedition."[48]

Despite similar skepticism among many Westerners with long experience in the region, yeti fever proved wildly contagious. The idea of an ape-man roaming the Himalayan snowfields became so widely accepted that virtually every expedition entering the region over the next twenty years reported tracks, sightings, or both.

In 1951, Shipton made his fifth attempt on the mountain, but again failed to summit. Several days later, while exploring a glacier, he and Michael Ward came across a set of large tracks, which Shipton photographed. One of the photos, showing four humanlike toes, was published in the *Illustrated London News* and soon thereafter in newspapers worldwide, creating a new sensation.

In Paris, Bernard Heuvelmans saw the photograph and read Shipton's account of the circumstances: how the two mountaineers had come upon the fresh tracks and followed them for nearly a mile, noting that whatever made them appeared to be walking on two feet, the prints being "slightly longer and a good deal broader than those made by our large mountain boots." A man on that scale would stand about eight feet high. "One could see quite clearly where the creature had jumped [a crevasse] and used its toes to secure purchase on the snow on the other side," something no human could do.[49]

Intrigued, Heuvelmans researched the historical record and found mentions of the yeti predating Howard-Bury's 1921 report. Apparently, for all the press coverage the snowman had received, no one had ever fully described it, scientifically or otherwise. If the yeti did exist, he thought, there must be physical evidence.

Heuvelmans wrote to Sanderson asking if he had any relevant information; Sanderson directed him to Franz Weidenreich and his study of *Gigantopithecus* at the Museum of Natural History. Heuvelmans read Weidenreich's book *Apes, Giants, and Man.* As he turned the pages, his breath caught in his throat. "This primate was not a giant ape," he read, "but a giant man."[50]

The implications were clear: *Gigantopithecus* was a real animal that closely fit the description of the yeti; it had lived in southern China; and Weidenreich had also discovered a connection between it and the fossils of apes found in northern India (close to the Himalaya). *Gigantopithecus* had also been relatively rare. To have survived predation by its fiercest enemy, man, Heuvelmans reasoned that the giant creature would have naturally retreated over the ages to the shelter of the high Himalaya, where it could have survived to the present—a simple and unique idea.

Seizing on the renewed scientific debate over the yeti's existence created by the publication of Shipton's photograph, Heuvelmans published his theory in May of 1952 in the Parisian publication *Sciences et Avenir,* presenting the idea that "the Snowman was a giant and biped anthropoid no doubt closely related to the *Gigantopithecus.*" He assigned the yeti a name, *Dinanthropoides nivalis,* "terrible anthropoid of the snows." "The layman may be surprised," he wrote (mindful, perhaps, of the controversy attending Haeckel's naming of the Missing Link), "that one should give an animal a scientific name on the mere evidence of some footprints and a description of a scalp. In fact this procedure is not only universal in palaeontology, but happens fairly often in zoology."[51] To buttress his case, Heuvelmans cited three examples of animals given names by scientists who had seen only skins and bones, failing to acknowledge that skins and bones were far more evidence than had ever been turned up in the hunt for the snowman of the Himalaya.

The many "discoveries" of exotic animals since the turn of the century fueled speculation that the yeti, fantastic as it seemed, might actually exist. The excitement generated by Shipton's photographs, together with Heuvelmans's theory (much discussed in zoologic and mountaineering circles), reached a peak in 1954, when the London *Daily Mail* launched an expedition to find the beast.[52]

The paper's team consisted of a reporter (Ralph Izzard), a mountaineer, a cameraman, several scientists, and a professional animal collector named Gerald Russell. A legend in wildlife circles, Russell had been a classmate of Ivan Sanderson at Cambridge. He accompanied Sanderson on his collecting expedition to the Cameroons and a few years later helped bring the first giant panda out of the wild. Russell, too, believed that the yeti might be a primitive species of human—a view shaped no doubt by his old friend Sanderson, whom he visited in New York just prior to the expedition.[53]

Talking late into the night, they explored different scenarios that might result from the search. Sanderson believed that finding "one of our own ancestors, thought to have been extinct for thousands of years," would have a profound effect on the human race. If "that creature turned out to be so intermediate in character and characteristics between man and beast as to be ineligible for either class," it could well shake the belief that humans are made in the image of God, whereas "the animals" are not. What would you do, he mused, "with a living creature that not even a scientist could say is either one or the other? [Would you] believe Holy Writ or Charles Darwin?"[54]

The *Daily Mail*'s broad syndication of the expedition reports to newspapers in more than twenty countries ensured that the project captured world attention. Sensitive to charges of publicity-mongering, team members stressed their plans to release the yeti if captured, after briefly studying and photographing the animal, and the fact that they were laying in nursing bottles and baby food in case they captured a youngster.[55]

Readers of the newspaper were told that reconnaissance by the team zoologist, Charles Stonor, had revealed the existence of two types of yeti: a larger, dangerous animal known as the *dzu-teh,* which Stonor determined was probably the red bear, and a smaller, more common creature—three to five feet tall, heavily built, and basically harmless—known as the *mih-teh*. In Stonor's opinion, the *mih-teh* was their quarry. "I cannot make out what it may be," he reported. "All descriptions point to an ape."

They set off in January 1954, with the *Daily Mail* team supported by three hundred porters. Four months of searching produced half a dozen sets of prints, both solo tracks and pairs moving together. Once the Sherpas faked tracks near the camp and laughed "uproariously" at Izzard's reaction.[56] The team also examined and photographed three purported yeti scalps preserved in Buddhist temples.

The expedition failed, however, to either see or catch a yeti. Returning to civilization, Izzard published a "word of warning to future expeditions":

> When we left England we had held [the] belief that it would be merely a matter of picking up the Yeti tracks in the snow and following them until we caught up with the animal. [In fact,] the Yeti is more likely to be met in a chance encounter round say, a rock, than by an organized search. A reconnaissance party of two or three Sahibs needs about 30 Sherpa porters to support it over a period of about three weeks. We found it impossible to introduce such a large body of men into an "empty quarter" of the Himalayas without disturbing all wild life within it. In such country there is no question of stalking an animal in the accepted sense of the term. . . . Often such a path, as at the Nangpa La, may cross the dead centre of a snow-field where a party is as conspicuous as a line of black beetles on a white tablecloth.[57]

Despite the team's failure, yeti mania raged. No sooner had the *Daily Mail* team left Kathmandu bound for home than requests poured in to the Nepalese government from climbing parties representing Switzerland, France, and Argentina to conduct searches of their own. Before long, a yeti-like creature called a Sasquatch was reported in North America.

· · ·

At the height of the yeti craze, in 1955, Bernard Heuvelmans published his cryptozoologic masterwork, *On the Track of Unknown Animals,* a 557-page tome about creatures "which may yet be found and are still unknown to science." His inclusion of what appeared to the casual reader to be scientific evidence, together with his stratagem of occasionally pointing up hoaxes, gave the book an aura of believability. In chapter 6, "The Not So Abominable Snowman," he detailed his argument for the yeti's existence, including his *Gigantopithecus* theory. Every pro-Bigfoot argument heard today is found here, including a verse from Genesis that is popular with contemporary Bigfooters: "There were giants in the earth in those days."

Reading the book, I thought of Henner Fahrenbach's talk at the Sasquatch Forum, where he described the Sasquatch in minute detail, with not a shred of physical evidence in support. Perhaps Heuvelmans's description of the beast inspired him:

> The snowman is a huge creature, half man, half beast; it lives in caves high and inaccessible in the mountains. The skin of its face is white; the body is covered with a thick coat of dark hair. Its arms, like those of the anthropoid apes, reach down to its knees, but its face looks rather more human. Its thick legs are bowed; its toes turn inwards—some even say they turn backwards. It is very muscular and can uproot trees and lift up boulders of remarkable size. The female can be recognised by her long breasts which she throws over her shoulders when she runs.

Heuvelmans's use of uncorroborated testimonies and "facts" lifted from the work of scientists who didn't agree with him is textbook Sanderson.[58] But the book reeked of science, and there were those who wanted to believe. If it took a book to persuade them, this was the one—an exhaustive argument that *something* almost beyond imagining lived in the Himalayan snowfields.

3

BLUFF CREEK

His fondness for sly jokes and malicious pranks, his powers as shape-
shifter, his dual nature, half animal, half divine, his exposure to all
kinds of tortures, and—last but not least—his approximation to the
figure of a saviour.

—Carl Gustav Jung, *On the Psychology of the Trickster-Figure*

Half a world away from the Himalaya, on the northern coast of California, Bozo the clown had just appeared at the Humboldt County Fair,
hula hoops were the new fad, and three thousand laborers were pouring
the concrete that would become the Trinity River Dam. A record heat
wave had aggravated some forest fires, but, all in all, 1958 was turning
out to be a good year.

In early October, the receptionist at the *Humboldt Times* in Eureka
looked up from her desk to find standing before her a bespectacled middle-aged man wearing a button-down striped shirt and freshly washed
blue jeans. In his arms he cradled a huge plaster footprint. Coupled with
his earnest expression, the sight reminded her of a clown with a gag gift,
and she had to force herself to keep from laughing aloud. He introduced
himself as Jerry Crew and said he'd come to speak with Andrew Genzoli, the editor, and she hustled down the hall with a smile on her face
to tell the editor, "You aren't going to believe what just walked in."

Genzoli and the rest of the newsroom were soon huddled around the
footprint cast peppering Crew with questions. He explained that he operated a bulldozer on a crew building a logging road along a stream

called Bluff Creek. The giant tracks had been appearing on the job site for months. He had got fed up with being ribbed by his coworkers about his mind playing tricks and made this cast to silence the doubting Thomases. He believed the tracks were real, and he wanted somebody to investigate.

Genzoli, who had received reports of such tracks before, treated the idea whimsically. Crew was offended. "If it were a bear," he said, "there would be claw marks, as well as other indications. But none of these exist." Construction equipment had been vandalized at the same time, and a drum full of diesel fuel tossed into the creek. His coworkers had taken to calling the creature Big Foot.

The cat skinner's vulnerability struck a chord with Genzoli, so he had a photo taken of Crew holding the cast. When the photographer suggested he smile, Crew answered, "Not on your life. If I did, someone would accuse me of trickery." The story and the photo ran on the front page of the Sunday edition with the headline "Giant Footprints Puzzle Residents along Trinity River." Crew's earnest expression lent the story an air of believability—and mystery—no one could have anticipated.

. . .

Crew's job site at Bluff Creek sat thirty miles inland from the Pacific on the fringe of possibly the largest stand of virgin trees in America. The U.S. Forest Service had divvied the forest into parcels and bid them out to sawmills that subcontracted with logging companies to cut and haul out the timber. One such company was a small gyppo outfit called Wallace Construction, run by three brothers from Washington State. They were experts in high-lead logging—using steel cables to lift logs through the air to surmount obstacles.

Ray Wallace, the middle brother, handled the company's business. A large man, well over six feet tall and stout, in his early forties, with a beak-like nose and an uncanny resemblance to the movie actor Slim Pickens, Ray had logged for twenty-five years and had the scars to prove it. Years before, a tree had rolled on him and broken his back and hip, which slowed him up. He never touched alcohol and was happiest cruising through the countryside in his Cadillac, promoting business deals. He even drove the Caddy to his job sites, filthy as they were. As one old-timer who worked for him put it, "He liked the flash."

Wilbur "Shorty" Wallace, reportedly the most trustworthy of the brothers, handled maintenance. Les, the oldest, was a religious man who leavened Ray's overabundance of BS with a rural beatitude and could usually be found operating a bulldozer.

In 1957 Wallace Construction contracted to build a main haul road along Bluff Creek, a job that entailed equal parts logging and road building. They began in the spring after the mud had set, removing the trees in the right-of-way, then grading the surface. Culverts were laid and dynamite used to push the road through the shale hillsides. Bluff Creek became a frenzy of trucks and heavy equipment, with diesel engines screaming, frequent explosions, and the jagged roar of chainsaws.

Wallace Construction payrolled in the neighborhood of fifteen men: cat skinners, high climbers, fallers, bull bucks, powder monkeys, riggers, choker setters, grease monkeys, and yarder operators. The work was dangerous, and the red dirt gouged up by the giant blades turned to fine dust that hovered in the hundred-degree air, coating the men in a grimy crust. The crew worked dark to dark, often seven days a week. Because the job site was remote, many of the men stayed in trailers and tents at nearby campsites.

Jerry Crew's job was "pioneering"—making the first cut for the road—which required him to work some distance from the main camp. At the end of each day, he left his cat parked at the head of the cut and returned to camp by pickup.

Crew was an affable guy and deeply religious—he would eventually start his own congregation—but life had kicked him in the gut and he was somewhat edgy. In his first year away on the Bluff Creek job, his wife's nightdress caught fire. Severely burned, she drove herself to the hospital. When she arrived, her fingers had to be pried from the steering wheel. Crew had no choice but to stay on the job while she clung to life. She died later that year, leaving him with three small children.

By the summer of 1958, the Bluff Creek road had been extended nineteen miles into the backcountry. Crew and his brother-in-law were living in a trailer at a campsite called Louse Camp, a thin patch of land along the creek. One night Crew's brother-in-law woke him up, saying something was shaking the trailer. At first Crew thought it was an earthquake. Peering outside, he saw what looked like a big animal, maybe a bear standing on its hind feet. They didn't open the door.

The next morning, going to work at first light, Crew discovered giant footprints. They came down a hillside at a steep angle, circled around his bulldozer, followed the road toward the camp, then cut off down a steep incline and disappeared back into the woods. They were much larger than a man would make, even a giant of a man. And they looked like human prints—but not quite. The width was nearly half the length of the foot. At first Crew thought it was a joke. Tracks like that, as deep as they were, couldn't possibly be real. When they appeared a second and a third time, he began approaching his rig each morning with apprehension.

Shortly before the giant tracks appeared on Crew's job site, the *Humboldt Times's* Willow Creek–based stringer, a grandmother named Betty Allen, had responded to two reports of similar tracks by publishing a plea for someone to make a plaster cast of the impressions to help identify the animal. Crew may have heard about the idea, because he asked a friend, Bob Titmus, a local taxidermist, to help him out. It's unclear who actually crafted it, but on or about October 5, 1958, Jerry Crew emerged from the forest with a giant plaster footprint.

Response to the story was immediate. "Within the past two days Associated Press, United Press International, national radio networks, San Francisco and Sacramento newspapers and college professors have been bearing down on the story of Bigfoot," Genzoli noted in his RFD column a few days later. In Canada, John Green saw the story on the wire at his newspaper office and drew the obvious connection with the Sasquatch. He left immediately for California without his coinvestigator, René Dahinden, who hadn't yet received Canadian citizenship and couldn't cross the border. At Bluff Creek he examined the tracks and talked to witnesses, including Titmus.

Odd acts of vandalism began plaguing the job site. Two workers on the Wallace payroll reported seeing a Bigfoot "bound across the road" in front of their car, "running upright like a man, swinging long, hairy arms." Reports became so numerous that parents began calling the *Times* to complain that their children were afraid to go into the woods. The sheriff's office quickly concluded that the tracks were the work of Ray Wallace, who had a reputation for high jinks. A deputy telephoned Wallace and told him the sheriff wanted to talk, hoping he'd confess and end the uproar. When the newspaper called Wallace for comment, he grew irate. "I'm not going in," he stormed. "If they want to put out a warrant, I'm going to sue them for slander!" The paper ran his denial along with his photograph, noting that Wallace wanted the reporter to know that he'd seen giant tracks himself and had plans to catch the beast.

Ray's brother Shorty supported him 100 percent. "This is no hoax," he averred. "We work from daylight to dark out here, by golly, and nobody's gonna work like that all day and then go running around the hills making tracks." The next day, Ralph Edwards, host of the popular NBC television program *Truth or Consequences,* offered a thousand-dollar reward for a "solution to Bigfoot."

Green had been home only a few weeks when he received a letter from Titmus saying he'd discovered tracks on a sandbar in Bluff Creek itself. Green promptly returned to California and spent several days with Titmus, camping on the creek and examining the new prints, which were noticeably different from those Crew had seen. Titmus pooh-poohed the idea of a hoax. "He was a person of very firm opinions," Green told me, "and he was satisfied that [the tracks] were genuine."[1]

Then winter blew in, closing the Bluff Creek road and precluding any further on-site investigation. As the new year approached, three months of inactivity threatened to turn the beast into a minor footnote in the annals of tomfoolery. But every success story has a maven, an individual capable of driving a social epidemic to its peak. Bigfoot—a goofy idea by almost everyone's reckoning—was no exception.

The following summer Ivan Sanderson turned his station wagon onto the Bluff Creek road, on the trail of what he believed might be the highlight of his career. His reputation as an expert in offbeat natural phenomena had soared in the last few years, in part because of his appearances on the *Long John Nebel Show,* a late-night talk radio program on WOR, broadcast from midnight to five A.M. from a studio in Manhattan.[2] Nebel's penchant for strange and offbeat topics—among them voodoo, witchcraft, conspiracy theories, teleportation, and ghosts—and his showmanship (he never hesitated to fake something if it was entertaining), leavened with appearances by famous personalities such as Jackie Gleason and Arthur C. Clarke, had earned the show a wide following. Sanderson, always introduced as a naturalist, was one of a group of freewheeling panelists who helped spice up the festivities. Another regular on the panel was a magician known as the Amazing Randi.

Speaking from Florida fifty years later, James Randi characterized Ivan as a "character" in every way. "By his own admission . . . a bit of a charlatan. Always expounding on weird ideas that were difficult to accept." He recalled visiting Sanderson at his New York apartment: "He was living in a jungle of his own [with] lots of animals, including a cheetah named Caesar. It was quite a tame cheetah, though Ivan said he never trusted it, quite."[3]

A decade-long wave of UFO sightings throughout the world, beginning in the early 1950s (a front-page story in the *Evening News* of London in 1957 described how a squadron of British Javelin jets chased a UFO over the English Channel), accompanied by numerous well-publicized reports from people claiming to have been abducted by aliens, provided a wealth of material for Nebel and regular exposure for Sanderson, who appeared frequently to discuss and debate the phenomena and pitch his own theories of what the objects might be.

Beyond radio, however, Sanderson's world was changing. The *Garry Moore Show* had been canceled, and his regular TV appearances seemed to be over.[4] He'd just inked a deal to write a natural-history book about North America when a cable arrived from Heuvelmans alerting him to a news report about a creature called Bigfoot in California. He quickly reworked the itinerary he'd made for a research trip related to the book to include a stop at Bluff Creek. Now, plunging through clouds of road dust on the edge of the wilderness, his imagination soared: "All along this mountainous trail, there are stumps of vast trees cut and hauled out, and the great dozers and crawlers clank and roar in the hot summer sunlight as they gnaw their way relentlessly into this timeless land."[5]

At the end of the road he found Jerry Crew atop his giant blade and, notebook in hand, began reporting the story. Over several days Sanderson interviewed the Wallace brothers, Betty Allen, and Titmus, who mentioned a Canadian named Green who knew of a similar animal in British Columbia called Sasquatch. Titmus also mentioned Tom Slick, who had contacted him about assembling an expedition to find the beast. Slick's name got Sanderson's full attention; he'd used the Texan's airplanes to transport animals from Africa and consulted for him on a yeti expedition Slick had financed in Nepal. He knew that Slick's craving for publicity could turn Bigfoot into a huge story.

Sanderson drove to British Columbia and talked with Green, who told him everything he and Dahinden had learned about Sasquatch. Inevitably, the subject of Slick arose, and Sanderson told them what he knew: Tom Slick had a consuming passion for discovering hidden animals and, as heir to a Texas oil fortune, the bank account to indulge himself (while a student at Yale, he had traveled to Scotland to look for the Loch Ness Monster). Slick had read Heuvelmans's book, met him in Paris, and come away convinced the yeti could be the Missing Link. In 1957 he had funded an expedition in Nepal to search for the animal. Having no luck on the first go-round, he financed a second, smaller search. The Canadians prevailed on Sanderson to contact Slick on their behalf to explore the possibility of a Bigfoot hunt.

A few weeks later, Green and Dahinden found themselves in the lobby of Wyatt's Motel in Willow Creek, meeting with Slick and Titmus. The Canadians wanted money to run their own search, but Slick told them that if he was putting up five thousand dollars, it would be his show. Ultimately they each signed a contract stipulating that, should Bigfoot be found, Slick would receive a hundred thousand dollars off the top of any revenue received. To manage in his absence—which would be most of the time—he appointed Titmus deputy leader. Thus was born the Pacific Northwest Expedition.

Thirty-seven years later, Dahinden recalled for me his adventures at Bluff Creek. "I still remember Wyatt's Motel," he said. "Standing out there . . . I signed the contract—in the back of my mind I said, 'Fuck you.' If I find the Sasquatch, I don't give a shit what you spent in the Himalayas. I'm gonna tell you I got one, I show you the pictures, and then we sit down and make a contract."[6]

Dahinden took an immediate dislike to Titmus, who sucked up to Slick shamelessly, nailed used sanitary napkins to trees as bait, and claimed to have discovered evidence in the form of mysterious hairs and droppings that turned out to belong to a moose, an animal not native to California, which Dahinden suspected might have come from a taxidermy shop.[7]

The professional expedition Dahinden expected didn't materialize. "Here we were," he said, "looking for the biggest mystery there is with some guy who had a jeep, the first time it got cold the battery didn't have enough power to start it when we were supposed to run the ridges in the snow twenty-four hours a day looking for tracks . . . and on and on and on and on and on. . . . We didn't even have a place down in the valley where we could go and have a shower."[8]

Disheartened, Dahinden boarded the bus and returned to Canada to spend Christmas with his family. As he was leaving, the December 1959 issue of *True* magazine hit the nation's newsstands featuring "The Strange Story of America's Abominable Snowman," by Ivan Sanderson.

The most popular men's adventure magazine of the era, *True* strove for a seamless blending of truth and fiction in its reporting: harmless fare, so long as readers did not take it too seriously. "The style we're after," one *True* editor said, "is essentially that of the short story applied to the fact field—something that can be told mainly in chronological sequence, working up to a climax and a denouement."[9]

This is exactly what Sanderson delivered: a tour de force of hyperbole, flavored with science-speak and infused with an air of mystery:

> Before you are tempted to scoff and put this story down, bear a few things in mind. [Bluff Creek] extends over one hundred thousand square miles, and *nobody* lives there. Apart from the higher ridges and mountain peaks, the ground area is completely concealed from the air by forest. It has never been properly surveyed or mapped. Yet, for all this, the area is well watered, overgrown with berries, full of small game, and never completely snowed in. Though it nestles in the midst of civilization, and is as fertile and livable as civilization, it is completely uncivilized.
>
> Almost anything could be living in there. From the evidence, something is. Will somebody please do something about it before it is too late?

The article unleashed a whirlwind of activity in Humboldt County. Nearly a thousand queries poured into the offices of the *Humboldt Times* from around the country. Andrew Genzoli reported the imminent arrival of "several well-organized expeditions . . . a Hollywood production company, and countless smaller groups that shunned publicity."[10]

Vehicles filled with hunters now patrolled the Bluff Creek road day and night. Desperate to stay ahead of the pack, Titmus used Slick's money to hire a bear guide named Ivan Marx to track the beast with hounds. When word spread that a real hunter had arrived on the scene, Marx found himself trailed by a string of cars whenever he drove out of camp. Dahinden, who had just returned after the holiday, found himself riding in the back seat surrounded by dogs while Marx nuzzled his new bride in the front.

Marx laughed when he recalled the experience for me in his rustic home in the shadow of Mount Lassen. "Very few of those [hunters] ever got off the damn road," he said. "Everybody was wanting Bigfoot to walk out in front of 'em. I mean, if [Bigfoot had] stepped down in one of our camps, people woulda hurt theirselves."[11]

When Slick began telling Titmus to hand over portions of the money he'd allocated to the Pacific Northwest Expedition to other hunters, Green and Dahinden realized that the Texan had only one objective: to have whoever bagged Bigfoot on his payroll.

Frustrated, Green quit the hunt and returned to Canada. Dahinden lasted only a few days longer. "I just threw up my hands," he said. "The Slick Expedition wasn't an expedition. It was three or four guys ... for a week or two ... staggering through the bush, wandering around. There never [was an] expedition. Ever! At any time! It just was a fuck-up."[12]

As Dahinden and Green retreated to Canada, a runner came pounding out of the gloom of the Himalayan night in Nepal's upper Chhoyang River Valley and handed Peter Byrne a crumpled letter. Byrne had been holed up for weeks in a cave with his brother Brian, living off yak's milk and cheese, the last remnant of Tom Slick's third yeti expedition, which the Texan had all but abandoned. The message contained an SOS from Slick instructing Byrne—if he so chose—to terminate the hunt and travel to the United States to take charge of the search for "a giant primate not unlike the Yeti," called Bigfoot.

Americans who meet Byrne today say he looks like he stepped out of a comic strip, dressed as he often is in safari clothes, replete with ascot and bush hat. But Byrne's attire is not an affectation. In an age when the human race has placed a camera on Mars, he is the living embodiment of a life that can now only be experienced via memoir. In his autobiography *Gone Are the Days,* Byrne recalls dispatching his first tiger—"an old cattle killer"—in the forest of southern Bhutan in 1948: "I took it ... alone and on foot with a clean, single shot to the neck that put it down at once. It was dead within five seconds."[13]

Byrne's fascination with the yeti began in Ireland, where he grew up listening to his father's stories about the snowman. He found his first yeti footprint in 1948, in northern Sikkim near the Zemu Glacier, while on holiday from a Royal Air Force assignment in India. After the war, he wrangled a job at a tea plantation in the jungles of north Bengal, close to the foothills of the Himalaya—as close to the yeti as a white man could get and still be gainfully employed. It was a place where, as Byrne put it, "the romantic legends and institutions of English colonialism still hung thickly in the air."[14]

Given a choice of becoming a "poodle-faker"—a name given to young English officers new in the country who preferred tennis and card games—or a hunter who spent his leisure time outdoors, hiking and camping and shooting tigers and boar, he chose adventure. "It was a good life," he recalled. "A very good life." It also gave him the opportunity to trek into the mountains and look for the yeti.[15]

In the summer of 1952, in the Casanova Bar at the Grand Hotel in Calcutta, he came to the defense of "a small, . . . impeccably dressed" little Nepalese man, who was being "stiffed by a German." Fisticuffs followed, and Byrne emerged the victor. The little man turned out to be the brother of the king of Nepal. Recognizing a bolt of luck when he saw it, Byrne quit his job at the tea plantation and, with the prince's help, obtained a hunting license to guide safaris into Nepal's fabled hunting grounds of Kailali and Kanchanpur.[16]

Byrne was fluent in Hindustani and by now had five years of big-game hunting experience. He found an agent in Los Angeles to promote safaris to the Hollywood crowd and went into the business of game guiding, pursuing his yeti search in the off-season. To raise money for a full-scale yeti expedition, he flew to Sydney, Australia, in 1954, arriving with a leopard for the Taronga Zoo. He announced to the press his plans for an expedition to start in the fall of 1956 and joked about arriving next time with a pair of yeti. Taking exception to the scale of the recently unsuccessful *Daily Mail* expedition, he proposed a search party consisting of two or three men traveling light.

Failing to raise the money, he returned to Nepal. At that point, fate brought him together with Tom Slick, who had been refused a permit by the Nepalese government to mount his own yeti expedition. With the prince's aid, Byrne secured the permit, and he and Slick, accompanied by Sherpas, hiked into the Arun Valley in northeastern Nepal. A month in the field yielded several sets of very promising footprints but no yeti.

A smaller search party, without Slick, the following year yielded a purported yeti hand, which Byrne claims to have smuggled out of a monastery. Study of the relic proved inconclusive.[17] Byrne convinced Slick to fund a third search, involving just himself and his brother Brian. And so it was, after three years in the Himalaya, that Slick's letter arrived, beckoning him to America.

In Willow Creek, Byrne took charge of what remained of the Pacific Northwest Expedition. By his own account, he was "a stranger in a strange land," and his appearance on the streets of the small logging community in bush jacket and safari hat did not go unnoticed. Several women in town were smitten.

The Slick-financed Bigfoot project limped along for two and a half years. Slick flew in from time to time to join the fun, usually accompanied by a guest du jour. Newspapers reported that Byrne had found a Bigfoot bed and three sets of footprints. The search ended abruptly in 1962 when Slick died in the crash of a small airplane.

. . .

So ended Bigfoot's first brush with fame: two years of excitement, followed by a gradual loss of steam as the beast retreated into the wilderness, apparently satisfied with the success of its protest against the threat to its habitat. But the affair was not over.

While Byrne was in the field, Sanderson took advantage of the brouhaha surrounding the events at Bluff Creek and published *Abominable Snowmen: Legend Come to Life,* an exhaustive global summary of the "evidence" regarding what he called ABSMs (Abominable Snowmen). "The fact is," he wrote, "we cannot draw a line between 'men' and 'sub-men' and in many parts of the world today all manner of intermediate forms—both individuals, tribes, and whole races—still exist." He promoted the book on radio and television, including on the *Tonight Show.*

The host, Johnny Carson, seemed genuinely intrigued. He held up the book, then introduced Ivan. "I have lots of questions about this," he said.

Sanderson explained that there were four different kinds of these creatures worldwide. Three of them were "distant from the type we have in
North America." The type here "appears to be about eight foot tall, covered in short hair ... small eyes close together ... and arms hanging
down almost to their knees."

"Could this be a hoax?" Carson asked.

"This has been going on all over the world for two to three thousand
years," Sanderson replied with a touch of incredulity. "What I would ask
is, 'Why should anybody go to the trouble?'"[18]

After a lifetime of moving toward a break with the scientific establishment that nurtured him, Sanderson had finally, irrevocably, done it:

> Sooner or later somebody always asks me: "You don't really think there is
> such a thing as an Abominable Snowman, do you?" My reply is always the
> same: "No. I believe there are hundreds if not thousands of unknown an-
> thropoids, of at least half a dozen kinds, running all over five continents."
>   ... I am firmly convinced that they range from extremely primitive hu-
> mans, without true speech, tools or knowledge of fire-making, and still in
> varying degrees, hairy, to one or two still undiscovered large apes in Africa.
> In between, some appear definitely to be Neanderthal submen such as in-
> habited Europe in the ice age but which have lingered on in eastern Asia,
> while others are even farther down the Hominid (Man) branch of the fam-
> ily tree, being what used to be called "Ape-men."[19]

Five years later Roger Patterson reprinted this article word for word in
his book, inspired by "Mr. Sanderson ... who has worked long and hard
in his search for the truth in this matter."[20]

4

THE BACKUP MAN

The woods of Arcady are dead,
And over is their antique joy;
Of old the world on dreaming fed;
Grey Truth is now her painted toy.

—William Butler Yeats,
The Song of the Happy Shepherd

The only irrefutable thing about Roger Patterson's film clip of Bigfoot is the image on the screen. The first few seconds of the scene are smeared, as if a finger had been depressing the camera's trigger while the camera waved wildly about. Then the shot steadies—as if the cameraman had put the viewfinder to his eye—and the Bigfoot figure appears, small in the frame, striding at an angle away from the camera. Frame-by-frame inspection reveals that, after about twenty seconds, the camera "hiccupped" for a frame or so (a malfunction that occurs when the photographer's finger slips off the trigger and briefly disengages the camera motor). Then the scene shifts ever so slightly (the background changes, and the figure appears at a slightly different spot in the frame), but the figure continues its retreat. Several seconds later, the figure enters an area of trees and shadow, and the film goes blank.

The film reveals neither who shot it nor who else may have been present. The only living thing seen on the film is the hairy figure. If Patterson did the filming, as he claimed, we know nothing of the whereabouts of his partner, Bob Gimlin.

In an interview Patterson and Gimlin recorded together in November 1967, less than a month after the filming, they described what happened next: as soon as Patterson ran out of film, Gimlin went after the beast on horseback. "I watched her until she went up the road about 300 yards," Gimlin said. "And she went around a bend in the road and that was the last I seen of her." Patterson yelled at him to come back, and Gimlin broke off the chase. "At this point," Patterson said, "my horse was I didn't know where, and the pack horse was gone, and my rifle was in the scabbard on the horse. And the tracks before down in there that we had heard about were in a set of three, and there was a bigger one there, and I thought that possibly there was a male close in. I was on foot without anything, and I yelled to Bob to come back and we would think the thing over."[1]

Gimlin rode off, found Patterson's mount and the pack horse, and returned with them to the film site. The two rode up the creek about a mile looking for footprints and discovered a wet track on a rock. From there the terrain became rough. Gimlin dismounted and followed the creature's most likely path on foot. About two hundred feet up the mountainside, he abandoned the chase. They returned to the truck, two miles away, loaded bags of plaster of Paris on the horses, and rode back to the film site. Then they cast a left and a right footprint.

Curious to hear what happened on that afternoon from the horse's mouth, so to speak, I drove to Yakima and knocked on Bob Gimlin's door unannounced. He received me as if I'd been expected, said, "Come on in," and offered me a seat in the living room. Carefully lowering himself into an easy chair, he said he'd got busted up by a horse and been in and out of the hospital recently.[2]

Looking younger than his sixty-five years, he was the Willy Nelson epitome of an old cowhand: short and slender, with clear eyes set in a taut, leathery skin. He spoke in a measured, deliberate manner that promised the straight facts. He recounted his childhood growing up on a farm in the Ozarks, riding anything with four legs. He'd done many things for a living, including a stint as a long-haul trucker, but he considered himself mainly a horse trainer. As taciturn as he appeared, he described an adventurous life, boxing and riding dirt-track motorcycles. He hung around with Bob Knievel before he took the name Evel and became a daredevil.

He met Patterson in 1956 or '57 at a rodeo. They shared a love of horses and physical fitness—he became an All-Navy welterweight during the Korean War, and Patterson boxed in the Army. Gimlin hadn't rodeoed much, but Patterson—who was into it big-time—encouraged him to keep at it, and they were soon traveling to rodeos together on the weekends. He described Patterson as "small but muscular . . . very robust and full of energy," speaking of him almost in awe. "We were really close friends," he said.

In the early sixties, Patterson contracted a lymph-gland disease, and Gimlin didn't see much of him for a couple of years. Then he got better. When they got reacquainted, Patterson was "really on to Bigfoot." In the years prior to the filming, they made a number of horse trips into the forests around Mount Adams and Mount St. Helens looking for the beast, often riding Patterson's horses—tiny Morgan cross-breed ponies—which Patterson trained to jump in the back of his Volkswagen bus like dogs.

Gimlin professed amazement at Patterson's ability to design and build things. He described a beautifully crafted miniature stagecoach Patterson built for his ponies to pull. Patterson also sang and played guitar.

In the mid sixties, Gimlin said, Patterson made several trips to the Bluff Creek area, and the folks down there knew him. That's how he came to get a call in the fall of 1967 from Al Hodgson, who owned the Willow Creek general store, alerting him that tracks had been found near Bluff Creek. That report led to the trip on which they made the film.

I asked him about the filming and he described it straight away. They traveled to Humboldt County in late September, in Gimlin's one-ton flatbed truck, hauling three horses. The first thing they did was drive into Willow Creek and talk to people Roger knew at the Forest Service office, and Al Hodgson at the variety store.

When they arrived at Bluff Creek, they found that the Bigfoot tracks they'd been told about had been reduced to big blobs of mud. Nevertheless, they set up camp by the creek. For about three weeks they scouted on horseback during the day and cruised the roads at night in the truck. They saw bear, bobcat, cougar, and deer sign, but no sign of a Bigfoot; Gimlin had yet to see a Bigfoot track.

The morning of the filming, Gimlin got up and told Patterson he was going for a ride. Patterson stayed in camp, saying he didn't feel well. Gimlin rode for a couple of hours, then his horse got a loose shoe, and he returned to camp. Patterson was gone when he arrived, but his horse was still there, which Gimlin thought was strange. Patterson returned later, saying he had taken a walk up the creek. They decided to do an overnighter and loaded up the pack horse.

Riding along the stream, they came around a big "downfall" tree and encountered the Bigfoot hunched down by the side of the creek. Both of their horses freaked—Patterson's flipped completely over—and the pack-horse bolted. In the confusion, Patterson managed to grab his camera. The creature was maybe ninety feet from them and walking away. Patterson yelled, "Cover me." Gimlin slipped off his horse with his rifle at the ready as Patterson followed the creature with his camera. After the film ran out, the animal went up and around a knoll, back down to the creek, then up a bank to the right and disappeared. It showed no hostility.

They'd both noted the animal was a female. The tracks reported in the creek only weeks before indicated there were three creatures of different sizes in the area, possibly a family, so they decided to stay together in case the male of the group, presumably larger, appeared.

They found the runaway packhorse and rode the three miles or so back to camp, loaded the horses with plaster of Paris, and returned to the film site. Patterson filmed Gimlin jumping off a stump near the Bigfoot tracks and walking his horse alongside them to compare the depth of the various footprints. After casting the tracks in plaster, they rode back to camp, loaded the horses in the truck, and drove to Willow Creek, where they talked with Al Hodgson at the general store. From there they drove to an airport near Eureka, on the coast, where Patterson "airmailed" the film to his brother-in-law Al DeAtley for processing. They arrived back at their camp on Bluff Creek around midnight.

I asked Gimlin for his impression of the animal. "About the best way I can think of to describe it," he said, "was like a large, well-muscled quarter-horse."

. . .

I left Gimlin's home in Yakima and headed back to Oregon. Approaching the state line, the road runs ruler-straight to the edge of a cliff, five hundred feet above the Columbia River. Perched on the lip of the gorge is a reproduction of Stonehenge built by a railroad baron. I stopped there and wandered among the huge stones, digesting what Gimlin had told me.

What I'd heard that afternoon differed in several ways from the joint interview in 1967. In that version two horses, not one, had run away; they'd ridden up the creek looking for footprints, and Gimlin followed the trail on foot; and the film site was two miles from camp, not three. Small details, yes, and that interview was thirty years old. But I'd looked at other accounts of the filming and found more irregularities.

In a joint interview with their hometown paper the week after they returned from California, Gimlin told the reporter that he could see the white gleam of the creature's teeth but could not tell whether she was snarling or smiling.[3] In another interview a few days later, he described the animal as "a large hairy creature with arms that hang . . . far down on its sides, below its knees."

"Were the breasts visible?" the questioner asked.

"They were visible."

"Were they covered with hair?"

"It was [completely] covered with hair, except around the face and nose. She was kind of slumped, and very heavily through the . . . well, her entire body was heavy . . . although I had no way of estimating her weight at that time."

"What kind of nose did it have?"

"It had a broad, flat nose."

"Like a gorilla's nose with the open nostrils?"

"No, no, not like that, the nostrils you could not see down . . . because she turned and she stood there for an instant . . . face on to me."[4]

Standing face to face with Bigfoot is a bold claim, especially with scientists and media listening carefully to every word you utter, as was the case with Patterson and Gimlin in the weeks and months following the film's release. Interviewed a few weeks later by Ivan Sanderson for a cover story for *Argosy* magazine, Gimlin abruptly backed away from it. When asked, "Did you see her, too?" he answered, "Yeah, Ivan. But way ahead and really taking off for the hills."[5] He made no mention of having stood face to face with the most incredible creature anyone had ever seen—a moment that, for most people, would have been life changing.

John Green and René Dahinden (who claimed to know more about Patterson and his film than anyone), writing about the affair, barely mentioned what Patterson and Gimlin did after shooting the film.[6] Peter Byrne's account of the filming added some detail to the story but basically regurgitated what he'd been told by Patterson and Gimlin.[7] Whatever happened in the creek bed, the one thing everyone agreed on was that Patterson and Gimlin first announced the existence of the film in Willow Creek, California, sometime late in the day of October 20, 1967.

With Patterson gone, it fell to Gimlin to carry on the story alone. As years passed, his retelling of the events opened the door to other interpretations. John Green interviewed him in 1992 and got essentially the same story I heard, but there were curious differences. In that telling, Gimlin caught two runaway horses, then tried to track the creature but "didn't have much luck. Then we decided it was getting late in the afternoon. . . . We wanted to get back and take plaster casts of the tracks and then go on into town to see if we had anything on film."

"So you cast the tracks the same day?" Green asked.

"Yes, we did," Gimlin replied. "In fact right that afternoon. By the time we got the tracks cast, it was getting late. It was almost dark by the time we got back down to the truck and got the horses fed and tied up. By the time we got into town at Al Hodgson's store, it was good and dark.

I imagine it was about 8:30 or 9 o'clock. Then we went on over to . . . *[reflecting]* . . . oh, whatever town that was to mail the film."

I found Green's question revealing. If one of Bigfoot's most famous proponents was unclear about what happened twenty-five years after the film appeared, it was reasonable to assume that Patterson's and Gimlin's story had never been vetted. A lot of water had passed under the bridge between the appearance of the film and my showing up on Gimlin's doorstep. He had probably described the circumstances surrounding the filming hundreds of times. Memories change, and human nature will inevitably embroider any story told once too often. Still, I found the discontinuities telling.

I found particularly odd Gimlin's mention of Patterson's being away from camp when he returned from his morning ride. The way he said it suggested that he was purposely leaving the door open to the interpretation that Patterson was hiding something from him.

In my book, rodeo riders and people who ride motorcycles with the likes of Evel Knievel are risk takers who crave attention. Gimlin had done both. When he told me he'd been a long-haul trucker and spent several months trekking solo across the Mojave Desert after the filming— both exquisitely solitary pursuits—a picture formed in my mind of an individual who'd wrestled life at both ends.

Just before leaving, I asked him how he felt about the notoriety he'd acquired from being Patterson's sidekick. "I'm not bitter," he said. "People will pick at you no matter what you say. There's a lot of barstool critics. But they aren't out there riding those hills."

5

THE KLAMATH KNOT

Here in Arcadia, dull human blood mingles with brilliant strains. . . .
Proudly antlered champions sing and tipple in the cafes, while on the
rooftops prophets perch, preening their iridescent wings. Cloven hooves,
pretty feet, furred paws, and fishskin sandals skim the golden dust.
Faith and Reason dance nude together, to the flute and tambourine.
They'll soon be wedded, bedded, merged, blessed with offspring.

—Alexander Eliot, *The Universal Myths*

I called Al Hodgson, the owner of the Willow Creek Variety Store in
Humboldt County, near where Bigfoot first appeared and Roger Patterson shot his film, and scheduled an interview. Willow Creek had become
the base camp for Bigfoot hunters over the years, and I hoped Hodgson
could provide me with insights missing from printed accounts.

Apart from meeting Hodgson, I had no agenda, other than an intense
curiosity to see the location where Patterson shot the film, and no good
reason to make the trip now, as it was winter and the road to the site was
closed. Looking back, I realize I'd heard the siren call that David Rains
Wallace describes so eloquently in his classic book *The Klamath Knot*. To
understand the mind of a Bigfooter, I needed to plunge into Bigfoot's natural habitat. Like Wallace, "I wondered if my motives for going into
wilderness might be more obscure, and more profound, than I had realized. While part of me was going into the mountains seeking the pleas-
ures of exercise, self-reliance, accomplishment, and natural history, it
seemed that another part was looking for things of which I had only a
vague conscious awareness, as though a remote mountain or desert re-

leases some innate human behavior, a kind of instinctive predilection for the mysterious."[1]

I spread out a map of the Six Rivers National Forest, which encompasses the Bluff Creek watershed; together with the adjacent Klamath National Forest, it covers nearly three million acres of backcountry and encompasses half a dozen or more mountain ranges, including the Siskiyous, the Marbles, the Red Buttes, the Salmon-Trinity Alps, and eight officially designated wilderness areas. The legend proclaimed it the "Galapagos of North America," an ecosystem dating back forty million years. It is one of the largest ancient forests left in the country, containing undisturbed climax stands of Ponderosa pine and Douglas fir, and Port Orford cedars that exist nowhere else. The tallest of these giants are said to host microstorms in their upper reaches in which bantam lightning bolts flash through tiny clouds stuck in the limbs.[2] The light beneath the big trees is green, the air a drifting haze of falling needles, spores, leaves, and feathers. Steep ridges cut through the landscape, covered with a jumble of vine maples, oxalis, salal, phantom orchids, sword ferns as tall as a man, and rhododendrons as big as a house.

The Klamath ecosystem is home to 281 species found nowhere else, including the Siskiyou Mountain salamander, Brewer's spruce, and the *Kalmiopsis leachiana,* a flowering plant endemic to the Siskiyou mountains, which once grew on an island in the Pacific Ocean.[3] The Humboldt marten, thought to be extinct, was recently discovered living in the Blue Creek watershed. Goshawks and owls hunt beneath the tree canopy. Under cover of darkness, silver-haired bats dart through the trees, and marbled murrelets ferry food to their young, nested on old-growth branches high above the ground. Below them roam blacktail deer, black bear, coyote, bobcat, Roosevelt elk, and an occasional mountain lion.

Bigfoot is not the only mystery here. Some lakes in the Trinity Alps are said to contain giant salamanders, called belly-whompers. A pioneer story tells of a traveler who stumbled on a small lake one early winter and saw something "dark and huge moving under the surface." He baited a hook with deer liver, tossed it out, and hauled in a giant lizardlike creature measuring eight feet, four inches long. Subsequently, scientists—including one of the world's foremost experts on snakes and lizards—have searched for these amphibians but come up empty-handed.

I headed south from Portland on a blustery day. Five hours later, Mount Shasta emerged in the distance, a white volcanic cone barely discernible against a gray sky, a foreshadowing of the country I had only read about. Shasta dominates the surrounding landscape. Often crowned by ethereal layers of lenticular clouds, the peak exudes mystery. Indians believe it's a bridge to the sky world, recalling the days when the cone spewed fire and ash. The ancient order of Rosicrucians believes it was the center of a land called Lemuria, a vast continent larger than North America, which sank beneath the Pacific twelve thousand years ago.[4]

New Agers embrace the mountain as a "power center." Occultists believe it sits atop the spiritual axis of the earth. The mountain is famous for reports of strange lights emanating from its slopes. UFOs are commonly reported in the vicinity, and one theory suggests the lights are spacecraft entering and exiting the mountain. Sightings of "hairy giants" in the vicinity are said to have occurred in the 1850s.

Snow appeared briefly as I crested the Siskiyou Pass but vanished during the long downhill run to California where, minutes after crossing the border, I turned onto the Klamath Highway, the route Patterson and Gimlin had followed thirty years before into the heart of Bigfoot country. The off-ramp had scarcely ended when the roadway descended without warning into a canyon, revealing the turbulent waters of the Klamath River rushing through a moonscape of granite cliffs and lava flows, diffused by a light fog. The forest suddenly vanished, leaving only scrub brush and scattered splinter pines growing at odd angles from angular stone surfaces glazed with a sheen of ocher and burnt umber. In film terms, it was a "smash cut," the kind of transition that leaves you breathless and wondering what the hell is happening.

Slowly the road climbed out of the gorge, revealing a rugged landscape with huge talus slopes, jagged peaks rising high above the timberline, and granite ridges soaring like the prows of gigantic ocean liners.

At Swillup Creek, China Point, and Schoolhouse Gulch, streams emanating from a thousand watersheds poured into the river, stoking its power as the road moved deeper into the Six Rivers Forest. I had entered the Klamath Knot. As one visitor put it, "Early explorers were stymied by these canyons. In 1828 Jedediah Smith and his party of fur trappers gave up in despair when they tried to follow the Klamath River upstream from its confluence with the Trinity River. The terrain was too rugged even for those mountain men, who had walked from Oregon to Los Angeles in search of beaver. They didn't find many beaver in Klamath Mountain rivers, which are generally too rocky and turbulent even for those ingenious rodents."[5]

The "knot" of basalt, feldspar, and marble stretched for miles, interrupted only occasionally by tiny settlements with buoyant names like Horse Creek, Happy Camp, Somes Bar, and Orleans—now looking sad and beleaguered. Weathered signs proclaimed the area a sportsman's paradise, but the fish are mostly gone and the game managed to the point where *wild* has lost its meaning.

Gaps in the underbrush revealed an occasional glimpse of an abandoned sawmill. Roadside clearings occupied by derelict motels and outbuildings appeared. Evidence of a once-flourishing Bigfoot trade were affixed to trees and old weathered boards: a sign depicting a cartoon Bigfoot holding a fishing pole, and that most ubiquitous of symbols, a big footprint, or, more often, several of them strung together to form a happy trail.

A sign for the Bluff Creek Campground appeared out of the mist, and I pulled into the parking lot. Despite the gloom and the pouring rain, I had to see the creek I'd read so much about. I walked to the edge of a narrow gorge where the stream, swollen with snowmelt, roared through a deep channel that passed under the highway, then crashed into the Klamath. The creek's roar mingled with wind gusts that tried to tip me over the edge. The sheer walls of the gorge were shrouded in fog. What little I could see of the country around appeared vertical as well: a series of cliffs staggered one atop the other disappearing up into the mist.

. . .

Bluff Creek once marked the division between the Karuk and Yurok peoples who inhabited the clearings and benches along the Klamath. The Yurok—dubbed the "Upriver People" by white settlers—believed they lived on an island, roughly circular, surrounded by ocean that rose and fell with an imperceptible rhythm on the primeval flood. They passed down stories of a character called the "world-maker," who had fashioned the sky after the pattern of a fishnet. If one paddled far out on the ocean to where the sky meets the water, it was possible to slip through underneath.[6]

Storytelling was the bedrock of both cultures. The Karuk men often stayed together in sweat houses where they made luck and hunting magic and decided about marriage and domestic affairs. The children were taught the important creation stories and the names of the rocks, the leaves, and the mountains, for each had its own spirit. They believed that all of nature possessed both feelings and consciousness.[7]

The Bluff Creek watershed is also the tribes' hunting ground and sacred area. On the slopes of a mountain in the center of the wilderness is a village, invisible to mortal eyes, that is the home of one of the oldest spirits. A smaller mountain, where the Indians still send their shamans to receive enlightenment and heal the sick, early settlers dismissively labeled Doctor Rock.

Native spirituality transcends the physical here and now in ways white people have never comprehended. The "healing spirit" they embraced was from the creation times, and their telling of creation stories was essential to release the healing medicines of the earth.[8] For these beliefs they were branded heathens.

In 1848 few Indians in Klamath country had ever seen a white man, but the next year gold was discovered there, and within a decade their society had been destroyed forever.[9] Entire villages were massacred by secret societies of settlers, and the Indians rose up against them. The army came in, put down the uprising, and herded the survivors to a reservation in the Hoopa Valley. Their languages and ceremonies were outlawed and hunting and gathering forbidden. Ceremonial regalia was confiscated, along with common everyday utensils, and shipped to the Smithsonian, relics of a Stone Age people.[10]

Bluff Creek lies only thirty miles as the crow flies from the town of Willow Creek, but for the uninitiated the drive can seem an eternity. Beginning where the small Indian outpost of Weitchpec perches high on a bluff overlooking the confluence of the Klamath and Trinity rivers, the highway suddenly takes refuge on the side of the Trinity River gorge, becoming, in the process, a one-lane road masquerading as two lanes, hanging on a rock face that drops straight down. In the raging storm I couldn't tell how far, but the opposite side of the canyon, glimpsed intermittently through the mist, appeared vertical, and I suspected a chasm below of mythic proportions.

On the inside lane, where there should have been a shoulder, there was none. Trucks materialized without warning around blind curves, leaving me awash in a hail of spray and gravel. The road slowly descended to the valley floor, where a sign marked the boundary of the Hoopa Valley Indian Reservation, a morose landscape of rusted trailers and abandoned houses.

Twenty minutes later I entered Willow Creek, population 1,050. In the center of town, posed on a pile of rocks at the junction of old Highway 96 and the Trinity Highway, in front of an abandoned tourist information booth, stands a tall wooden statue with a sign identifying it as a near-life-size rendition of a male Bigfoot, known in the native vernacular as Oh-Mah. The beast's shoulders and torso are massive and shapeless, with arms hanging almost to its knees. The nose looks surprisingly human above a distinctly simian upper lip, and the flattish head sports a pageboy haircut framing a low, protruding brow that hides the eyes.

I called Al Hodgson from a pay phone in front of Bob's Shopping Center, and he told me to stay put, he'd be right down. As I hung up I saw, in huge letters high on the facade of the adjacent building, the words

"Hodgson's Department Store": Al's place, the epicenter of Bigfoot gossip for four decades. I peered through the window. Carpenters were at work tearing it apart.

Al arrived, a slender, pleasant man in his mid-sixties, with pinched features and the subdued air of a clerk. A plush high-crowned hat perched on his head with the brim turned up in back gave him the look of a slightly worn Robin Hood. He explained that he'd leased his store to a clinic, and renovation had just started. We walked inside, where men were ripping beams from the ceiling with loud screeches and much splintering of wood. Al looked around for a few moments in silence. "We were here thirty-eight years," he said, looking at me like he half-expected an answer. His eyes softened, and he turned back to the destruction at hand. "Boy, they move fast. We just moved our stuff out yesterday." It looked like he needed a moment alone, so I beat a hasty retreat outside.[11]

When he rejoined me, I was staring at the Oh-Mah. "When that was first carved, it was probably the most photographed thing between Eureka and Redding," he said softly. "That was the same year as the Patterson film—that'd be the latter part of '67. A young man by the name of Jim McClarin was carving it just at that same time that Roger Patterson was taking his film. 'Course, that animal was a female, and this one here is not." He lowered his voice to a whisper. "McClarin told me there were certain things he would have changed if he had seen the film first." I asked what those might be, and he leaned a bit in my direction. "I don't know exactly, breasts maybe."

Al had donated his store's fixtures and memorabilia to the China Flat Museum, a rustic building located behind the Oh-Mah, and we wandered over to take a look. Inside, a merry group of seniors were busy reconfiguring Al's display cases and stitching a quilt with embroidered native wildflowers to be raffled off, they explained, during Bigfoot Daze. My puzzled reaction set the ladies laughing, and Al explained that they'd started the event to bring in tourist business. "One time we had a Ferris wheel and everything," he said. "There was three or four thousand people out there at midnight just walking the streets, hanging out."

Featured prominently near the museum entrance was an illuminated glass case containing five Bigfoot plaster casts. Until last week they'd been displayed in Al's store. He pointed out his three favorites, starting with the first one that got him hooked in 1961. "I was still skeptical then. I still have a bit of skepticism. But when Betty Allen and I found this one, it was a little bit different thing; we hadn't seen fresh tracks before."

I was surprised to learn that one of the casts was only a few years old, and sightings were still common. A lady had seen a Bigfoot recently at a place called Burnt Ranch, just east of town. "She told me she was in the back seat of a car, and the people up front driving were busy talking," Al said. "She happened to look up this little canyon, and there one was standing right in there. Well now, did she or did she not see one? I have no reason to doubt her. She was mad, too. She said, 'I told 'em I saw Bigfoot and they wouldn't go back!'"

He first heard about big footprints in the area right after returning from the service. "I remember my brother saying we ought to go over and help catch that ape that people were talking about, but I wasn't interested. But, later, other people told me they'd seen tracks back then, too, so this puts an entirely different slant on it."

I asked about Jerry Crew, and Al said he had died the year before. He characterized him as deeply religious but high-strung. Crew might have got taken in, he said, but he wasn't the type to lie. He knew Green and Dahinden, too. Green was a fixture at Bigfoot Daze for a few years, he said. "Some of these people I've run into I don't trust too much, but John Green I trust implicitly. I don't think he stretches the truth at all."

Al took Polaroids of the casts in their new home, and I took a few shots of him, and the ladies ribbed him about it. We called it quits and made plans to meet again before I left town. Outside, it was nearly dark, and the Oh-Mah, backlit by a streetlamp, metamorphosed into a silhouette as Al disappeared into the rain.

I walked into the Willow Creek Motel and found a huge plaster footprint on the counter. Through a door I could see the motel family sprawled in front of a television. A woman appeared when I rang the bell and slid me a registration card. I asked if the cast was from an actual track. "I don't really know," she replied. "Our son got that at a garage sale a few years back. Cost him five bucks."

The heater in my unit had two settings, off and tropical. What looked like junk-store furniture—including the television—was probably new in the fifties. Fiddling with the flecks of color on the TV screen, I realized a lot of Bigfoot hunters had probably stayed in the same room, sitting at the dinette table cleaning their weapons, the air pungent with the smell of bore oil and damp wool. How many, I wondered, believed in the beast because of casts like the one on the counter? Plaster Bigfoot tracks look cartoonish, but they do represent an imprint left by something. To actually see an animal's print in the ground can be startling. The few times I've seen tracks in the wild were cause for all present to gather round and envision the unseen creature.

On a film shoot in Mexico years ago, Arriflex camera in hand, filming a party of birdwatchers moving across a jungle stream in deep shadow, I suddenly glimpsed a flash of color in the bankside mud. It was a quetzal feather (think Montezuma's headdress) four feet long and generating an spectrum of iridescent colors despite an almost total lack of daylight. Below the feather were two large paw prints. Our guide, Don Pedro, solemnly pronounced them jaguar—and very fresh. The birders exchanged furtive glances, and I found myself peering into the gloom anticipating a snarl, a sudden leap, and the flash of white fangs.

John Green recounted a similar experience at Bluff Creek with Bob Titmus while examining footprints that appeared to have been left by something enormously heavy:

> At some time just a few days before, something had been on that sandbar making those marks in the ground, and whatever had done it was as real as the tracks. If it couldn't have been a man, then there had to be an animal that was heavy almost beyond imagining, and that walked upright like a man. It was years before I could accept that proposition emotionally, but on a logi-

cal basis it was inescapable. Something had made the tracks, and it had to be either a man with a machine or an animal. Both explanations were ridiculous, but one of them had to be true.[12]

A few credentialed scientists have gone absolutely mad on the subject of giant hominid footprints. Notable among them was the late Grover Krantz, a physical anthropologist at Washington State University, who wrote a book titled *Big Footprints* that set forth an exhaustive case for the beast's existence. Much of Krantz's reasoning stemmed from his analysis of footprint casts. His book is a classic of the pseudoscience genre: a bewildering jumble of comparative photos and information, including charts of human and animal prints and body types, probable hominid phylogeny, contrasting striding gaits, overlapping support phases, shoulder widths, pressure mounding, and push-off mounds. Krantz claimed that the presence of what he concluded to be dermal ridges on several casts he inspected—the patterns of fine parallel ridges like those of human fingerprints and handprints—were proof of Bigfoot's corporeal existence. He went so far as to deliver a paper at an international biology conference proposing that the plaster casts of two such footprints he had examined warranted assigning Bigfoot a scientific name.[13]

Reports of giant footprints in North America have been found in journals, books, and newspapers dating from the early 1800s, predominantly on the West Coast. The characteristics of the tracks reported through the years are remarkably consistent: they are rarely larger than eighteen inches long and nine inches wide and seldom smaller than eleven by six.[14]

This historical similarity can support opposing hypotheses. To those inclined to believe in Bigfoot, it lends the prints an air of credibility, evidence of a species with normal variations for size, gender and age; for non-Bigfooters, such uniformity suggests the work of hoaxers who adhere to the familiar to ensure their handiwork is not discounted out of hand. Too large a track would suggest an animal too big to escape detection over the millennia, and too small a print would lack the desired shock and awe.

The footprints of exotic animals (Bigfooter books teem with examples) are strange-looking indeed, but they possess an unmistakably lifelike quality. Not so with Bigfoot prints. Even Ivan Sanderson—who deduced that a 15 ¾-inch-long Bigfoot track translated to a size 21 shoe, but thirteen sizes wider than a EEE—admitted that they looked "a bit ridiculous." Photographs of Bigfoot, he wrote, have shown that "they walk with their feet pointing straight forward," not turned out as most humans do. All in all, he could explain the tracks only by saying that certain characteristics of the giant prints "are definitely not typically human. . . . [They] simply do not fit into a pattern."[15]

. . .

I turned off the TV and made a note to take photos of the Oh-Mah statue. Oh-Mah being a name well known to Bigfooters (likely because of the statue's longtime notoriety), prior to the trip I'd done some research trying to pin down its origin. As with so much Bigfoot lore, the facts were elusive. Various sources claimed the word was of either Yurok or Hupa origin (the Hupa tribe being the historical inhabitants of the Trinity River area south of Bluff Creek).

I e-mailed Ray Crowe, director of the International Bigfoot Society, and asked him about Oh-Mah. He replied that the word came from the Hupa. "That's their specific word for Wild man of the Forest. Each tribe around the [Pacific Northwest] anyway, has its own particular word for Bigfoot. As with the Yakima [tribe], calling it a Sealitik, or the Coleville a Skanican. Generally [the Bigfoot] are referred to as Stick People, or literally stick equals tree, or forest . . . the forest people."[16]

Crowe's claim that every tribe in the Northwest had a name for Bigfoot sounded far-fetched. But after talking with several anthropologists and reviewing an ethnographic study of Native Americans published by the Smithsonian Institution, I found he was right. Nearly every tribe on the Northwest coast has stories of a giant hominid—often several. What these peoples described to researchers, however, was a mindbending assortment of creatures, differing both physically and behaviorally. None of them could remotely be mistaken for a real animal.

Stick People turned out to be a recurrent, generic term. A researcher named Elmendorf, who worked with the Twana tribe on the shores of the Hood Canal in Washington in the late 1930s, described the Stick People he was told about as giants who lived in the forests, had odorless bodies which enabled them to walk up to game and kill before the animal scented them, could climb vertical cliffs, and were usually invisible—characteristics similar to those of other humanoid spirits described by tribes on the West Coast.[17]

As for the name Oh-Mah, Peter Byrne told me it was Yurok in origin. He first heard the name in 1960 from Dorothy Alameda, a Yurok Native American he met on the Hoopa Reservation, who recounted for him how her grandfather had watched an Oh-Mah defecate in a stream. She also told him that her father saw one while riding a horse in the mountains east of Hoopa.[18]

The anthropologist Thomas Buckley, who studied the Klamath River tribes intimately for many years, identified several varieties of manlike creatures in the Yurok spiritual bestiary. One has a name that sounds like Oh-Mah and characteristics that led him to classify it as a devil. Buckley calls it a "not terribly important figure" in the tribe's spiritual hierarchy. "While generally humanoid, it is bigger, stronger, hairier, and meaner . . . than an ordinary human being and lives in areas considered uninhabitable by humans. . . . [It] is a monster insofar as it is not a human being, yet is too humanoid to be fully an animal."[19]

In the early 1970s Bigfoot became a subject of interest among Northwest anthropologists due largely to the efforts of John Green, who wrote two books pushing the idea that the oral tradition of Sasquatch-like spirits among the tribes of the northern Pacific Coast offered strong evidence that Bigfoot was a real animal. Believing that scientists were willfully ignoring the subject, he posed a challenge: "Anthropologists must have heard a good deal about the hairy giants of the mountains, at least in the role of characters in legends. I have seen two or three of these legends in books but to my knowledge they have never been assembled or studied as a group so that the area they cover could be determined and their content compared."[20]

Green's books caught the interest of Roderick Sprague, the editor of *Northwest Anthropological Research Notes,* a scholarly journal published by the University of Idaho. Sprague responded directly to Green's criticisms in an editorial and concluded with the announcement that "the editors of Northwest Anthropological Research Notes will welcome and view favorably for early publication any reasonably scientific paper dealing with the Sasquatch phenomenon."[21]

The anthropologist Wayne Suttles, an expert on Northwest Coast Indians, took up the challenge. In a study that analyzed a century's worth of field research involving the tribes where the term "Sasquatch" originated, he concluded that it was impossible to separate the "natural vs. supernatural in Coast Salish thought," but his conclusions were clear. "I am still unconvinced that there is a real animal there," he wrote in a paper published in 1972. "I must admit that I will be delighted if it turns out that there is, but for that very reason I must be critical in looking at what is said to be evidence."[22] Those who see such creatures, Suttles explained, be it in Tibet or British Columbia, are "simply allowing their memories to translate baffling or disturbing experiences into a language provided by their heritage of folklore."[23]

Oh-Mah, then, served the same function for the Indians along the Klamath River as Sasquatch did for the tribes in British Columbia or, for that matter, native peoples elsewhere: to help people achieve psychological balance and harmony with nature.[24] It was a living part of native spirituality, dwelling at the margins of their physical world, appearing in sweat houses or on vision quests, acting as a bogeyman to soak up fears and adolescent cravings, one among many beings of forest and water that provide, as the ethnologist Claude Lévi-Strauss put it, "a ready-to-hand means of conceptualizing relations between human groups."[25]

. . .

Outside the motel, rain fell in buckets. I phoned a man named Max Rowley, touted as a local historian. Max had worked for the Forest Service for thirty years. I figured if anybody had seen tracks, it would be him.

"I personally am not a believer of Bigfoot," he said in a tone suggesting he'd had such conversations way too many times. "I think it was a hoax from the beginning. It's just my personal thought, but when you get in this country here it's about fifty-fifty, people that believe and people that are nonbelievers. I was with a Forest Service crew in that very area, Bluff Creek, in the early 1950s, and we were surveying some of these roads that's in there today—six or seven years ahead of when they actually constructed the road—and we never saw any tracks or anything like that. And I was the guy that was out all the time in it, you know."[26]

Most of the nonbelievers in town like himself, he said, were convinced that Ray Wallace had started the whole thing. He characterized Wallace as a "real nice person," a successful businessman and a good citizen. But he knew some guys who'd come down from Washington State with Ray when he moved to Willow Creek, who had gone to high school with him, and they said faking tracks would be "a typical thing he would do." Max had heard one story: when the Wallace brothers were having problems with fuel thefts from their job site, they left the tracks hoping to scare the culprits away, and the trick just backfired. I asked him about footprints that were found occasionally after Wallace moved away in the early sixties, and he opined it was probably just somebody wanting to carry on the Bigfoot tradition, "maybe someone who didn't even know Ray."

I drove to a restaurant called Cinnabar Sam's, attached to a garage with a sign advertising "Bigfoot Rafting." I ordered dinner and sat in the corner. The place had been built to resemble an old mill, and the walls were covered with strange pioneer tools and old photographs of nameless people. The pictures were black and white and brown, and the walls were made of old gray wood. Outside the rain fell sideways.

The next day I planned to ask Al about Roger Patterson, Al being the first person Patterson had told about the filming. I walked across the highway and entered the Forks Lounge, pausing for a moment to get my bearings in the dim light. Except for two old fellows at the bar who turned in unison to stare, the place was empty. I gave them a nod, ordered a beer, and retreated to a booth near the pool table. The room was as dingy and damp as the motel. If the walls could talk, "Your Cheatin' Heart" would have been blasting from the jukebox, and the place would have been crammed with hirsute Bigfoot hunters moving through a swirl of cigarette smoke and ordering Budweisers and Jack Daniels with water back from tables awash in ashtrays and drinks. A map would have been spread out on the pool table, a stub of a finger tracing a likely plan of attack, a group in the corner passing around a 50 mm shell while those at the table near the cigarette machine admired a Bowie knife. Speculation on the beast's habits would have been the reigning topic of conversation—that and the question of how best to put down an eight-hundred-pound animal. For the most part, these were serious men. Your average weekend deer plunker didn't belong. Matter of fact, anyone who didn't believe in the animal had just as well keep it to himself.

The next morning, over pancakes, Al Hodgson told me that he had first met Roger Patterson when he dropped into his general store in the summer of 1964. He said he was on his way to Los Angeles to promote a toy he'd invented, and he'd heard Al had cast a Bigfoot print and wanted to check it out. In the course of the conversation, Roger revealed he had Hodgkin's disease, and Hodgson recalled telling his wife he didn't think they'd see him again.

Patterson visited Willow Creek a few more times, but Hodgson couldn't remember any specifics. He did remember giving Patterson a call a couple of weeks or so before he shot the film to tell him that tracks had appeared near Bluff Creek. Patterson told him he might come down. Hodgson didn't know if he had until Patterson called on the afternoon of October 20.

"It was about 6:30 on a Friday evening," he said. "My wife and I, we'd just closed the store and got home and I was out with the barbecue and she hollered at me, 'Roger wants to talk to you.' I got on the phone and he said, 'Al, I got a picture of the son-of-a-buck.' So I told my wife, 'Roger's got a picture of Bigfoot,' and she gave me the biggest horse laugh you ever heard, and we went down to the store and talked to him." Normally Roger was calm and soft-spoken, Hodgson said, but that day he "was high, walking on air."

Hodgson paraphrased what Patterson told him: he and Gimlin had surprised the animal in the creek, and he was lucky to get off his horse and get his camera. Patterson showed him a stirrup that his horse had fallen on, and Hodgson could see where it had been bent. Hodgson then called Syl McCoy at the Forest Service, and they all went to his office and talked there for a couple of hours. Relating all this, Al had hardly mentioned Gimlin, so I asked him if Gimlin had been there, and he said, yes, Bob was there but he didn't remember him saying two words. After breakfast, Hodgson and I stood on the porch overlooking the parking lot and watched it rain. I told him that come spring when the snow melted, I'd be back to visit the film site.

Before checking out of the motel, I made one more phone call. When Hodgson mentioned Syl McCoy, I recalled a photograph showing McCoy and Titmus together, holding up plaster casts the way hunters display their trophies. McCoy had died some years before, but his wife, Mary, still lived in the area. I called her, and we talked about old times. "Titmus was very enthusiastic about his belief in Bigfoot," she said. "He was the one who got Syl interested." She remembered that Syl and Titmus once climbed into a tree together and waited, hoping to get a photograph when Bigfoot walked by. When I asked about Ray Wallace, she said that Syl knew him, but "didn't hold him in much high opinion. He thought he was kind of a BS'er. Everybody thought he was a prankster. That's the kind of guy he was before he came out with all this Bigfoot stuff. I just don't think there's too much there in his stories."[27]

I asked if Syl said anything to her about the afternoon when Patterson came into town with the film. She said I should talk to her son David, who had been there. He happened to be in the room, and she put him on the phone. I recounted for him Hodgson's version of events. David said he was a teenager at the time, but his memory of that afternoon was vivid. He remembered Patterson describing how his horse had reared and he had fallen off and was lucky to grab his camera and get a shot.

"Patterson was so excited," he said. "That's what excited us. His talk. My immediate impression was, this guy's tellin' the truth. And there was so many fakes goin' around that I was skeptical all the time."

"Fake footprints?"

"That's right."

He remembered Patterson holding a small round metal can with the exposed film in it. "He was real nervous about gettin' it developed right away before something happened to it," he said. "And from [Willow Creek] he drove to Eureka." I asked if maybe he was mistaken about Patterson's not having yet been to the airport. He said no. "They came from Bluff Creek and were on their way to go over the hill. They had it right there with 'em. In fact, it wasn't a real long meeting at all because [Patterson] wanted to get this film developed right now."

He thought for a moment. "You know what? When you talked about how you understood that Al Hodgson was there . . . I don't think Al was there originally when me and dad met with 'em. It might have been after [Patterson] came back that [he] met with Al. And I just remember . . . I might not have been there when they [all] went down to the Forest Service station and talked later like you said happened. I might have been home. Me and Dad were there sooner, 'cause Dad had his Forest Service uniform on, so I knew it was still work time. I just remember [Patterson] bein' so excited. I couldn't believe how excited he was. He just swept you away with his excitement!"

"Do you remember anything about Gimlin?"

"No."

"His partner?"

"Nope. I don't remember anything about him."

I pointed the truck west up the Trinity Highway toward the ocean, the route the cowboys said they had followed to the airport to ship the film for processing. The narrow, twisting road climbed steeply into the clouds. Within a few minutes I reached the Lord Ellis Summit of the Coast Range and crossed over the Mad River. Half an hour later I arrived at the junction of Highway 101 and turned north to follow the coastline toward home. Elapsed time from Willow Creek: fifty minutes. Had I turned south on 101, the Eureka airport was at least another ten minutes farther on. That makes a round trip from Willow Creek to the coast and back a minimum two-hour drive.

Al Hodgson told me that when he met with Patterson and Gimlin at six-thirty, they told him they had just delivered the film to the airport to be flown for processing. As they would have had to pass through Willow Creek to get there, that would have put them at the airport at five, five-thirty. Counting back from there, they would have passed through Willow Creek for the first time at about four-thirty, probably earlier. This jibed with David McCoy's recollection of the cowboys showing up at his father's Forest Service office, with a canister of film in hand, in the mid- to late afternoon.

In two interviews—at a conference at the University of British Columbia in 1978,[28] and talking with John Green in 1992—Gimlin said that because of all they did that day documenting the tracks after the filming, it was dark even before they left for town. At that time of year, according to Al Hodgson, in that neck of the woods it got dark at about seven o'clock. If Hodgson and McCoy were right—and they both seemed absolutely clear in their recollections—to reach Willow Creek in the late afternoon, the cowboys would have had to depart their Bluff Creek camp while the sun was high in the sky.

I didn't have a theory of what might really have happened up on Bluff Creek, or when. The one thing I was sure of was that Patterson's and Gimlin's story was a total fabrication.

An hour later I entered Redwood National Park. Fog had reduced visibility to the point that driving was dangerous. I pulled into a popular tourist stop called the Trees of Mystery and parked near the colossus of Paul Bunyan and Babe, his blue ox—ironically, the only other American mythical figure as famous as Bigfoot. I remembered visiting here as a kid and being embarrassed by a person masquerading as Paul hiding in the statue, pestering passersby with amplified questions. Today, all I could see was Paul's beard hanging out of the mist above me.

Inside the gift shop is an Indian museum, its walls covered with sepia-toned photographs of Native Americans, including an exhibit of the work of the photographer Edward S. Curtis. Curtis spent many years traveling among the local people and taking their pictures in circumstances he felt represented their true aboriginal ways. The label beside his picture reads: "Through sacrifice and dogged pursuit he was admitted to secret societies, instructed in ancient legends and entrusted with timeless truths." There were photographs of Indians with deer and fish, but no pictures—not even a mention—of Bigfoot.

At Crescent City, the highway swings east and drops into the Smith River Canyon, which drains the mountains north of Bluff Creek. As with the canyon of the Klamath, the landscape is composed of great slabs of rock. The canyon is narrower than the Klamath's, but bulky and muscular, like a power lifter on steroids. The gorge seems hewn from a single gigantic piece of granite: the walls are so steep, the boulders so monolithic, and the river currents so powerfully thick that the effect is both awe-inspiring and foreboding, as if the river were a moat anchored by huge ring rocks of the type used by zoos to keep the animals from getting at the public. The far side of the river might well be a fantasy land like Jurassic Park, where animals from deep in the human imagination came to life.

PART II

OBSESSION

6

MOUNTAIN DEVILS

There is a time in life when you just take a walk: And you walk in your
own landscape.

—Willem de Kooning, *Sketchbook: Three Americans*

The few people who have written about Roger Patterson have said little
of substance about him, other than to describe him as a promoter. John
Green, who rubbed up against him sporadically for six years, described
him as "plainly a man given to obsessions."[1] The assessment is apt. From
the information I gathered, the only thing more remarkable than
Patterson's shooting a film of Bigfoot would have been for him not to have
done so.

Roger was one of six children. All four of the Patterson boys were
tough, a trait they inherited from their father, Clarence Clayton, better
known as "C. C.," who was a boxing champion in the navy. C. C. grew
up on a cattle ranch in South Dakota homesteaded by his father, which
C. C. inherited. In the depth of the Depression, the government took possession of the ranch. Times were so tough that even the feds couldn't afford to feed the cattle, so they ran what they could over a cliff and shot
the rest—an act that rendered the Patterson clan homeless.

The family moved to the Methow Valley in Washington State, where
Roger was born in 1933. A nomadic period ensued as C. C., often away
from home, shuffled between jobs in the mining industry, moving the
family around the country for several years before settling on a hard-

scrabble ranch outside Yakima, Washington, in a valley filled with orchards, a stone's throw from the Yakima Indian Reservation.

C. C. built a bunkhouse on the property with a boxing ring in the middle and beds for the boys around the outside. He hung a sign over the door that read, "Smokers and boozers are losers—abstainers are gainers" and started them sparring. "You're gonna be two things in this world," he told them. "You're gonna be good fighters and you're gonna be saddle bronc riders." He bought them cowboy hats and boots, which they wore even to school. By the time Roger learned to walk, C. C. had turned his older brothers into prizefighters, matching them up against refugees from the Dust Bowl weeknights at a downtown Yakima ring.

When World War II erupted, Loren and Lester, the oldest boys, enlisted. C. C., age forty-eight, did the same, despite the fact he'd served in the navy in World War I. He opted out of the shore duty offered him, signed on as a chief machinist's mate, and shipped out to the Pacific. Five months after Pearl Harbor, his ship went to the bottom in the battle of the Coral Sea. Roger was nine years old.

By any standard, Roger Patterson was a remarkable kid, driven by an inner fire and possessing phenomenal physical strength and agility coupled with a strong creative streak. With his father dead and his brothers gone to war, he became resourceful early, working with his brother Glenn in the orchards to help support his mother and sisters. He picked up the guitar early and stuck with it. He learned to draw.

He was also exceptionally agile. When Loren returned from the service and saw his twelve-year-old brother do sixteen back handsprings in a row and a one-armed handstand atop a twenty-foot pole, he talked his brothers into forming a tumbling act like they'd seen at the Capitol Theatre in downtown Yakima, and for several years the Patterson boys staged tumbling exhibitions to earn extra money. "You could throw [Roger] out of a helicopter and he'd land on his feet," his brother Lester told me. "He was just a little man, but he was always the dominator."[2]

I spent an afternoon with Lester at his home in Washington State, a stone's throw from the Columbia River, across from the Hanford Nuclear Reservation, where Lester worked for forty years. Nowadays Lester—close to eighty—rents rodeo stock, runs a bulldogging school, and raises what he calls "four-wheel-drive" quarter horses that can stop on a dime. Watching Lester, short and whipsaw-tough like his youngest brother, race around his ranch kicking up a trail of dust on a three-wheeler was like watching Roger himself.

Lester showed me pictures of the acrobatic troupe, remarking on Roger's confidence and independence. He played high school football despite being only five foot three, and became notorious for doing one-arm pushups and pulling wheelies on a motorcycle in front of the school.

A friend, Bill Pearl, introduced him to body building. Pearl turned out to be a phenomenon, winning, in short order, the titles of Mr. America, Mr. Universe, and Mr. USA—the Arnold Schwarzenegger of his day, and proof that hailing from Yakima was no impediment to success. Roger, too, became obsessed with weight lifting, winning titles in his weight class, and built up his neck, biceps, and calves to a uniform eighteen inches around. Lester said he was "quite a showman" when it came to lifting weights. "People called him muscle-bound, but not to his face." He developed a passion for health food, eschewing meat for huge helpings of vegetables and carrot juice.

In the early fifties Roger enlisted in the army and was sent to Germany, where he became part of a tumbling act and toured Europe staging acrobatic exhibitions. A photo from the time shows him square-jawed and handsome, oozing confidence alongside his two partners, all dressed in satin costumes furnished by the U.S. Army.

Discharged in 1955, Roger returned to Yakima, joined his brothers on the rodeo circuit, and was soon making a name for himself riding bulls and saddle broncs. He bought a black Cadillac convertible (missing a fender) and drove his brothers to rodeos. Lester claims they made more money riding rough stock than they ever could picking apples.

Roger disdained fulltime work, jumping from one odd job to the next. He worked sporadically for his brother-in-law, Al DeAtley, who operated a paving business; he did some roofing, handled deliveries for a parts company, and sold manure to gardeners. Tapping his artistic streak, he made and sold drawings of rodeo scenes. Brimming with ideas, he would tackle virtually any kind of project, but always doing it his way and never staying with any one thing too long.

In his book *The Making of Bigfoot,* Greg Long compiled interviews with Roger's family, friends, and acquaintances. Together they paint a portrait of a short man who willed himself into being extra large, with "more guts than the law allows"; who dressed nice, combed his hair, and always wore a cowboy hat and boots. Several people called him a creative genius. A good friend observed that his "mind was always working" and that he "loved to talk." Another called him a "born entertainer" with "bright eyes," who enjoyed making people laugh. Others remembered him as cocky, like a bantam rooster, and domineering toward women—who were to be seen, not heard. Several people said he could be hardheaded and had quite a temper. A rodeo buddy recalled that he got "real upset" if somebody didn't believe what he was saying. His brother Glenn recalled him fondly as "an aggressive little guy that never backed down from nothing."[3]

In 1956 Roger married Patricia Mondor in the Tampico Grange Hall on the outskirts of Yakima. His passion for rodeo remained undiminished, but Patricia thought it too dangerous, and with a baby on the way, he began looking for a stable enterprise. Working in a shed behind his house, he built a two-wheeled cart designed to be pulled by a pair of long-haired goats. He made everything himself, working almost entirely without tools (which he couldn't afford). The craftsmanship and beauty of the cart amazed everyone who saw it. Roger parlayed the cart into a deal to build and operate several miniature wagons as a promotional gimmick for a meat-packing house. Lester recalled the miniature red stagecoach Roger built, perfect to the last detail, filled with children and pulled by a team of six black Shetland ponies.

Roger muddled along with the wagon-rental business for several years but never gave it his full attention. His interest was always taken up with the next project, the one just over the horizon. As Lester put it, "Roger was always looking for the unusual. Things that had never been tried."

Of all Roger's talents, Lester said, his most remarkable was a genius for inventing things. To illustrate his point, he led me to the corral and fired up a practice device Roger designed for team ropers: a metal frame with an electric motor, attached to a pair of wooden legs shaped like a cow's hindquarters that moved forward, then back, as a cow would kick, over and over—the object being to lasso the legs. Forty-five years later, Lester's students still use it. "He was the guy who could tell you how to build anything," Lester said. Roger also invented a toy he called a "roll-a-hoop," built along the lines of the hula hoop, and a device to support the limbs of heavily laden fruit trees that he christened the "prop lock." He put the name on a sign atop his minibus and drove around the Yakima Valley to pitch the device to orchardists.

The invention business being all expense and no income, Patricia became an expert at stretching a dollar. Despite the hard times, Roger was undaunted. Ideas came easily to him, and he talked them up incessantly, confident he'd soon find the one breakthrough every inventor dreams of. And so, at the height of the Christmas season 1959, he opened the December issue of *True* magazine and read "The Strange Story of America's Abominable Snowman."

To someone who had toured the world performing feats of strength and agility, and rode truck-size bulls that could turn on a dime and kill a man, the eye-catching paragraph in big type just below the title no doubt stood out: "Somewhere in the wilds of California there is a gigantic creature which walks on its hind legs, leaves huge human tracks, and is scaring hell out of everybody. What is it? Nobody knows—yet."

He took to the phone, calling people whose names appeared in the article and peppering them with questions. Pursuing the Indian connection noted in the article, he visited with friends on the Yakima reservation who told him about a race of hairy, wild people called Sehlatiks who had been cast out by the mountain tribes long ago but could still be found in the wilderness surrounding Spirit Lake in the shadow of nearby Mount St. Helens. Before long he was riding horses into the hills of southwestern Washington looking for Bigfoot.

For some time Roger had been experiencing fits of coughing, swellings, and fevers. Red patches appeared on his skin, accompanied by a deep, unrelenting itch. His doctor couldn't tell him what was wrong, but he'd recently watched his mother die of leukemia and suspected cancer might run in the family. When he started coughing up blood, he and Patricia knew it was serious. A clinic in Seattle finally delivered a diagnosis of Hodgkin's disease. The doctor told him he had only a year to live—two at the most.

Distrustful of traditional medicine, he intensified his already Spartan diet, increasing his intake of vegetables, downing huge quantities of carrot and grape juice, and gorging on vitamins. His strength continued to ebb, and his buff physique melted away. There were periods when he was robust and chipper one day, bedridden the next. Unable to work, he struggled to pay the rent and sank into depression. But as one year turned to two, the good days became more pronounced. The symptoms didn't disappear overnight but, inexplicably, he rebounded.

Roger rarely talked with Lester about that first brush with cancer. "I got it whipped," he once told him. Underneath, Lester could see he remained troubled. "I think that Rog got a different perspective on life, that life *is* precious. Before he was a wild man. He thought he could do anything. After that sickness he became more serious." Serious was not the half of it. The further I dug into Roger's story, the more I realized logical assumptions about the man didn't apply.

Diminished by his illness, Roger focused more and more on the idea of capitalizing on Bigfoot. Initially, he entertained the idea of capturing and displaying the animal, but after several fruitless trips in the wilderness, he began envisioning a book. As a business proposition, the idea of becoming the world expert on Bigfoot wasn't half bad. The beast had received national exposure—global, if you counted the yeti—so the controversy guaranteed publicity. And much of this international mystery had played out in California, relatively close to Yakima—an important factor for a cowboy on a budget.

Bernard Heuvelmans had faced the same situation as he contemplated advancing his yeti thesis: no one had come forward—scientist or expert of any sort—to explain it and develop a full picture of the animal. And this creature—if it existed—had to be truly extraordinary. In a way, the lack of firm reports made the idea doubly exciting: any animal wily enough to stay hidden this long must be totally unlike any other on the planet. From what Roger had read, it might even be the Missing Link.

There came a point when Patterson locked totally onto Bigfoot, probably some time in 1964. Evidence for the animal's existence, however, was resoundingly absent. Other than footprints—which proved nothing, actually—no physical proof had ever been found. Sorely in need of something to show around, he went looking in California, the scene of the reports in *True* that first caught his attention.

Patterson publicly acknowledged making only one trip to Bluff Creek, but he actually made several, the first shortly after his cancer went into remission.[4] On one occasion he hauled two mountain ponies to the area in his minibus. Another time he employed a dozen pack horses to haul in audio equipment and batteries, and played the amplified call of a distressed rabbit, hoping to lure Bigfoot into a trap (how he acquired such a recording is a matter of speculation). The one trip he did write about, ostensibly in 1964, resulted in the discovery of giant footprints. A cast he made from one of the tracks became the vital evidence he needed to solidify his credentials as a Bigfoot expert.

In his search for money to support the hunt, Lester recalled, Roger developed an investment routine to show to "rich guys" that included a film of him in Mexico darting a wild bull with a tranquilizer rifle, grabbing the stunned animal by the horns, and waltzing it before the camera, announcing this was how he would bring Bigfoot out of the woods.[5] Legend has it that in his search for money Patterson approached the trucking magnate J. B. Hunt and the cowboy star Roy Rogers. Whether this was true or not, one person close to Patterson told me, "One of the most impressive things [about Roger] was calling people. He had more guts than a government mule."[6]

Living hand to mouth as he did, with no obvious means of support, where Patterson found the money to pay for his trips is puzzling. The likely source was his brother-in-law Al DeAtley, whose paving business was prospering. Patterson was especially close to his sister Iva, Al's wife, and she may have made sure her brother was provided for.[7] It is also possible that Al, a shrewd businessman, may have seen—like P. T. Barnum—the potential to capitalize on Bigfoot through the efforts of his multitalented brother-in-law. Judging by the remarkable lengths Patterson went to sell Bigfoot—and the ultimate payoff—it was a good bet.

Although Patterson became famous for the film he made at Bluff Creek, he centered most of his investigation on Mount St. Helens in Washington State. Growing up with the peak sitting on the horizon like a part of the neighborhood, then learning that it had a history of giant humanoids, he may have felt that something more than coincidence was at work. Perhaps fate had put him in Yakima.

Mount St. Helens has been called the Fujiyama of America. It is the youngest of the nine major peaks in the Cascade Range, which stretches from California to Canada. In Patterson's day, its majestic dome emerged from a solid cloak of green to a height of 9,677 feet. People often remarked that on a clear winter day, the mountain resembled a freshly made ice-cream cone.

From the right angle, the entire mountain could be seen mirrored in Spirit Lake, a deep-blue jewel that took its name from an autumn phenomenon in which human-size wisps of fog rise from the surface and whirl like dervishes. The Indians believed they were the demon spirits of departed chiefs angry about the coming of the white men. Spirit Lake didn't need demons to gussy it up, but something about the place, with its legends and otherworldly beauty, invited speculation that all was not as calm as it looked.

In 1847, the French-Canadian artist Paul Kane set out by canoe from Fort Vancouver, located across the Columbia River from present-day Portland, to travel downstream to the Pacific. He kept a journal in which he described camping on what is now called Sauvie Island and visiting with the Multnomah Indians who lived at the mouth of the Lewis River, which flows into the Columbia from headwaters high on the mountain. Kane painted a now-famous picture of Mount St. Helens belching fire, which he visualized from the Multnomahs' campfire tales. The Indians had many superstitions about the peak. Kane, curious for a closer look, asked them to guide him up the Lewis, but they refused. Near the head-waters, they said, lived the Skookums, a race of giant, hairy cannibals, and the river and its surrounding forest were forbidden territory; no tribes ventured up there.[8]

Settlers heard the tales and passed them on. As the population there-abouts grew, reports of giant, vaguely human creatures living near the mountain began creeping into newspapers. The most famous report oc-curred in 1924, when a group of miners working a deep canyon on the mountain's eastern flank claimed they were attacked at night by giant apes who rained boulders on their cabin. The miners' story—borne out by the discovery of huge footprints—sparked pandemonium. Law officers and vigilantes stormed the mountain armed to the teeth.

Years later, a retired Forest Service supervisor, Harry White, recalled getting a call from a fellow ranger who found himself caught in the mid-dle of the excitement. "Why, Harry," the ranger shouted through a tinny connection, "the woods is full of people. They're armed with rifles and shotguns and pistols, and they're shooting at anything that moves. I'm afraid that somebody is going to get hurt!"[9] No apes were found, but the canyon became "Ape Canyon," and the story was enshrined in the mountain's official Forest Service history.

Patterson located and interviewed Fred Beck, one of the miners in-volved in the incident, and began exploring the mountain on horseback. He was particularly taken with Ape Canyon. Viewed from either end, the long, deep fissure—once known as Thousand-Foot Canyon—ex-udes mystery. In the mid-sixties it was an easy and spectacular ride across the mountain's southern shoulder, passing through patches of wild strawberries, twisted bonsai pines, blue lupines, and red Indian paint-brush, to the canyon's lip, where the walls were vertical and a stream flowed through the middle like a scene from Shangri-la.

Before the mountain's catastrophic eruption in 1980, much of it was ringed by a single, narrow road that connected a handful of tiny communities. Everyone in the area came to know the little cowboy on the lookout for Bigfoot, including several grizzled forest veterans who claimed to have seen either the beast or footprints or knew someone who had.

Early in his investigation, Patterson was encouraged by an incident involving a couple fishing on the Lewis River, who reported to the sheriff that they had seen a giant, beige-colored creature walking on the bank. A logger named Charlie Erion, who owned a farm on the river, went to the site with his son and found hundreds of huge humanlike tracks. The couple's story and Erion's discovery made the newspapers. Patterson showed up at Erion's place a few weeks later and peppered him with questions. Erion told him of several other reports.[10] They became friends, and Patterson took to using Erion's place as a way station on his journeys to and from the mountain, occasionally staying overnight.

By 1965, Patterson's financial situation was such that he desperately needed to finish the book. A friend drove him to British Columbia, where he met John Green for the first time and obtained permission to reprint Green's Sasquatch articles. (Green described him during that visit as looking "skinny and very frail." He learned later that Patterson had just finished a session of cobalt radiation treatments.)

As he neared completion of the manuscript, giant tracks appeared again on Charlie Erion's farm. Patterson cast one in plaster and put a photo of it in the book with a description of the scene: "We could see where the creature had come down from the foothills, stepped over a four-foot fence, walked across the plowed field, stepped over a five-foot gate into an alfalfa field. Eventually, it had come back over the gate, ate some berries, then returned to the hills. Charlie said that his dogs had barked [that night] and that the cattle had all come up close to the ranch out-buildings."[11]

Thirty-five years later, I asked Erion's son, Jim, about the first tracks that had appeared on the riverbank in 1963.[12] "I was a go-gettin' little kid back then," he said. "And I bailed off that boat, and sure as hell, there they were, and, boy—you should've heard this from my father. He said it was like a cartoon character: My hair stood straight up, my eyes got great big, and I just went, 'Holy shit.'"

"Could they have been bear tracks?"

"Absolutely not. There were distinctly five toes, they were very clear."

His dad didn't report the second set of tracks to the press because the neighbors had razzed him about the first incident, but Jim clearly remembered Patterson's showing up and casting them. He remarked several times on Patterson's sincerity. "He seemed to take everything in a kind of scientific matter," he said. "As intent as he was into [Bigfoot], I just can't see his faking it."

I remembered John Green's maxim that people who see evidence time and again are suspect, which made me think that maybe Charlie had planted the tracks. Then again, with Patterson being locally famous as a Bigfoot hunter and a friend of Charlie's, if you wanted to create a stir, what better way than to plant a string of footprints on Erion's property?[13] Possibly Patterson made them himself, or had some hand in it.

In any case, discovery of the tracks coincided neatly with the book's release. Patterson called them "new evidence of the existence of the Giant Hairy Ape around the Mt. St. Helens area in Washington state."[14] He took the manuscript to a small publishing company in Yakima, who printed the book on credit. The printer and a local entrepreneur who had taken a liking to Patterson purchased an ad for the book in the Boy Scout magazine *Boys' Life*. Orders flooded in. Patterson kept the cash but didn't pay his printing bill, and the printer refused to print anything more until he settled. Patterson's go-for-broke mentality had finally brought him to a dead end.

In the spring of 1966, Patterson ran into a high school acquaintance named Glen Koelling, fresh out of the navy. Patterson sold him on investing in the hunt for Bigfoot. Intrigued by Patterson's entrepreneurial energy and touched by his circumstances, Koelling assumed the printing debt and paid him cash for the book's copyright. They formed a partnership called Trail Blazer Research, and Koelling opened an office for the enterprise in downtown Yakima.

Over the next few months, Koelling spent thousands of dollars and all his time promoting the book. Sales skyrocketed, but as the weeks rolled on, he found it impossible to get Patterson's attention. "Roger's number one interest was Bigfoot," Koelling told me. "He was so intense talking about it, sometimes he'd just wear you out." He recalled book signings where Patterson got caught up talking with a purchaser about Bigfoot and lost track of time. Other buyers waiting in line, with books in hand to be autographed, eventually just put them down and left.[15]

Unbeknownst to Koelling, however, Patterson was busily promoting the book in his own way. The releases of both editions of the book were preceded by reports of tracks and sightings in the Yakima paper and, on at least one occasion, the local TV news. One report involved a group of orchard workers who watched a Bigfoot cross a busy road during a shift change. Several days later, a high school kid encountered a "huge man covered with silvery white hair" on a road during a lightning storm. According to his longtime friend John Ballard, Patterson also blanketed Yakima with Bigfoot posters. "Roger put them up, or he asked people to put them up," Ballard said. "I knew they were his posters because I saw them in his house one day."[16]

Faking Bigfoot tracks or running across a road in an ape costume is harmless fun. But the particulars of Patterson's story raise questions about his mental health. To produce a facsimile of what a Bigfoot might sound like, he recorded himself screaming on audiotape while sitting in the bell tower of a church with a bucket over his head. On another occasion, he had an enormous metal cage fabricated and hoisted into a tree as a Bigfoot lookout. Witnesses recalled him sitting in the cage at night blasting his recorded Bigfoot screams into the dark, hoping to attract the beast.

Patterson's friends didn't see his actions as any of their business. When Ballard was asked if he ever thought maybe Patterson was faking Bigfoot sightings, he replied, "Oh, yeah. . . . [Roger] was always so enthused about Bigfoot when I talked to him . . . I didn't want to ask him. . . . It was something he was doing that he could make some money on, more power to him. . . . If people are that gullible, and he was that cunning, let him have that money."[17]

About the time Koelling moved to Yakima, another of Patterson's high school friends, Jerry Merritt, moved back to town from Los Angeles, where he had been a successful rockabilly musician. Patterson had kept in touch and traveled to LA to see him. Merritt bought a house near him and installed a recording studio, and they hung out, played music together, and schemed ways "to make money."[18]

Patterson envisioned a Hollywood-type film about Bigfoot. Merritt—who knew show business, a little about TV, and some Hollywood agents and lawyers—encouraged him. Merritt connected Patterson with a couple whose son played in a band Merritt managed, and they loaned him seven hundred dollars. The contract stated the money was for: "expenses in connection with filming *Bigfoot—America's Adominable [sic] Snowman.*"

Meanwhile, back at Trail Blazer Research, Koelling was struggling with flat book sales and a cash bind stemming from a membership gimmick Patterson had included in the book's first edition, in which he solicited subscriptions to a quarterly newsletter. Orders poured in from kids who had read about the club in *Boys' Life.* Patterson had pocketed the money but ignored the newsletter. Koelling had to refund thousands of dollars.

"Roger had no concept of money or how to handle it. Or operating a business," Koelling said, sounding exasperated. "Roger's thing was Bigfoot, pure and simple. "He didn't understand paying bills if he could go look for Bigfoot. He wanted to get an expedition up and go after [it]. I mean, spend time out in the fields. . . . And he needed horses, he needed trailers, he needed cameras, he needed wranglers, you know, food and all the other things that went with it."

When Koelling began receiving bills for camera equipment and other expensive items Patterson had bought without Koelling's knowledge, he realized he was in deep water. Unbeknownst to him, Patterson had begun shooting his film and was scrambling to pull it off however he could.

I learned of Patterson's first film from the Bigfoot archivist Larry Lund, who showed me a photograph of six men mounted on horses, who turned out to be the cast. I recognized Patterson and, after a closer look, Gimlin, wearing a long dark wig and a solemn expression, playing the part of an Indian. Patterson directed the shooting in the hills near his home, using a cameraman from the local TV station. "We just dug up a dollar here and a dollar there," Merritt said. "Whatever Roger could scrape up."[19]

The plot involved a hunt for Bigfoot. Patterson staged horse stunts and a campfire scene with Merritt playing the harmonica, filmed for three days, and then ran out of money. Desperate, he and Merritt drove to Hollywood and made a pitch to a showbiz type of Merritt's acquaintance, pleading for cash to finish the film, but they struck out. "He was very sick at this time," Koelling said, "and he was running panicky a little bit because of his illness as far as getting everything done that he wanted to get done. . . . There was a desperation in his voice."[20]

Friends noticed burns on Patterson's neck that they assumed were from radiation treatments, though he rarely talked about it. They watched worriedly as he slugged down oats and raisins mixed with alfalfa tablets and honey, and winced when he undertook a long regimen of enemas. Outwardly he seemed to take the "blood thing" as just one more challenge and maintained he could beat it. But time was not on his side—and he knew it. Green and Dahinden visited him at his home just after the new year. Green noted that he seemed anxious, talking incessantly about the Yakima sightings and his inventions.

The book had stopped selling, and Koelling's life savings were gone. In the spring of 1967 he threw in the towel, rejoined the navy, and left Yakima forever. Two months later, Patterson emerged from Willow Creek with his famous film in hand.

In *The Making of Bigfoot,* Greg Long identifies the man he believes wore the suit in Patterson's film as a friend of Patterson's named Bob Heironimus. Long's interviews with Heironimus and others close to Patterson make a persuasive case that the west Yakima crowd was well aware of Patterson's Bigfoot shenanigans, and—though times and locations are vague—Heironimus did, in fact, wear an ape suit at Patterson's behest. It's impossible to be certain that Heironimus is telling the truth, but I think Long may have it right.

Heironimus claims that Gimlin (on Patterson's behalf) offered him a thousand dollars to drive to Bluff Creek, meet up with him and Patterson, don the suit, walk in front of the camera at Patterson's command, and then return to Yakima, dropping the film in the mail on the way (for processing at a film lab, probably somewhere in California). Long also offers a plausible date for when the film was shot: several weeks, perhaps as long as a month or more, before the October 20 date claimed by Patterson. Heironimus also described features of the ape suit that only someone who had worn such a costume could know.[21] It all adds up. After all, *someone* was in the suit, and Patterson's clock was ticking. The making of the Bluff Creek film was the act of a desperate man.

I drove west through Yakima toward a small line that bled off the edge of the county map, labeled Cottonwood Canyon Road. The city disappeared, replaced by rolling hills of brilliant golden brown, peppered with ranchettes. I wanted to find the corral where the Patterson boys had practiced rodeo, but I had no idea where to look. Perhaps it was gone. Knocking on doors, I located an old gentleman named Gerald in a house overlooking the canyon.

Gerald had gone to school with the Patterson boys and later rodeoed with them. He vividly recalled the family's losing their father. "God, I'll never forget that," he said. "When you know somebody, and they're gone, and then you get word . . . boy! Left their mom with all those kids. Jesus. It was a tough go.[22]

"After the war, all the Patterson boys were into rodeo," he said. He pointed to a rundown corral in the distance, along the main road. "Right there. The old Reed Thompson place. That's where we rode the horses, 'cause it had bucking chutes. Course, there were no houses around then. This was all country. Doc Rider, he used to have five or six horses out here, and Patterson would break 'em and work with 'em. You got to be on the ball to do that. He was a little short guy but, man, he was strong."

"Tough?"

"Oh, God. Nobody messed with him."

"Didn't drink or smoke or any of that?"

"No. He didn't believe in it. He trained and ate good. Once in a while he might have a beer, but that's it. A lot of times he'd go in a restaurant and order a hamburger without the hamburger."

Patterson and Gimlin occasionally borrowed Gerald's stock truck to take their horses into the hills to look for Bigfoot. "God, he spent a lot of time on that damn thing," he said. "He was really into it.

"Roger always had time for you. That was one thing that helped him. He had a lot of friends. Course, in those days, everybody was wantin' to see him catch somethin'. I always told him, I said, 'God, get out and find that damn thing. If you find that thing, I mean, you got it.'" Gerald's eyes grew misty. "He had a real good funeral. A lot of people there." He stared at the corral for a while. "Sometimes I walk down there and just think . . . about the good times. . . . I always wanted to see him make it because, you know, I'll never forget his dad in that damn war."

Shadows were lengthening when I stopped at the tottering old corral where the Patterson boys had practiced long ago. The roof over the hay shed had collapsed, and weeds stood waist-high in the arena. A column of gnats spiraled in a shaft of sunlight. But for a snuff can poking from the dirt and a plastic bag caught on a rusted piece of barbed wire, it looked like a scene on a postcard.

The Patterson boys materialized across the way, shoving Buggylight into a chute; the horse was banging the rails and blowing, its coat white with sweat, Patterson balancing himself catlike on the fence, poised to ease himself down, the horse anxiously twisting, trying to spot the next antagonist on its back.

René Dahinden told me he "probably talked as much to Patterson as anybody," and, in his opinion, Patterson saw Bigfoot as "just one more money tree to be shook."[23] But, he added, "When it came to Sasquatch, I never found him to exaggerate or lie or anything else." Therein lies the nexus of the Bigfooter conundrum: an inexplicable blindness to the vagaries of the *human* animal, a state of mind that can only be explained by the adage that people believe what they want.

The same myopic thinking has obscured Ray Wallace's involvement with the events that begat Bigfoot at Bluff Creek in 1958. With the exception of Ivan Sanderson—who understood the value of never qualifying a colorful source, and characterized him as "hard-boiled and pragmatic"—everyone who ever met Wallace during that period described him as a hoaxer.

When I first seriously became interested in Bigfoot, I visited Wallace at his home in the small logging community of Toledo, near Mount St. Helens. He turned out to be a large, impish man in his seventies with a shock of white hair and a twinkle in his eye. At my mention of Bluff Creek, his eyes lit up. "Hey," he boomed, "the Indians down there know more about Bigfoot than anybody. They called them Tee See At Coe; that stood for 'giant people.'"

Before long I knew how best to observe a Bigfoot, their favorite food, and what to beware of. "Don't make any noise to where the Bigfoots'll hear ya," he cautioned, "or you'll get killed. They can throw rocks like a bullet and kill deer and elk three hundred feet away on the run."

Wallace knew his stuff. The Te See At Coes he spoke of were the same spirits known to the Puget Sound Indians that Wayne Suttles identified in his cultural study of the Sasquatch. Beyond that anthropological tidbit, however, things got strange. Wallace informed me that, shortly after moving to Humboldt County, he'd recorded the sound of a young Bigfoot screaming in a cave. He charged into the living room, grabbed an old record album, and played me a song titled "Bigfoot," a vocal number rendered in a serviceable country baritone (by someone other than Wallace) in which the screams he'd recorded were incorporated into the chorus. The album cover showed a Bigfoot and a cougar posed together on a log. He handed me an "affidavit" attesting the screams had been analyzed on a K-101 Dektor Counterintelligence and Security, Inc., Psychological Stress Evaluator. He mentioned that he'd put the screams (in what form I didn't ask) on three thousand 45 rpm records and sold them at Hodgson's variety store in Willow Creek during Bigfoot Daze (probably at the height of the initial frenzy, around 1960).

When I mentioned Patterson, he swiped at the air as if to dispel a bad odor. "Shit, old Patterson, he didn't have nothing, man," he said contemptuously. "He didn't have five cents—only a line of gab. He went down there to Bluff Creek three or four times and never seen a doggone thing and he came back and he was questioning me and a pumping me.... He didn't even have a camera. He wanted to borrow my camera. And I said, 'Hey! That camera's worth ten thousand dollars. Have you got ten thousand dollars to leave here case Bigfoot tears it up?'"

He hobbled into the back room and reappeared with some cases, which he threw open to reveal an old 16 mm sound camera. I knew the camera from my days as a news photographer—an Auricon CineVoice, worth a substantial amount of money in its day. "I had that made to order in 1953," he said. He added almost in passing that he'd shot film of a Bigfoot. At the time I thought he was pulling my leg, but several years after the interview, I watched a film with the Bigfoot archivist Larry Lund. Lund said he'd acquired the film from Wallace, who told him he shot it in 1957. It turned out to be a series of lingering shots, taken from a distance, of a Bigfoot—looking suspiciously like the creature on the album cover—wading ankle-deep in a bog grabbing fish. What Wallace did with the film, if anything, I never discovered.

Then he started talking about flying saucers.

In the years since I interviewed Wallace, I've often wondered how a person so completely nuts in one regard could also carry on a successful business, contribute positively (and generously) to his community—he got kudos in Willow Creek as a Little League coach—and be, in so many other respects, normal. Wallace was officially outed as the original Bluff Creek hoaxer after his death in 2002, when his nephew described to a newspaper reporter how Ray—aided by his brother Wilbur, also known as Shorty—faked the footprints using a set of carved wooden feet with which the nephew posed for a photograph.[24]

It could almost be said that fake footprints were in Wallace's blood.

He was six years old and living near Mount St. Helens in 1924 when the "mountain ape" panic hit and armed posses charged into the forest—big news in an area that didn't get much. His boyhood friend was another joker named Rant Mullens. Wallace mentioned Mullens to me (in a story about some kind of falling-out involving a pair of fake Bigfoot feet), but the story made no more sense to me at the time than his rambling on about a four-hundred pound guy named Lard Smith who never got out of his pickup because he couldn't. Later, in a newspaper archive, I found an interview given by Mullens shortly before his death, in which he recounted how, as a boy, he and an uncle had carved huge feet out of wood and used them to make tracks on the mountain to keep the St. Helens ape legend alive. He also loaned them out. He said the feet had been used over the years from the wilderness of British Columbia to the Mount Shasta area of Northern California.

"I have to laugh," he told the reporter. "All these experts are saying, 'The prints show Bigfoot was 900 pounds,' or something. These higher educated guys are dumber than anybody. I was born and raised in these mountains. I've worked these woods all my life and I've never seen a damned thing I didn't understand. Anybody who'd believe in that Bigfoot stuff'd have to be pretty damned hollow between the ears."[25]

Apparently, Wallace and Mullens, indoctrinated as boys into the culture of "mountain apes," had done their best to keep the joke alive. Patterson reported in his book that when he visited Wallace, Wallace played him the Bigfoot screams. But he wrote nothing about any film. I can't imagine that Wallace didn't tell him about it; there's a good chance he projected the film for him.

So Patterson wasn't the first to shoot film of a Bigfoot—or replicate what the beast might sound like. At the very least, Ray Wallace left Roger Patterson considerable food for thought.

.   .   .

Back in Cottonwood Canyon, Buggylight rises upward in slow-motion, all four feet leaving the ground, Patterson's spurs raking the bronc's shoulders, his free hand high in the air. HOOF STRIKES mingle with SHOUTS from his buddies ringing the corral. Their dying friend had drawn the toughest ride there was, and if he'd set his mind on Bigfoot, what the hell. The damn thing might actually exist, so let's give ol' Rog some juice. As for naysayers, any information about Bigfoot was relative, "facts" being simply somebody else's opinion. This camp had their own opinions about the beast, the bottom line being, unless you're an outdoors person you wouldn't understand—there's lots of country out there where no one ever goes.

Magic hour turned the canyon to gold. I snapped some pictures and headed toward town, curious to see where Patterson grew up. In the forties, the Wide Hollow area of Yakima, where the Pattersons lived, was country. Today it's the suburbs, with spacious avenues leading to giant intersections bristling with gas stations and mini-malls. The Patterson home, a gray house at the corner of Seventy-second and Tieton Drive, was gone. Near as I could figure, the lot where it once stood now boasts a Starbucks.

I bought a latte and watched the traffic roar by, wondering what Patterson would think of all this progress. He would probably have followed his brother Lester's cue and bought a place in the country. And some horses. Definitely horses.

I thought about Lester at his ranch in the low, dusty hills near the Hanford reach. After an hour of reminiscing with me about his brother, he'd gone silent, watching a dust devil spin across his bulldogging corral. Roger had been a spark in his life, but he'd been gone for thirty years. I had no idea whether Lester believed in Bigfoot or not, but it didn't make any difference. I was simply curious about his brother's obsession. Maybe Lester sensed this. "There was one incredible thing about Roger that always amazed me," he said firmly. "His eyes. They were like deep, deep pools of water. You could look in his eyes and there was absolutely no fear of anything."

7

SHOW TIME

"The time has come," the Walrus said,
"To talk of many things:
 Of shoes—and ships—and sealing-wax—
 Of cabbages—and kings—
 And why the sea is boiling hot—
 And whether pigs have wings."

—Lewis Carroll, *Through the Looking Glass*

In the fall of 1967, René Dahinden stepped off a bus in Willow Creek into a driving rain, depressed and anxious after a fruitless week in San Francisco trying to persuade the newspapers there to buy photographs of Bigfoot tracks he'd taken the week before near Bluff Creek. "I got divorced that summer and I was really emotionally upset," he recalled when I interviewed him decades later at his home outside Vancouver, British Columbia. "That really hit my pride."[1]

The news he had just received from John Green in Canada couldn't have been worse—or more poorly timed. Not only had his obsession with the hairy ape-man torpedoed his marriage, but now, apparently, someone else had found the animal first. He trudged to the general store and frantically interrogated Al Hodgson to find out exactly what had happened, but all Hodgson could say was that Roger Patterson and Bob Gimlin had stopped there the previous afternoon and told him they'd surprised a Bigfoot in Bluff Creek. Patterson had managed to film the animal for several seconds before it disappeared into the forest, and he wasn't even sure if the film would turn out. The irony for Dahinden was that the very tracks he had just photographed probably belonged to the same animal Patterson saw.

Hodgson thought the cowboys might show up at the store again, but then the phone rang. It was Patterson calling from Orleans, two hours away, to say that he and Gimlin were on the Klamath Highway, heading home to Yakima. A storm had driven them from their camp, the road had washed out, and they had to leave while they could. They wouldn't be coming through Willow Creek. Dahinden wanted to drive to the site and check out the tracks, but Hodgson couldn't rustle up anyone willing to take a rig into the mountains during the first big storm of the season.

Patterson had apparently called a newspaper in Eureka and described what happened, and the story was on the wire. Ivan Sanderson phoned from New York to ask about it, and Hodgson told him what he knew.

Dahinden jumped on a bus, arrived in Portland the next morning, and flew from there to Yakima—his first airplane flight. The trip cost him $14.50 (he had saved the receipt all these years). Twenty-five minutes later, he was in Yakima. "We took a taxi to Al DeAtley's place. Patterson was there, and DeAtley and John Green. So we looked at the film and talked to Roger, and that was it. Then we hopped in Green's car and drove home."

"What did you think when you saw the film?"

"Other people ask me that," he said, "and, you know, looking back on it, the film was just like it came out of the camera. You see this little goddamn thing running across the screen—blurry, exactly as the people described it—Sasquatch."

Dahinden and Green convinced Patterson to screen the clip in Vancouver, where they had established relationships with the press and with scientists at the University of British Columbia. In the process they received some media attention themselves, as in the old days. But the media's focus had shifted. It wasn't about them anymore. And it wasn't long before the relationship between the two men began to change as well.

Green and Dahinden had always been ships passing in the night:

Green, a family man with a newspaper to run; Dahinden, suspicious and bull-headed, with no professional skills, who put Sasquatch before all else—including family. Green seized on the media buzz generated by the film clip to begin a book about his experiences hunting Sasquatch. Dahinden would, of course, be mentioned, but Green certainly didn't need his help to write it.

Dahinden had no such fallback. Anti-intellectual to the core, he had only one option—fieldwork. But what did that mean? The hunt for Bigfoot had never been a hunt in any common sense of the word. His experience on the Slick expedition had showed that baiting didn't work. Nor could the animal be scared out of the bush, no matter how many men were employed. And Bigfoot tracks—on the few occasions they appeared—led nowhere. No one was even sure if the animals were active during the day or the night.

Patterson's experience was no help at all. He had simply been in the right place at the right time, camera in hand. It had been pure luck, and Dahinden didn't feel that lucky. On balance, as far as Sasquatch hunting went, the future held nothing for the acerbic little Swiss, who feared he would be left watching as the ape-man drama unfolded without him.

The Vancouver screenings launched Patterson on a roller-coaster ride of publicity and deal-making. Within hours of the film's screening, calls for him were coming into Yakima from producers and agents on both coasts. DeAtley quickly assumed the role of Patterson's business manager.

Almost immediately came an offer for Patterson to appear on a Los Angeles TV talk show, and he flew to LA, accompanied by DeAtley and Gimlin. After the TV appearance, DeAtley arranged a press conference that sparked interest in the clip from several film producers. Believing they were poised for a home run, the threesome went to an attorney and formed an equal partnership called Bigfoot Enterprises.

Patterson's film was the epitome of tabloid television, but the genre hadn't yet been invented. Without such programming, producers didn't know how to use the clip. Or maybe Patterson and DeAtley's demands were seen as unreasonable. In any case, leveraging a few seconds of film into a full-length production proved futile, and they returned home empty-handed.

A few weeks later, the threesome flew to New York to screen the clip for *Life* magazine at a meeting arranged by Ivan Sanderson. Arriving in Manhattan, they learned that the magazine had arranged to show the film to scientists at the American Museum of Natural History, where they faced the indignity of being excluded from the screening.[2] Patterson later told Dahinden he felt like the entire office staff was present, looking and giggling. "I had the feeling that when they came into that room they were doing it only as a favor to *Life* magazine and that they already had their minds made up."[3] The clip was projected once; the scientists emerged a few minutes later and pronounced the film "not kosher" because it was "impossible," whereupon *Life* withdrew its interest.[4]

Anticipating *Life's* decision, Sanderson had preemptively pitched the story to the editor of the popular adventure magazine *Argosy*, a close friend, and received assurances that the magazine would run the story if *Life* passed it up. The same evening, Sanderson orchestrated a deal with *Argosy* for exclusive rights to Patterson's and Gimlin's story.

The magazine mounted the film as a cover story to go head to head with *True,* which had loaded its recent issues with UFO reports. Sanderson was ebullient. He had recently formed the Society for the Investigation of the Unexplained and—capitalizing on a wave of UFO sightings in 1966—published a book, *Uninvited Visitors: A Biologist Looks at UFO's.* Now, with the Bigfoot story, he found himself the magazine industry's reigning king of pseudoscience. He took the film's defense as the most serious challenge of his career, building his story around an analysis of the film by several respected scientists (all of whom couched their responses in guarded terms).

Sanderson's obsession for detail bordered on the pathological. Patterson later remarked to Dahinden that, at one point in New York, he got fed up and told Sanderson that "if he didn't keep his goddamn mouth shut and his finger off my goddamn film I'd throw him out the door or window or some goddamn thing."[5]

"Sanderson just drove him nuts," Dahinden said. "Of course [Sanderson] wanted to get his name out there, too. He was the big winner on that one."

Argosy hit America's newsstands in February 1968, with a cover photograph showing the cowboys posed on horses against a mountain backdrop and Gimlin dressed like Cochise, his long hair wrapped in a headband, reins in one hand, a rifle in the other. The headline screamed: "EXCLUSIVE! First Photos! CALIFORNIA'S ABOMINABLE SNOWMAN. Gimlin and Patterson: How we found and photographed it." The editor at *Argosy* was deliriously happy.

The *Argosy* story made Bigfoot a household word, but Patterson's hope that it would open doors in Hollywood quickly faded. Despite his now-testy relationship with Sanderson, Patterson broke down and called him to ask for his help in finding a buyer for the clip.[6] Writing later of the affair, Sanderson said he made one call to the science and natural history division of the British Broadcasting Corporation (BBC), and a documentary highlighting the clip was quickly green-lighted. Within weeks, Bigfoot Enterprises had a deal with the BBC. No money changed hands, but Bigfoot Enterprises retained rights to distribute the film in North America. Two weeks later a BBC film crew flew to America and commenced production of an hour-long documentary.[7]

Soon after the *Argosy* story broke, Patterson received a call from Ron Olson, who worked for a company called American National Enterprises (ANE), a producer of true-life nature films with titles like *Alaskan Safari* and *Vanishing Wilderness*. ANE had pioneered a distribution technique called "four-walling," which involved bypassing theater chains by renting screening venues—auditoriums, small halls, and independent theaters mostly in rural towns—directly from the property owner; the owner kept the concessions, and American National kept the box-office receipts. Olson, who had been interested in Bigfoot since he was a kid, believed that the footage, incorporated into a feature-length film and distributed using the four-wall method, would do great box office. He went to Yakima and met with Patterson and DeAtley. When he learned they had rights to use the BBC film in America, he hit on the idea of using that footage as the core of a "test" to convince ANE to fund a full-fledged feature.

The ANE board financed the test. Olson shot some extra scenes and changed the soundtrack. But the test film didn't play well with audiences, and the ANE board opted out. Undaunted, DeAtley decided to finish the film with his own funds and four-wall it himself. Olson signed on to help.

Olson revamped the storyline to cast Bigfoot as the focus of a scientific investigation conducted under the auspices of an organization called Northwest Research, headed by Patterson, and recut the film. Bigfoot Enterprises unleashed the movie—*Bigfoot*—on the rural West in the fall of 1968, beginning with cities along the Interstate 5 corridor in Oregon and Washington. Before the opening in each town, Olson saturated the area with radio and TV ads that featured an interview with Patterson—identified as a researcher—in what looked like a news story. In the larger venues, they brought him to town before the ad blitz for interviews with news departments and talk shows.

For the premiere, Olson rented the Spokane Auditorium and advertised a personal appearance by the filmmaker himself. They sold ten thousand tickets in two seatings and sold 640 of Roger's books at intermission. After the film, Roger went out on stage and answered questions. The audience loved it. Believing they had a hit on their hands, they rented the Portland Coliseum.

Skeptical theater managers were surprised to see hundreds of customers lined up at the box office. Full houses were common.

A lot of money was coming in (DeAtley has admitted to personally making several hundred thousand dollars from the film), but people close to the action agree that an awful lot was also going out.[8] Whatever money filtered down to Roger Patterson wasn't near enough. Debt followed him from the start. On his return from filming at Bluff Creek, he was arrested on a warrant issued by Shepard's Camera Shop, seeking return of the film camera and payment of a five-month rental fee, and he was lodged briefly in the Yakima jail.

Gimlin was cut out of the deal early. During the editing of the film, DeAtley informed him that Bigfoot Enterprises needed money for expenses. Gimlin replied that he had none and hadn't expected to pony up any, his wife was unhappy, and he wanted to drop the whole thing. DeAtley gave him seven hundred dollars and said, "You're out." Gimlin considered a lawsuit but didn't have the money to file one. He withdrew almost completely from the scene, keeping an especially wide distance between himself and the press.

From the first showings of Patterson's film in Vancouver, it was clear that the mainstream press wasn't buying Bigfoot. A story in the Yakima paper a few days after the screenings set the tone of future coverage: "Dateline Vancouver. B.C. (AP) 'Scientists and reporters have viewed a 20-second *[sic]* film of a large hairy animal, but remain largely unconvinced that it was the legendary Sasquatch mountain giant. . . . About 40 persons attended the second showing of the day, at a downtown hotel last Thursday night, and few appear convinced by the film. . . . [M]ost scientists at the earlier showing, held at the University of British Columbia, would make no comment on the film.'"[9]

A profile of Patterson in *National Wildlife* magazine found him chafing at the idea that people thought he'd hoaxed the film. "Is the photograph real? The photographer says it is, and to say otherwise is to call him a liar. Naturally, he is sensitive about the careless use of that word. What's more, he's getting a little testy about it, because he's been questioned by both believers and disbelievers several hundred times, and he's tired of it."[10]

Patterson clung to Northwest Research—which he referred to as a "clearinghouse" for reports—as a lifeline to reputability. Reports by honest citizens were the heart of his belief, proof that what he was chasing wasn't just a dream, but a belief that was shared by others.

Overwhelmed by the spike in Bigfoot reports following the *Argosy* story, Patterson hired an assistant investigator, a tall, slender young man from Idaho named Dennis Jenson. Jenson had no idea what the job entailed; the ad he'd responded to had simply said, "Communication skills and backwoods experience necessary."

Jenson today lives with a naked parrot he refuses to call a pet in a cabin near the scene of many of his Bigfoot adventures; he is a thicker, grayer bulldozer of a man than the one in photos from the spring of 1968. When I asked for his reaction when he heard what the job actually entailed, Jenson stuck a wad of tobacco under his lip and said he thought it a bit strange, but the weirdness factor got him excited. "The only thing I knew about Bigfoot was what I'd read in *Argosy*," he said. "I didn't go in this thing as a believer." He moved to Yakima and immediately found himself on the road, traveling to the site of every halfway plausible report.[11]

For long trips, he drove an old postal van Patterson had outfitted with bunks, a tack room, and space for Patterson's three ponies, which Jenson characterized as "the meanest, orneriest mountain ponies you ever seen." They were small animals that Jenson, at six-four plus, "didn't feel quite manly" riding. His longtime companion was Patterson's German shepherd, Reb. He cruised thousands of miles in the van emblazoned with the words "Northwest Research" on the door, horses in the back, tailgate piled with hay bales, spare tires on top, towing a smaller four-wheel-drive pickup, with Reb riding shotgun.

One Bigfooter described Jenson's appearance at his home "like mountain country coming into the city"—a "show and a half" that amazed the neighbors. The best part of the job, according to Jenson, was the hippie girls hitchhiking. "It was the 60s," he said with a grin, "and the highways were full of them."

.   .   .

Something about Patterson's film didn't sit right with Dahinden. Two people had been to the film site to check out the cowboy's rendition of events, and both assessments made him dubious. After seeing the footage at the screenings in Canada, Bob Titmus had driven immediately to Bluff Creek and spent three days roving the scene. He claimed to have picked up the beast's trail and followed it to a point eighty feet above the creek, where it sat in the ferns and watched the cowboys go about their business. His findings sounded like those of a seasoned tracker, but Dahinden had never liked Titmus and knew he'd faked evidence before. John Green visited Bluff Creek the next spring with the Arcata Bigfooter Jim McClarin, comparing frames of the film with McClarin's movement along the beast's path. But Dahinden was leery because Green had made the trip for the purpose of reporting it in his book and unabashedly supported Patterson's claim.

Born out of wedlock in Switzerland in 1930, placed in an orphanage as a baby, and raised in foster homes and institutions, Dahinden had always found trust a foreign concept. He struck out on his own at an early age and hitchhiked through Europe. A program to naturalize immigrants in exchange for a work commitment brought him to a farm in Alberta, Canada, in 1953.

The hot news in the province at the time was the *Daily Mail* expedition's search for the yeti. Before long, word came of a similar creature in North America. "Dateline Vancouver, British Columbia—At the same time as the *Daily Mail* Yeti expedition is entering upon its hunt for the Abominable Snowman in the Himalayas, similar big game is alleged to have been sighted in the high snow-covered mountains of the Fraser Valley Canyon and behind Kitimat on the Northern British Columbia coast."[12]

That news item changed Dahinden's life forever. Years later, he sent a letter to his two boys recounting his life and describing his feelings on first hearing about the animal. "I could scarcely imagine such a thing," he wrote. "Wouldn't it be something if [Sasquatch] really was true. . . . Looking back, it seemed that maybe I'd been searching all my life for a chance like that, a chance to really accomplish something."[13] The very next year he moved to British Columbia, married a woman named Wanja who had followed him from Sweden, and took up the hunt that would occupy the rest of his life.

Six years later, in the wake of Tom Slick's chaotic "expedition" at Bluff Creek, he took over a boat-rental business on Harrison Lake in British Columbia, trying to begin a normal life, but several mysterious incidents in the province screamed "Sasquatch!" to him, and his obsession festered.

"In the back of my mind, I was just kind of like a bird dog shaking," he told me. "I wanted to go out there."[14]

He moved his family to the village of Lumby, found work in a sawmill, and started a business recovering lead shot from the skeet ranges at Vancouver gun clubs, a ploy that allowed him summers apart from his wife and boys to continue the hunt in earnest. Sasquatch had become a full-blown obsession. Even thirty years later, he couldn't admit he'd put his family second. "I tried to make a living up there in Lumby," he said. "Shit, sometimes I didn't have twenty-five cents to rub together. So, tough times, but we always had food."

·   ·   ·

Just as Dahinden loved tramping and keeping to himself, John Green, an inveterate journalist, loved gathering information and telling people all about it. With Sasquatch, the extraordinary nature of what he was hearing and the number of reports seemed to indicate something unique. Too many people had spoken up—in many cases, courageously so, considering the ridicule they'd endured—and they couldn't *all* be lying or mistaken about what they'd seen. Tom Slick's Bluff Creek expedition had been discouraging but not demoralizing. The idea of a worldwide army of hoaxers was utterly preposterous. As long as reports continued to mount, Green would be there to collect and file them meticulously away and keep the idea alive among the faithful.

·   ·   ·

In the fall of 1967, in response to the challenge posed by Patterson, Dahinden and Green hit the road once again on the trail of Bigfoot, only to be knocked off stride by Patterson's film—taken at a spot not five miles from the road on Blue Mountain where they had just spent a week examining giant tracks themselves.

The following spring, after the initial excitement over the film had abated, Dahinden trekked into British Columbia's primitive Garibaldi Provincial Park, ostensibly to look for Sasquatch. A photograph from the trip shows him on a mountain ridge holding his pipe, admiring the view. Countless photos and videos taken over the next thirty years showed him in equally wild places, for, whatever anguish he may have felt in dealing with people, the wilderness cleansed it all away. The first time I met him, he brought out photographs he had taken of mountains, clouds, and wilderness vistas, and described trips to several wild places: what he'd seen, how long he'd stayed, and the weather. He named the trees he'd seen by species.

On this trip, two months in the wilderness produced no sign of the beast, but his enthusiasm remained undiminished. He knew Green and Patterson were fielding more reports than ever, and though Patterson had a film, he still hadn't found the animal. Judging by the attitude of the scientific community and the media, only one thing would satisfy critics: a body.

He talked Green into partnering to buy the Canadian rights to the film clip from Patterson and DeAtley, incorporated it into an audiovisual program with nature scenes and footprint photographs, and set out to exhibit the presentation in the provinces. While Patterson jetted about making personal appearances and Green watched sales of his first book climb (and began writing a second), Dahinden lugged his lackluster presentation through the cold of a sub-Arctic Canadian winter, struggling to break even and stewing over the idea that he had got the short end of the stick and had his thunder stolen by a film that, the more he thought about it, might not even be real.

In December 1968 came word that Ivan Sanderson and Bernard Heuvelmans (visiting from Europe by happenstance) had just returned from Minnesota, where they had examined a mysterious frozen carcass. The body, which had been exhibited in fairs and circus midways in the Midwest for two years, was known as the Iceman. After two days photographing and sketching the figure—which reposed in a freezer under plate glass (no touching allowed)—they had concluded that the body was a real life form with "Neanderthal" characteristics. Rumor had it that Heuvelmans was preparing an article about it for a scientific journal, and that Sanderson—who had just been appointed science editor at *Argosy*—was writing it up as a cover story.

Brad Steiger, a well-known paranormal investigator at that time, wrote to me about a phone call he had received from Sanderson at the height of the Iceman affair. "I remember Ivan calling me [up]. . . . It was late at night. He must have been calling from an outdoor pay phone. The wind was howling in the background, and I could barely hear him. 'My boy,' he said, 'I have found that for which I have searched all my life. Proof of a Yeti, a Bigfoot!' Then he explained that both he and Bernard had examined the thing and were convinced it was authentic."[15] The buzz surrounding the Patterson film, together with news of the Iceman, made Bigfoot an especially hot topic in the Midwest, so DeAtley and Olson took *Bigfoot* east to Colorado, Nebraska, and Utah, and made plans to open big in Iceman country in Wisconsin and Minnesota.

In February 1969 Heuvelmans published an article in a Belgian scientific journal claiming that the corpse represented an unknown species of man. In April, *Argosy* ran a cover story about the Iceman under Sanderson's byline. "Found in Wisconsin: 'Living Fossil,'" the headline shouted. "Is this the missing link between man and the apes?"

Bigfoot sightings escalated. Desperate to remain a player in the expanding drama, Dahinden put the lecture business on hold and took to the field. His first stop was Skamania County, Washington, on the Columbia River near Mount St. Helens, where he checked out a report by a man on his way to fishing early one morning, who watched "an ape-faced, dark-colored creature" cross the fog-shrouded highway in front of his car, leap a steep bank, and disappear into the bushes. Four months later, he drove to Northern California and talked to a man outside Oroville who said he was burning rabbit guts in his backyard when he looked up and saw an apelike creature beside the outhouse. Several other reports scattered throughout the Northwest during this time described generally the same animal: tall, hairy, and bipedal. The Oroville ape was said to have another feature: flat breasts that hung down to her navel.

Meanwhile, in New York, Sanderson, flushed with success over the

Argosy story, arranged through an acquaintance at the Smithsonian to have Patterson's film screened for the institution's staff in Washington, DC. The viewing did not go well: the film was greeted with "massive skepticism."[16] Sanderson, apparently clueless about this development, sent photographic enlargements from the clip to the editors of *Life International* and sold them on the idea of running the very story their domestic counterpart had previously rejected. A few days later he received a reality check:

> Dear Dr. Sanderson:
>
> Regretfully, I have concluded that LIFE's International Editions should not use the Sasquatch pictures.
>
> In my telephone conversation with you, I had got the clear impression that the Interior Department and the Smithsonian Institution had displayed great interest in the photographs and that they had undertaken or were undertaking investigations. But, at my instance *[sic]*, a representative of our Washington Bureau has talked with a number of persons at Interior and the Smithsonian who would be concerned with such a matter and has found no one who supports that impression. Frankly they scoff at the responsibility of *[sic]* the Sasquatch's existence, and display considerable annoyance at the suggestion that they are pursuing the affair. They could be wrong, of course, but they make a convincing case.
>
> So, I am returning the photographs with thanks herewith.
>
> Sincerely,
> Henry Moscow
> Editions Editor

December found Dahinden in the microscopic town of Bossburg, Washington, near the Canadian border, inspecting what appeared to be the tracks of a badly injured Bigfoot that someone had dubbed Cripple Foot. The prints had been identified by Ivan Marx, the bear hunter who had run his hounds for Tom Slick a decade before and was now living in Bossburg in a tar-paper shack with a pet cougar caged in the front yard.

Patterson and Jenson soon arrived on the scene. Jenson was worn out physically and mentally. He'd been on the road for months and was having problems getting reimbursed for his expenses. That situation was the result of the *Bigfoot* film exhibition enterprise's having been stopped in its tracks by the Smithsonian's widely publicized unmasking of the Iceman as a hoax only days before *Bigfoot* was due to open in the north country, leaving DeAtley with thousands of dollars in prepaid publicity and venue rentals that went up in smoke when audiences failed to show.[17] The revelation also dried up book sales and demand for Patterson's appearances.

Despite this turn of events, Patterson had stayed focused on his "investigation," seemingly oblivious to the fact that hunting Bigfoot cost money. In making the film he had thrown down a gauntlet, announcing to the world that he believed in the beast. His cancer had returned with a vengeance, and, coupled with the skepticism surrounding the film, it made for a witch's brew. The result was tragically predictable.

"Roger's health was never good from the first time I met him," Jenson recalled. "He always had a yellow color to his skin. He was dead serious about capturing [a Bigfoot]. And he knew he was going to die. When we were on the road together, at nights we talked about how he might not be able to 'root one out of the woods' before he was gone."

Patterson returned to Yakima to rest, leaving Jenson in Bossburg to protect his interests against Dahinden and a growing number of voyeurs attracted by the excitement. The bars in nearby Kettle Falls soon reverberated with the same arguments heard in Willow Creek a decade earlier. His financial problems mounting, Patterson received a call from an Ohio businessman, Tom Page, inquiring into the possibility of partnering on the hunt.

Page was a confirmed Bigfooter. In 1960 he had talked to the Himalayan Scientific and Mountaineering Expedition, led by Edmund Hillary, about joining their team, but his background running a building-supply business in Dayton wasn't quite the experience they were looking for. Page had been thinking about starting a hunt of his own when he learned about Patterson. He had deep pockets and wanted a front-row seat for the action. They arrived at an arrangement whereby Page paid Northwest Research a retainer to be kept informed of every break in the search.

I asked Page about his relationship with Patterson. He said that he sensed Patterson had a funding crisis at the time he called, or he wouldn't have heard him out. He added that he found him easy to talk with and stressed that Patterson always dealt with him straight up. It never entered his mind that he was hoaxing anything.

Page and Patterson arrived in Bossburg in a helicopter that Dahinden perceived as a form of class warfare. The disparity between the obvious affluence of Patterson's camp and Dahinden's resources—consisting of himself, two volunteers there simply for the excitement, and Green, back home in Agassiz, busily writing—added to Dahinden's frustration and embitterment about everything and everyone involved in the hunt.

Jenson hadn't met Dahinden and was taken aback by the coarse little Swiss. René was "a little bit crazy," Jenson said. "He always had an axe to grind and a wrong to be righted."

The hunt for Cripple Foot devolved into bona fide lunacy, with a prospector who claimed to have a Bigfoot trapped in a mine shaft, opposing parties of Bigfoot hunters in helicopters, light planes and snowmobiles criss-crossing the frozen hills in wild searches, and escalating offers to the prospector to reveal the beast's whereabouts. "It was kinda cutthroat back then," Jenson recalled. "Everyone was after the prize."

Patterson was in a downward spiral, his symptoms worsening. Broke again and frantic for a breakthrough, he received a letter from a U.S. airman stationed in Thailand who claimed to have evidence of a Bigfoot imprisoned there in a monastery. He wanted to check it out and convinced a leery Page to send Jenson, who had spent time in Southeast Asia in the marines. Jenson made the trip and concluded the airman was mentally unbalanced. Shortly after his return, another letter arrived from the airman containing new information that Patterson believed warranted a second trip. He called Page and described a plan to smuggle the Bigfoot out of Thailand in a DC-3 and fly it to Alaska, then on to Madison Square Garden or Yankee Stadium for exhibition. Page said no.

In desperation Patterson called Ron Olson, who had returned to his job at American National Enterprises, and sold the company the theatrical rights to the clip for what Olson described as a pretty good sum of money. Patterson used the cash to fly with Jenson to Thailand. They had difficulty locating the airman, and when they finally tracked him down, he admitted that the Asian Bigfoot was an illusion.

Patterson was devastated. "He didn't do much after that," Jenson said. "And I was done, too. Tired of traveling. Patterson and me were just kind of done with each other." The episode also marked a turning point for Tom Page, who called it quits with Northwest Research.

Chemotherapy and cobalt treatments were taking their toll on Patterson. One of his eyes and his mouth drooped on one side, and he was deeply depressed. He began drinking a green concoction made of comfrey and popped handfuls of vitamins. His wife was paralyzed with grief and worry. Money had been coming in from subscriptions, book sales, rights and appearance fees, and the film circuit. Now there was nothing. Creditors were relentless. "I think Roger was just grasping at straws at that time," Jenson said. "Thailand took the heart out of him." All Roger got for his troubles was a tiger skin.

Back in Bossburg, the prospector had faded from the scene, and the furor over Cripple Foot had just died down when Ivan Marx let it slip to a local reporter that he had captured the beast on movie film. The Bigfoot hunters who had previously besieged the town and then left now returned with vigor. Dahinden viewed the film and pronounced it a fraud. Green viewed it and pronounced it authentic. Then into the midst of the uproar marched Peter Byrne.

Ivan Sanderson working on a book illustration
during a jungle expedition, ca. 1938. Courtesy Ivan T. Sanderson
Collection, American Philosophical Society.

Peter Byrne talking with villagers in Nepal, 1957. Courtesy Peter Byrne.

Jerry Crew's photo introduces Bigfoot to the world, October 5, 1958. Courtesy *Times-Standard*, Eureka, California.

"Animal Man" Ivan Sanderson (right) and TV host Garry Moore
display jungle animals, ca. 1958. Courtesy Ivan T. Sanderson
Collection, American Philosophical Society.

———

Roy Wallace in Willow Creek, California, 1960.
Courtesy Peter Byrne.

René Dahinden searching for Bigfoot in hills above
Bluff Creek, California, 1960. Courtesy Larry Lund.

The first Bigfoot Daze parade in Willow Creek,
California, 1961. Courtesy Al Hodgson.

———

Roger Patterson displaying Bigfoot casts, ca. 1969.
Courtesy Dennis Jenson.

René Dahinden (left) and Roger Patterson with Patterson's mountain ponies, Yakima, Washington, 1967. Courtesy Erik and Martin Dahinden, © Dahinden.

John Green measuring Bigfoot stride on
Blue Creek Mountain Road, California, 1967.
Courtesy John Green.

Frame from Roger Patterson's
Bigfoot film, reportedly shot on October 20, 1967.
Courtesy Erik and Martin Dahinden, © Dahinden.

Ivan Sanderson in his home office, ca. 1965.
Courtesy Ivan T. Sanderson Collection, American
Philosophical Society.

———

Roger Patterson answering audience questions
after a screening of his film *Bigfoot,* ca. 1968.
Courtesy Dennis Jenson.

From left, Dennis Jenson, Peter Byrne, and Don Byington on the hunt for
Bigfoot near Bossburg, Washington, ca. 1971. Courtesy Peter Byrne.

Roger Patterson's backer, Tom Page, near Oroville,
California, 1969. Courtesy Dennis Jenson.

Roger Patterson (right) and Dennis Jenson investigating yeti report
with monk in Thailand monastery, 1970. Courtesy Dennis Jenson.

René Dahinden at the Patterson film site on Bluff Creek, 1985.
Courtesy Larry Lund.

Ray Wallace at home in Toledo, Washington, 1996. Photo by the author.

———

John Green at home in Harrison Hot Springs, British Columbia, 1995. Photo by the author.

René Dahinden at home outside Vancouver,
British Columbia, 1997. Photo by the author.

Peter Byrne at the White Grass Plains Reserve,
Nepal, 2005. Courtesy Peter Byrne.

Jay Rowland touring the Bluff Creek drainage, California, 1996.
Photo by the author.

Bigfoot sign on the Klamath Highway, 1996.
Photo by the author.

BIGFOOT DAZE

Yes, I've lived my life and I've took a chance,
Regardless of law or vow.
I've played the game and I've had my dance,
And I'm payin' the fiddler now.

—Bruce Kiskaddon, "The Old Night Hawk"

After Tom Slick's death in 1962, Peter Byrne returned to his safari business in Nepal. But after five years of slogging through the jungle, what seemed at first like "an exciting and exhilarating occupation" that allowed him to spend several months of each year on holiday became an increasing discomfort. His clients were, for the most part, wealthy Americans looking for trophies, and, as he wrote in his book *Tula Hatti,* big-game hunting "brought out the worst" in many "who seemed to think they could drink all day and hunt at the same time . . . and expected to be allowed to shoot everything in sight, from porcupines to pythons, from monkeys to mongooses."[1]

In the winter of 1968, he closed his safari business and set out to turn his former hunting ground into a wildlife preserve. Putting the touch on his clients, who included American tycoons, heirs to banking and oil fortunes, and members of the British peerage and Asian nobility—such as the maharaja of Baroda—he formed the International Wildlife Conservation Society and established the Suklaphanta (White Grass Plains) Wildlife Reserve in Nepal.

Exactly what happened next is unclear. Patterson's film appeared while Byrne was in Nepal, and Byrne had only heard of it. But having spent more than two years of his life in California searching for the creature, of course he was interested in the clip. The safari business had taught Byrne that money was no barrier for rich sportsmen who craved adventure, and Bigfoot was arguably the biggest adventure on the planet. The game was surely afoot, but to conduct what he came to call "the ultimate hunt," he needed backing.

As Byrne tells it, he ran into a "one-time oil man named C. V. Wood, who had been an associate of Tom Slick's," by accident while visiting New York in 1970.[2] Wood asked Byrne to check out both Marx's clip and Patterson's and give him an opinion on whether they were real. Byrne flew immediately to Washington State.

Byrne's entry onto the scene with his reputation as a big-game guide, coupled with his worldly panache and smart English accent, confounded Dahinden and Green, as did Byrne's idea of a proper "hunt." They simply had no frame of reference for such a person. And why would they? After all, how many exotic big-game guides were left in the world? After thirteen years of fruitless searching, they had no more of a clue how to find Bigfoot than they'd had in 1956. Byrne represented experience, connections, a plan, and the obvious wherewithal to carry it out. And now hunting Bigfoot allowed Byrne, now reborn as a conservationist, to remain a trophy hunter without using bullets. For two guys "without a pot to piss in," as Dahinden put it, Byrne presented a formidable challenge.

"So I went out [to Washington State], and there were two pieces of footage," Byrne recalled, when I interviewed him at his home in a leafy forest in Portland. "One was shot by this man called Marx in northern Washington. And the other was Patterson's. I saw both of them. And Marx's footage was good. Very good. I didn't know what to make of it."[3] Dahinden hadn't believed Marx's film for a second, and he didn't think Byrne did either, being of the opinion that the Irishman had prolonged the affair simply to keep his backers on the hook.[4] Then again, Dahinden wasn't absolutely sure of anything. Only one thing was certain: Bigfoot fever was in the air.

Media coverage of the ape-man had increased exponentially since Patterson's film exploded on the national scene, and Bigfoot experts were coming out of the woodwork. In the summer of 1970, a flamboyant Floridian named Robert Morgan talked *National Wildlife* magazine into financing a Bigfoot expedition to Mount St. Helens under his "command." Morgan told the magazine's executives that he had experienced an epiphany near the mountain in 1957, when he had come face to face with the creature. "It was the most manlike-looking gorilla I'd ever seen," he said. "And he had the most knowing look on his face. And when I tried to report it, it was treated as a joke." Accompanied by an archaeologist, a biologist, a cinematographer, and the magazine's managing editor, Morgan spent two weeks combing the mountain with a "sound device," which he declined to describe in detail "except to say it has a high-pitched bell tone."[5] It must have been effective; he found three sets of tracks.

The resulting magazine article concluded with a look ahead: "What's up for Part 2 of the expedition? Plans are to attract [Bigfoot] to drugged bait, then follow the sleepy creature perhaps with the aid of a trained Labrador Retriever until close enough to shoot it with a drug-filled dart. If successful, the captive will be flown to the Smithsonian Institution in Washington, D.C. where it will be available for scientific study."[6]

Meanwhile, Peter Byrne reported back to Wood that "both [Marx's and Patterson's] films, at first glance, looked very interesting and at the least deserved further investigation."[7] They struck a deal for Wood, in partnership with two associates, to fund a three-year Bigfoot search project, to be headed by Byrne under the banner of his International Wildlife Conservation Society.

Byrne returned to Bossburg. He hired Dennis Jenson, who had recently left Patterson's employ, and set up a base of operations not far from Marx's shack. His mission was to determine the authenticity of the two film clips, and then, if either appeared genuine, to undertake an organized search similar to the one he had conducted for Slick in Northern California. True to his new conservation ethic, Byrne issued a press release stating that the intention of the society was "to endeavor to find one of these primates and, using a harmless tranquilizer, immobilize it for examination. The examination, which would be done by scientists, would in no way harm the primate and, after its completion, the creature would be released and allowed to go free."[8]

Jenson didn't share Byrne's sanguine view of Marx's film. All these years later, he laughed when recalling chapter 2 in the Bossburg saga. "Ivan Marx, bless his soul. . . . He would lie to you just to fuck with you. But he did it with such flair you'd laugh like crazy. I knew the film was a phony when I saw it."[9]

First, however, Byrne had to get his hands on the films. Marx wanted twenty-five thousand dollars for his. Reluctant to hand such a sum over to a man with a wild glint in his eye, Byrne negotiated a compromise, putting Marx on retainer as a Bigfoot hunter, in exchange for which Byrne was allowed to send the master copy of the film, sealed in a metal canister, to his attorney in Washington, D.C., "to be held in trust" until its authenticity could be verified.

Byrne then turned his attention to the Bluff Creek film. "I went to see Patterson three or four times at his house," he said. Patterson was very angry at that time, bitter about not being accepted. "Who the hell are you? You're just another person coming here to laugh at me," Byrne remembers him saying. "That was his attitude. No one believed him. People laughed at him. And he'd had problems with Gimlin. Arguments about the money. Eventually, I got him calmed down, and he showed me the film."

Byrne was deeply impressed by what he saw. Whereas the Marx film had a slapstick quality, the Bluff Creek film felt like TV news, shot live on the scene, with a figure glimpsed in haste, not hanging around to be observed. Impressive as it was, however, at the moment Patterson's clip was secondary to Marx's footage, which, if real, placed the beast in the hills above Bossburg.

Alas, it was too good to be true. After three months of investigation, Byrne concluded that Marx's film was bogus. He published his findings in Sanderson's *Journal of the Society for the Investigation of the Unexplained,* along with frames from the film. "For your interest," Byrne wrote, "the 'creature' in these pictures, which is either Ivan Marx or another man in a fur suit, is no more than six feet in height." He also noted that a month before the film, Marx had been spotted buying old fur coats at a Goodwill store in Spokane.

Going to Marx's shack early one morning to confront him, Byrne and Jenson discovered that the woodsman had loaded up his household and left town in the dead of night. Byrne called his attorney and told him to open the film canister. Inside was a roll of Mickey Mouse cartoon footage.

United Press International picked up the story immediately. "I realize we've got a rather large blob of egg on our face by admitting this," Byrne was quoted as saying.[10] "But this same film fooled a lot of expert photographers and at least two television networks who had sought to purchase rights to the film." Despite the embarrassment, the story reported, Byrne was unbowed, announcing that he would now take the hunt to the "wilderness country" in Oregon and Idaho as well as Washington. "I led three major expeditions in the Himalayas in 1957, '58, and '59, as well as two other small expeditions in 1948 and 1952," Byrne said. "I am convinced such a creature exists."

To complicate matters, Byrne was soon summoned to Los Angeles by his benefactor, Wood, who said that he'd heard from Marx that Byrne had declared he would not shoot any Bigfoot he found. Recounting the episode, Byrne recalled that "Wood, never having mentioned this previously, . . . now told me that . . . he wanted a definite commitment from me that I would shoot one when I got the chance, in that he wanted a mounted one as part of an exhibit at his new resort. . . . I flatly refused to agree to shoot one, and sometime about mid-April, Wood and company pulled out, and the project's funding ceased." Wood's resort was Lake Havasu City in Arizona, the new home of London Bridge, which Wood had just shipped from Britain stone by stone and reassembled as the centerpiece of a world-class tourist attraction. A stuffed Bigfoot would have been the pièce de resistance.

The saga of Bossburg was finally over.[11] Byrne had lost his backers, Dahinden had alienated everyone on the scene (including Green, who Dahinden believed had sided with Patterson), and Patterson had lost his dream. A year later, however, Marx appeared on the television show *You Asked for It* with a second movie, showing a white Bigfoot filmed in a snowstorm.

In the months preceding his death, Patterson, often too sick to travel, had begun asking the film distributor Ron Olson to check out Bigfoot reports. Olson did what he could and soon found himself overseeing Patterson's entire operation, such as it was. When Olson and Patterson first got involved, the collaboration was simply "a chance to produce and market a potentially lucrative film." The relationship ultimately became much more. Olson came to admire Patterson's adventuresome spirit and the fact that he thought big. And he wasn't all bluff; he rode broncs and he boxed. At the same time, "he was a congenial, quiet guy who would just as soon not talk about his film and who never made a penny off it in his life. . . . In four years of knowing Roger . . . if there had been a flaw in the guy's personality, that if he even had the possibility of faking something like [that], I believe I would have detected it." Patterson reassured him on his deathbed that the film was real.[12]

Tom Page recalled Patterson's last year as very rough; the closer Roger got to being incapacitated, the more frantic he became. His decline devastated everyone around him. One man who met him at the time recalled that his voice sounded "kind of like his neck being squeezed and strangling."[13] Finally, he couldn't get out of bed, and Page did interviews for him.

The week before Patterson died, Peter Byrne went to his home and found him "sitting in his garden in the sun. He looked awful, he was just a skeleton." Patterson told him, "Peter, we should have shot that thing. Then people would have believed us."[14]

Near the end, Patterson's brothers visited him together in the hospital. He wanted to arm-wrestle them all. They let him win, and he thanked them. They reminisced about their rodeo days, how they'd go into a bar and lay on a big arm-wrestling wager pitting little Roger against some unsuspecting tough guy. Roger always won.

Gimlin saw Roger for the last time in the hospital, shrunken and helpless, covered with bruises. They talked about horses, and Roger doubled over in a fit of coughing, painful to watch. The toughest part of being laid up, he said, was not being able to get out and investigate leads. He said he'd heard of another report from Oroville, then laughed and added that he wasn't sure the old guy down there who'd made that first report about the Bigfoot by the outhouse wasn't just a little bit touched.

He'd said he was sorry about the money and promised they'd get it squared away. A long silence ensued. Then he said: "I worry about Patty and the kids. She's gonna need a hand." The remark struck Gimlin deeply.

Roger Patterson died on January 15, 1972. All the people I've talked with who knew him said he maintained right to the end that the creature on the film was real. When Tom Page learned of Patterson's death, he was pleased that Patterson hadn't recanted and said the film was a fake. Integrity being so strongly valued in the West, it would have left a legacy of deceit for his family.

Roger Patterson created a wave but never saw it break. At his death, sightings and footprints were increasingly common, but the beast had not yet attained tabloid supremacy. He might have believed the animal would eventually be caught or killed, or he might not. The fact was, if Bigfoot never did show up, no one could call him a liar—not directly, anyway. You could always argue the beast might just have gone extinct, and no one would ever know. For the Bigfooters of the world, Patterson's fierce and abiding determination to find the beast in the face of almost universal derision lends a powerful certainty to their cause. It is simply inconceivable, they say, that anyone who believed so deeply in something could have faked it.

9

CRYPTID WARS

The mind of no man is a unit, but is a community of mental states that influence one another.

—Charles Fort, "Talents," in *The Collected Works of Charles Fort*

Thirteen months after Roger Patterson's death at thirty-nine, Ivan Sanderson died of cancer at the age of sixty-two. In many ways, their relationship was familial. Both lost their fathers at a young age. For a brief time, when Patterson first began the ape-man business, they were like father and son. If Sanderson provided the hype, Patterson provided the substance. Without Sanderson, the beast might well have languished in obscurity forever. Without Patterson, the myth wouldn't have endured. His rugged defense of the film and unflagging belief in the animal captured the imagination of many who met him. He enlarged the Bigfooter community as well as divided it, but his faith infected them all. Now, with both men gone, the hunt entered uncharted territory.

At the time of Patterson's death, Peter Byrne had moved himself and Dennis Jenson to The Dalles, a small Oregon town on the Columbia River, strategically centered in Bigfoot's realm. A sighting on the outskirts of town in the summer of 1971 had stirred up excitement in the area, and he'd struck an arrangement with Tom Page to continue the search, similar to Page's deal with Patterson.

Publicity surrounding Byrne's arrival in Oregon under the banner of the International Wildlife Conservation Society sparked a flurry of reports of sightings and footprints. Not one to pass up an opportunity, he began writing a book about his search for the ape-man—now twenty-five years long—while he looked for more substantial funding to continue the pursuit. Using Patterson's film as the centerpiece of an investor presentation, he convinced a group of wealthy New Englanders calling themselves the Academy of Applied Science to fund a Bigfoot search, as they'd recently done for a group of British searchers who needed help finding the Loch Ness Monster. In the spring of 1974, Byrne established the Bigfoot Information Center in a trailer topped with a sign reading "Bigfoot Exhibition," flying a flag emblazoned with a big footprint. The center functioned as both a Bigfoot reporting center and a casting agency for Byrne, who fielded requests for interviews and documentary appearances from the moment he opened his door.

None of these developments escaped Dahinden, who watched the beast's popularity soar. The craze was driven in part by syndicated TV programs featuring Bigfoot and other natural mysteries, created by producers like David Wolper and Alan Landsburg.[1]

Sightings and footprints were now being reported from Texas to Nova Scotia. Dahinden disdained so-called professionals like Byrne, who had turned the beast into a tourist attraction, and Robert Morgan, who spiced up his television persona by shaving his head commando-style and running his Bigfoot "expeditions" like military campaigns. What most disturbed Dahinden was the scientific community's near-total refusal to even acknowledge the ape-man, which he experienced firsthand when his attempts to talk with scientists directly resulted in unreturned phone calls, broken promises, and outright evasion. When he did hear back, the results were predictable:

Dear René,

You ask me why I reject the idea of a pre human *Giganto pithecus* type bipedal anthropoid living in the wilds of British Columbia.

I have actually hunted and collected higher vertebrates in British Columbia for the past 35 years, for the National Museum, the University of British Columbia and the provincial government. My work has taken and still takes me into all of the habitats that occur in this ecologically widely diversified province. I have time and again hunted, trapped and collected practically every species of higher vertebrate that lives here. I've never encountered a "Sasquatch" or any concrete evidence thereof. Neither have the hundreds of game biologists and Conservation Officers that work and have worked in our wilderness areas for decades. Further, there is no palaeontological evidence that any anthropoid creature ever lived in North America prior to the coming of contemporary man.

I believe all of the foot prints, films, etc., to be faked.

Sincerely,
Charles J. Guiguet,
Curator of Birds and Mammals[2]

John Green shared Dahinden's frustration. His first two booklets, *On the Track of the Sasquatch* (1968) and *Year of the Sasquatch* (1970), had sold well enough to allow him to back off from the newspaper business and devote himself full-time to writing about the ape-man. He published his books himself and traveled the West selling them from the trunk of his car. The more people he talked to, the more enthusiasm he stirred up about the beast, and the more incredulous he became that scientists were ignoring the testimony of hundreds—if not thousands—of people.

When he published his first book, he had on record approximately 250 reports of "people seeing a two-legged, hair-covered creature or finding huge human-like tracks," including several accounts he found in provincial newspaper archives.[3]

In *On the Track of the Sasquatch,* under the heading "A Sasquatch Caught," he reproduced an account—now enshrined in the Bigfoot canon—describing the capture of a "half man and half beast" creature near Yale, British Columbia, in 1882.[4] The animal—dubbed Jacko by its captors—was "something of the gorilla type, standing about four feet seven inches in height and weighing 127 pounds. He has long, black, strong hair and resembles a human being with one exception, his entire body, excepting his hands, (or paws) and feet are covered with glossy hair about one inch long." The creature was said to possess extraordinary strength and occasionally uttered a noise which was "half bark and half growl." A doctor advised withholding raw meat from the creature, as it might "have a tendency to make him savage."[5]

In the spirit of Ivan Sanderson and Bernard Heuvelmans, Green peppered the book with jabs at the establishment: "I have found that scientists generally take some pride in being sceptics and seem to feel that this justifies doing nothing themselves to look into a matter about which they nonetheless lay claim to some special competence. The proper attitude for a 'sceptical' scientist, I gather, is to insist that the layman find some way to prove him wrong before he will condescend to pay any serious attention."[6]

Two years later, Green had five hundred reports in his card file and was trying to make sense of his data, looking forward to the day when a computer could crunch it properly. "It may be possible," he wrote in *Year of the Sasquatch,* "to [one day] relate Sasquatch appearances to such things as altitude, lighting conditions, weather, phases of the moon, etc. . . . There could be a correlation with the maturing of certain types of plant food or the movements of other species of animals."[7] His data showed that the creatures appeared in certain places more at one time of the year than others, suggesting that they migrated. And there was "considerable evidence" they were more active at night.

Many of the reports Green collected were so detailed it seemed impossible that anyone could have made them up. "It seems pretty plain that the Sasquatch, like their human cousins, will eat just about anything," he noted. "They will steal food on occasion, and will raid garbage cans. . . . Whether or not Sasquatch are a danger to livestock or hunt deer, is not yet established to my satisfaction." Comfortingly, they posed no danger to humans. "More than one has followed close behind a man in the woods, but without molesting him. There are several reports, although I know of none that has been traced and investigated, of Sasquatch taking food and leaving things in exchange, and two accounts of injured men being carried back to camp by them."[8]

The data suggested many things, but the most impressive aspect of Green's research was the sheer number of people who claimed to have seen *something:* "Any report could be wrong, but it must be remembered that if even one of the 500 is correct, then Sasquatch do exist and all the other reports do not have to carry the burden of proof."[9]

Fed up with do-nothing North American scientists, Dahinden took Patterson's film, along with plaster casts, footprint photographs, and tape recordings of eyewitness accounts, to Europe to solicit scientific opinion there. At his first stop, in England, he showed the film to John Napier, recently relocated from the Smithsonian and now a professor of primate biology at the University of London. Napier's assessment set the tone of the trip: "The upper half of the body bears some resemblance to an ape and the lower half is typically human. It is almost impossible to conceive that such structural hybrids could exist in nature. One half of the animal must be artificial. In view of the walk, it can only be the upper half. . . . I was puzzled by the extraordinary exaggeration of the walk: it seemed to me to be an overstatement of the normal pattern, a bad actor's interpretation of a classical human walking gait." A colleague of Napier's who specialized in the human gait concluded that the creature stood no more than six-foot-five and walked like a human. He found the footprint length, which was given as between fourteen and fifteen inches, to be "totally at variance with its calculated height."[10]

Dahinden moved on to Stockholm, Helsinki, Berne, and Geneva, where he met with anatomists, paleontologists, zoologists, primatologists, and specialists in biomechanics. Opinions did not improve. In Moscow, he showed the film to two enthusiastic members of a "snowman" research team, Dmitri Bayanov and Igor Bourtsev, and explosively unloaded on them his frustration with scientific opinion, and not being able to get his head clear about whether the film was real. The outburst left the two men bewildered. Bayanov later sent him a letter taking him to task for having doubts about the ape-man's existence: "I want to ask you why the film is still 'driving you crazy'?"[11]

I chatted with Dahinden one day in the shed at the Vancouver Gun Club that he called home, a spare and extraordinarily neat space, filled with shelves bulging with materials accumulated over fifty years of Bigfooting, each item—and it looked like thousands of books, magazines, clippings, photographs, and casts—sealed in its own plastic bag. When I asked him about the trip to Europe, he started waving his arms. "Nobody gave a shit," he said. "I met some of the biggest scientists in Europe—world-famous in their field: Napier, Schultz, Brunholg. And I looked at 'em and I looked at the screen, I listened to 'em, I said: 'Are we watching the same piece of film?' I stood there with my goddamn mouth open. Number one, they didn't see what was there, and number two, they saw things I didn't see. They are supposed to be the high priests in our society. They looked at the film and they see whatever the hell they wanta see! Totally an emotional response to this thing."[12]

His cool reception in Europe notwithstanding, he couldn't shake the idea that he was onto something big. But he found it hard to separate the question of the beast's existence from questions surrounding Patterson's film. "You see, that was my big thing," he said. "That damn film. Because I realized: if the film was real, if I couldn't crack it, then we have proof that the Sasquatch exist. Period! End of discussion!"

At this point he began actively investigating the film, an activity that led him thousands of miles up and down the West Coast digging up material about Patterson. "Every deal he made, I knew about it," he declared. "Somehow, in some fashion." Dahinden's investigation of Patterson lasted for years, interspersed with periods of collecting shot at the gun club and the endless task of checking out sightings and footprints. Talking with him that afternoon in Vancouver, thirty years after Roger Patterson produced his film, I wasn't sure but that he might still be at it.

Shortly after Dahinden returned from Europe, a writer named Don Hunter appeared at his door, researching Bigfoot for the *National Enquirer*. Captivated by Dahinden's stories and the "treasure trove" of archival material the acerbic little Swiss had squirreled away, Hunter dashed off a query to a large Canadian publisher, proposing to write a book about the beast in collaboration with "the world's best-known Sasquatch hunter."[13] He received a contract back in the overnight mail. I asked Hunter about the experience of working with Dahinden. He let out a sigh. "Jesus," he said. "He was a hard guy to work with. We had some fallings-out. We both walked away a couple of times. 'Fuck you,' that kind of stuff. He was abrasive. But, at the same time, I admired him and respected him.

"We sat in that shack of his there at the gun club and watched the film over and over. And I interviewed him at length." Hunter described himself as "a skeptical newspaper guy." But the more he looked at the film, "the more real it seemed." He remarked that René felt the search for the creature should have been purer. "He had contempt for anyone who even looked like a phony. I also found he was the greatest skeptic of all. I never heard him say he believed in the animal absolutely."

As the book's publication date neared, Dahinden began worrying about the future. For all his years chasing Bigfoot, he had little to show. Despite the publisher's enthusiasm, he knew the book wasn't going to make him rich, and a sequel seemed unlikely. He wasn't a writer like Green or a photogenic media figure like Byrne. An assiduous—some would say compulsive—collector of anything and everything having to do with the beast, Dahinden sensed that his future lay in the accumulation of archival items related to the search: films, photographs, audiotapes, and casts of footprints. As a writer had already lifted two of his footprint photographs from one of Green's books without permission, he knew that collecting would involve legal issues, but the growing number of writers and television producers climbing on board the Bigfoot bandwagon strongly suggested that owning the trophies from the hunt could be lucrative.

The upcoming release of his book may have given him a rush of power, for the plan he devised was utterly Machiavellian. Having received the news of Patterson's death while traveling in Europe, along with a rumor that medical bills had left his family deeply in debt, Dahinden surmised that Mrs. Patterson's defenses were down and that the rights to Patterson's film might be up for grabs. Also aware that Gimlin had been shafted by Bigfoot Enterprises, Dahinden invited Gimlin to travel with him to Toronto and appear at a news conference accompanying the book launch. On the flight, Dahinden told him he would bankroll a lawsuit against Mrs. Patterson to recover what Gimlin was owed, in exchange for half of whatever Gimlin might receive. Gimlin initially balked but finally agreed. Three years later, Gimlin won the suit, received a retroactive one-third interest in the assets of Bigfoot Enterprises, and gave half his interest to Dahinden.

Dahinden remained forever unrepentant. He cursed Mrs. Patterson's lawyer. "They knew they had no case," he said. "And I felt sorry for her— a widow with three kids, you know. But never feel sorry for somebody when you sue them. Just pound the shit out of them, flatten them out so they never can rise again. That's what Mao Tse-tung said, you know. If you have an enemy, destroy 'em so he never can rise again." When I asked him to justify his legal crusade, he answered without a trace of remorse: "I thought, this goddamn film is, in all probability, real. And I wanted to get my sticky fingers on it."

In fact, he wanted more than that. He described to me how, even as he was fighting Mrs. Patterson in court, he approached Glen Koelling, who owned the copyright to Patterson's book: "'Glen,' I said, 'what are you going to do with this book? You're not going to publish it, are you?' He said, 'No, not now.' So I said to him, 'Look, you invested five hundred dollars, I give you five hundred dollars. At least you get your money back.' He said, 'Okay.' So I went to my attorney, he drew up a piece of paper, I give him his money—so I own the Patterson book."

His next tactic was to go after companies who'd used the film clip on television but never paid for it. "It was time the court put a stop to this [piracy]," he said. "Just how many times can those rights be sold?" Lawsuits proliferated.

Dahinden's book *Sasquatch/Bigfoot* was published in 1973 and did moderately well, cementing Dahinden's reputation as a Sasquatch expert—a two-edged sword. Shortly after the book's release, Harvard University held a symposium titled "The Bigfoot-Sasquatch Phenomenon" and asked Dahinden and Green to participate via telephone. As they listened in, halfway through the introductory lecture, a student dressed in an ape suit burst onto the stage and began to stalk the speaker, who, having received a tip, pulled out a toy pistol and fired at the intruder. The sponsors later apologized to Dahinden and Green for the conduct of one Professor Trivers of the biology department, whom they characterized as "unnecessarily harsh and accusatory, in fact downright arrogant."[14]

. . .

Other parts of Patterson's legacy passed to different hands. With the consent of Al DeAtley and Patricia Patterson, the film distributor Ron Olson took over the operation of Northwest Research, which had languished during Patterson's incapacitation, moved it to his home base in Eugene, Oregon, and changed its name to the North American Wildlife Research Association. Eschewing a salary and relying on memberships to keep the operation afloat, he worked full-time compiling reports, soliciting volunteers to join the hunt, and organizing several small expeditions.

A trap Olson and his crew built out of giant planks and telephone poles in the Rogue River–Siskiyou National Forest in Oregon still survives.[15] They baited it with an animal carcass. The plan was: when Bigfoot grabbed the meat, a trap door would fall, sending an electronic signal to a lookout stationed in a nearby cabin. Olson snared several bears but never caught a Bigfoot.

Olson pursued the hunt for a year before returning to his old job working the exhibition circuit for ANE. He continued to lobby the company to produce a Bigfoot film. The board remained hesitant, but every so often something would happen to revive their interest. In 1974, for example, the Smithsonian Institution produced a documentary probing the secrets of Bigfoot, the Abominable Snowman, and the Loch Ness Monster. CBS preempted *Gunsmoke* in prime time to run the program, and sixty million viewers tuned in. *TV Guide* noted the broadcast as a peculiar milestone: "A humble documentary, that [beat out] all other network shows that week, including all of the Top-10 regulars."[16] Unable to deny such overwhelming interest in the subject, ANE finally agreed to let Olson shoot his feature.

Dahinden's view of the CBS documentary was colored by the fact that the program's Bigfoot segment featured Peter Byrne. Through the grapevine, he learned that Byrne would also soon be appearing in a Bigfoot miniseries and had begun negotiations to appear on another highly publicized Robert Morgan "expedition."[17] When producers for LA-based Wolper Productions, who had been grooming Green and Dahinden for a featured role in another major documentary, abruptly decided to feature Byrne instead, Dahinden began to take things personally.

In 1975 Byrne published *The Search for Bigfoot: Monster, Myth or Man?* and Dahinden's smoldering resentments burst into flame. The simple mention of Byrne's name sent him into fits of cursing. "I got a copy of [Byrne's book]," he told me with a tone of incredulity. "I looked at it and I said, 'That sonofabitch stole one of my footprint photos.' The same track which I photographed up on Blue Creek Mountain in 1967, August 29. [I could see the] kick-back by the big toe and all kinds of other little things. I couldn't believe it." Byrne's book also contained the reports prepared by Russian researchers that Dahinden had obtained in Moscow.

Predictably, Dahinden launched a legal barrage against Byrne. The validity of his claims is unclear, but his motives weren't: he wanted to put the Irishman out of business. He appeared at Byrne's information center in The Dalles and, according to anecdotal reports, caused a near panic. (Dahinden later claimed he entered the premises believing that his copyrighted photographs were being displayed illegally.) Byrne called the police for help getting him out of town and persuaded a judge to issue a warrant for his arrest. Byrne later told an acquaintance he feared Dahinden would set fire to the center.

Three years after Patterson's death, Ron Olson released a feature-length film under the ANE banner titled *Bigfoot: Man or Beast.* Using the same scientific hook he used to market *Bigfoot,* he devised a story-line involving members of a Bigfoot research party determined to capture the beast for science on a pack trip deep into a mysterious wilderness. The film comes to a frightful end when a Bigfoot terrorizes the expedition at night.

Olson spent several years exhibiting the film around the country. He planned to make millions with the film but says it lost money. In 1978 he showed it in Orlando, Florida, where he was interviewed by a reporter. "Until the day he died," Olson said, "Roger maintained steadfastly that what he captured on film was exactly what he stumbled across that day on horseback."[18] It was only a matter of time until Bigfoot was captured, he added. Search parties were still scouring the wilderness, following up on "hundreds of reports" that were flowing into his "headquarters hotline." But it was a daunting task. "The Pacific Northwest is so big and uncharted, anything could be living there."

In the spring of 1978, the University of British Columbia Museum of Anthropology organized a symposium titled "Sasquatch and Related Phenomena." Nearly two dozen scientists attended. John Green, who had just released his fourth book, *Sasquatch: The Apes among Us,* was asked to deliver the keynote speech. Dahinden also appeared, accompanied by his crowd-shy "partner," Bob Gimlin. Byrne also showed up, unannounced, with a camera crew who proceeded to set up lights in the auditorium. Outraged, Dahinden and Green threatened to leave and take Gimlin with them unless Byrne and his crew were ejected. They prevailed, and the invaders packed up and left.

Gimlin could hardly believe it. He had tried for a decade to distance himself from the Bigfoot scene, only to be pulled back in, pestered with legalities, and made a partner to lawsuits—one of which had clearly hurt Patterson's family. Now he was party to an internecine squabble, all because he'd once agreed to help out his rodeo buddy. Shortly after the conference, he instructed his attorney to turn all his rights and percentages over to Dahinden.

Dahinden was uncharacteristically sheepish about this turn of events. "I phoned [Gimlin] and kept him informed what I was doing, and I felt like I was harassing him," he said. "I mean, he was my business partner, you know. He just didn't want to be bothered. So he says, 'I turn it over to René. He did all the work, and I just don't want to be bothered.' So my attorney told me, and I said, 'Did I dream this?' He said, 'No, I just drew up the papers to get signed, and I'll send them to you.'"

Apparently money also entered into the picture. Dahinden told me he paid Gimlin a "significant sum" for "expenses" associated with the deal but didn't elaborate. Another source corroborated the expense payment and mentioned an amount that was, indeed, significant. In the end, perhaps Gimlin did get at least part of his due.

Three months later Dahinden was in Portland for a court hearing. The occasion may have had something to do with Byrne, as the legal landscape between them was by now tangled; but the particulars are essentially beside the point. One morning he found a note on the door of his motel room from an acquaintance, asking to meet him at a nearby restaurant. What happened next Dahinden described in a police report:

> 10:10 AM: I stepped outdoors . . . and walked toward the restaurant. I got to the entrance of the lot. Peter Byrne stepped out from my right from behind a vehicle. He walked toward me about ten feet or so. As he came close to me he said "Dahinden, we have *[sic]* enough of you, now." I said to Byrne, "I will not talk to you, there is a court order out about that. If you want to talk to me, talk to my attorney. I will not talk to you without a witness." I reached into my shirt pocket getting my attorney's business card out, holding it toward Byrne. At the same time I attempted to walk by him toward the restaurant.[19]

An altercation followed. Court documents issued two weeks later show that a pending charge in Wasco County (The Dalles) against René Dahinden (at the behest of Peter Byrne) was dismissed "in light of the recent assault on Mr. Dahinden by Mr. Byrne in Multnomah County" (Portland), and that charges pending against Byrne stemming from the preceding incident were dropped. Shortly afterward, Peter Byrne closed the Bigfoot Information Center and returned to Asia to work on elephant conservation. René Dahinden retired to his home at the Vancouver Gun Club, where he continued to collect lead shot and royalties from the rights to the Patterson film.

PART III

REASON AND TRUTH

10
THE GOBLIN UNIVERSE

If you see me disappearing down a mental rabbit-hole from time to time you will know where I am headed. I will be traveling unwillingly into the Goblin Universe.

—John Napier, *Bigfoot: The Yeti and Sasquatch in Myth and Reality*

I attended my last Bigfoot conference in a planetarium. Several speakers spoke of the beast in metaphysical terms, an uncomfortable development for many attendees. For example, Henry Franzoni, a computer consultant, suggested that Bigfoot might be a purely mental phenomenon, citing as an example his own ability to communicate telepathically with his cats.[1]

A "native legend speaker" from a coastal tribe in British Columbia told of seeing a "Bukwas" at night on a beach. "They're very rare," he said. "As our legends tell us, they live in an invisible house deep in the forest so we can't find them." An excruciatingly calm older gentleman named Mr. Cotton, with snowy-white hair and matching beard, spoke about his experiences living on other planets and became so wrapped up in his tale that it took the moderator several minutes to get him off the stage.

Jack "Kewaunee" Lapseritis spoke about the "Sasquatch people," whom he described as "paraphysical, interdimensional nature people that are profoundly psychic." I knew of Lapseritis but had never met him. Early in my investigation, I was given his name and wrote him a letter asking for news of recent sightings. A year later I received a reply, my first inkling that the hunt had transmogrified into something very odd:

Dear Mr. McLeod,

I apologize for the delay in responding but I'm just completing the last chapter of my book based on 40 years of Bigfoot research and what I discovered (which has nothing to do with the monster hunts that short-sighted researchers have been on all during this time). To them, ego and money and fame are more important than the truth.

Enclosed are maps marked with active (Bigfoot) areas for the summer. No guns or cameras! They'll know and won't come around. Camp for 1 or 2 weeks in a place, sit and read, study nature, meditate, and do other "non-threatening" things and you may have a good chance to encounter one.

Very sincerely,
Kewaunee[2]

During Kewaunee's talk, several of the audience walked out, clearly disgruntled. Asked to comment on Lapseritis for a documentary, René Dahinden spoke for the old school. "We know all about Lapseritis," he said. "He had 235—or 500 by now—Sasquatch encounters . . . in his mind! I'm not interested in Sasquatch in his goddamn mind. I'm interested in Sasquatch in the bush on the ground. How many Sasquatch he has in his mind, I don't want to hear about it!"[3]

The tensions in the Bigfoot movement came into sharp contrast during a panel discussion titled "The Great Debate: Conventional vs. Paranormal." Speaking for the paranormal supporters were Franzoni, Cotton, and Lapseritis. They faced off against a full-time Bigfoot investigator, the vice chairman of a cryptozoological society in Arizona, and a Bigfoot buff who made his living as a comedian. The panel elicited puzzlement and outrage. Several audience members made it clear they resented being associated with "the lunatic fringe." "What they are and where they came from," declared one frustrated Bigfooter, "is rather irrelevant because, until this animal is proven to exist, it doesn't matter where they came from."

Lapseritis remained unfazed. "Just because you have eyes you believe that you can see," he said. "I've seen both physical and nonphysical Sasquatch. And I've seen the space ships that were there—and they *were* there—and there's some connection, and I'm not going to ignore that or plead ignorance."

The Bigfoot investigator looked grim. "The situation is," he said slowly through clenched teeth, "we either have a new undiscovered animal out there, or we don't! The only way to prove it is to find solid physical evidence. To me, it's a simple question: yes or no? There's no . . . between."

"We cannot prove anything in actual fact," Mr. Cotton replied calmly. "We cannot even prove we exist. As far as hallucinations are concerned, we do not know if a psychotic person is actually hallucinating or that they may be seeing a reality which we cannot see."

"But if you don't start with the assumption that it is one reality that we all share," exclaimed the comedian, "there's no reason to be having this discussion at all, because nothing means anything."

The highlight of the event was a tribute to Dahinden by the symposium's sponsor, Kokanee Beer, acknowledging his role as the world's greatest Sasquatch hunter in a series of beer commercials, for which he won a top acting award in the Canadian advertising industry. The spots were projected on a huge screen amid laughter, cheers, and thunderous applause, and Dahinden took a bow. The man who had spent a lifetime railing at others for not giving Sasquatch the serious attention it deserved had achieved his most lasting fame by spoofing it.

Forty years of dealing with Bigfooting's daffy underbelly had left Dahinden deeply angry and indestructibly tactless. But he could also see humor in the chase and laugh at himself. A close friend characterized him as a "charming asshole." He saw thousands of footprints but never discovered one himself, and he was constantly overshadowed by figures like Roger Patterson, John Green, and Peter Byrne. They all made money off the beast while he lived hand to mouth, tracking every lead and getting nowhere. No steady paycheck, no Bigfoot film, no Irishman's gift of the gab.

Nevertheless, something about wilderness and the mysteries Dahinden imagined in such places took possession of his life. He set off on adventures into the woods driving a delivery van he converted to a camper, towing a trailer holding his motorbikes. Every few years for three decades he returned to Bluff Creek. By day he roamed the ridges; at night he enjoyed sitting by a campfire eating a rib-eye steak, boiled red potatoes, salad, and a beer, followed by brandy and a skinny cigar. As the moon rose, he would crank up Pavarotti on the stereo until the soaring tenor reverberated through the forest.

Approaching his seventieth birthday, he visited the home of his friend Larry Lund, bringing with him a copy of Patterson's film. Lund threaded it on a viewer and got caught up looking at it frame by frame. After watching him for a while, Dahinden piped up, "Larry, what do you think? Do you think Bigfoot really exists? Do you think Patterson could have fooled all of us all this time?" Lund couldn't believe his ears. "All the years I've known René," he said, "that one time he came as close as I've ever heard him say that he had a serious doubt."[4]

At the symposium, Dahinden's tribute ended with a prize drawing, and I won a Kokanee Beer T-shirt.

René Dahinden died in April 2001. I remember having coffee with him inside his shed at the gun club. He was staring at a poster on the wall of the famous frame from Patterson's film in which Bigfoot looks over its shoulder at the camera. "You know," he said, "I sit here and drink my coffee and read or whatever, look at it there. You have to know what you're looking at. Bloody muscle masses moving there. . . . You know the ones on the back of the knee, the big muscles there, breasts bobbing up and down. . . . What you understand on TV is nothing. You have to really look at the 16 mm over and over and over. . . ." He paused for a moment. "You're a filmmaker," he said. "You can picture it." He held up his hands, palms out, and closed his eyes. "Picture the forest: tall trees, foggy in there, kinda dark, you know, in there. . . . And you see this nebulous thing flittering through the bush. You say, 'What the hell was that?' You know it looks like a Sasquatch . . . but!" He opened his eyes, stared at me for a moment, and shook his head quizzically. "That's the Sasquatch today. You know what I mean? This problem has really nothing to do with Sasquatch as such, it has to do with people!"

Held together by the hollow camaraderie of the Internet, contemporary Bigfooters lack the prickly, outdoorsy quality of the old guard who made the first twenty years of the hunt such earthy history. But for the isolated outbreak of tracks, or the occasional lone, hairy figure observed crossing a dark road, sightings and footprints—never reported in great numbers even in the beast's heyday—are now rarely reported at all.

The most exciting development in the Bigfoot world is the Skookum cast, brought out of the southern Washington woods in the summer of 2000 by a group calling itself the Bigfoot Field Researchers Organization (BFRO). Their discovery is detailed on their Web site.[5] The story began when a BFRO team of ten plunged into the Gifford Pinchot National Forest outfitted with a boom box to broadcast a tape of putative Bigfoot vocalizations, a supply of "pheromone chips" and fruit for use as bait, a "high-sensitivity microphone," and a "thermal camera" to detect the heat signature of large mammals at night.

They searched for six days and nights and found "potential Sasquatch tracks," heard "unusual sounds," and detected "bipedal movement" in several locations. The playing of the Bigfoot tape elicited "return screams from up to two Sasquatches."

On the evening of day 6, they left fruit and peanuts along a road where screams had been heard. On day 7 they hit pay dirt: a large depression in the mud at the edge of a shallow pool. They preserved the imprint in plaster. Once it hardened, several people were required to lift the cast from the mud.

Soon afterward, John Green and Grover Krantz came to see the Skookum cast. Jeff Meldrum, associate professor of anatomy and anthropology at Idaho State University, and Krantz's heir apparent as the world's preeminent Bigfoot scientist, posted his analysis of the evidence on the Web:

> The imprint of what appears to be a large animal's left forearm, hip, thigh, and heel was discovered Sept. 22 in a muddy wallow near Mt. Adams in southern Washington state by a Bigfoot Field Researchers Organization expedition in the Gifford Pinchot National Forest.

After the cast was cleaned, extensive impressions of hair on the buttock and thigh surfaces and a fringe of longer hair along the forearm were evident. Meldrum identified what appear to be skin ridge patterns on the heel, comparable to fingerprints, that are characteristic of primates.

"While not definitively proving the existence of a species of North American ape, the cast constitutes significant and compelling new evidence that will hopefully stimulate further serious research and investigation into the presence of these primates in the Northwest mountains and elsewhere," Meldrum said.[6]

After studying the BFRO Web site, I made a few inquiries and found several oddities in the circumstances surrounding the cast. For one, by the BFRO's own admission, there were no giant footprints in the vicinity. For another, the group just happened to have 250 pounds of casting plaster on hand to form the cast. But the most revealing aspect of the affair is the fact that the expedition was staged at the behest of an Australian production company that had contacted the BFRO seeking material for a film about Bigfoot. Some dubious observers have dubbed the plaster evidence the "butt cast."

. . .

After Dahinden's death, I returned to British Columbia to talk with John Green and see how the loss of his old partner had affected him.[7] Today, except for the look of the cars and an ATM or two, the small farming community of Agassiz, where Green took over the *Advance* newspaper in 1954, still resembles a scene from the fifties. But the ghost of the letters "Agassiz Advance," visible at the top of an old storefront on Pioneer Avenue, was a reminder of how much has changed: the building was being turned into a craft gallery. On the trip to Green's home in Harrison Hot Springs a few miles away, I saw his legacy hanging, literally, all around, in the form of signs announcing "Sasquatch Provincial Park," "Sasquatch Campground," and "Sasquatch Springs RV Resort."[8]

Green, in his seventies, presents an unruffled exterior, but he has a couple of hot buttons. One is Peter Byrne, of whom even a passing mention made him apoplectic. "I should make clear," he said sternly, "if you're planning to write about Peter Byrne as if he was a part of the Sasquatch investigation on a real basis, I'll stop talking to you right now." I quickly redirected the conversation to his old partner.

"The split between René and me was very fundamental," he said. "We had a lot of fun in the early days. We didn't have any serious arguments. We started out together trying to get this thing. But after a while it became clear to me that the odds of being able to do it ourselves were zilch, and I became much more inclined to work with other people, and, you know, share things. To him, sharing information that he and I had been involved in together was a real betrayal. René, to the end of his life, was still trying to be the guy who got the Sasquatch." He had more to say about Dahinden, none of it good. Whatever had happened between them, the rift was total and irreconcilable.

When I asked about the status of Bigfoot today, he perked up; his enthusiasm for the hunt was obviously undimmed. "In Florida these things are really under pressure, because they're paving the whole damn state," he said. "There's a much better chance of encountering one there than there is here, where the animals have 99 percent of this country."

He then launched into a detailed description of the BFRO body cast. He considered it perhaps the most important piece of evidence ever to support the existence of Bigfoot. "One of the heel prints from the big cast," Green said, had been examined by a noted physical anthropologist, Darius Swindler, who opined that it "can't be from anything other than an enormous higher primate."

As I bid Green goodbye, I asked how he felt about the nearby territorial park being named after Sasquatch. "You're asking about whether I have a legacy," he stated soberly. "Sasquatches were well known in British Columbia long before I got involved. But when I saw a great big sign saying Sasquatch Valley in Ohio, that made an impression."

Later that day, standing on the shore of Harrison Lake, where I began my pursuit of Bigfoot at the Sasquatch Forum, I pondered the new era of Bigfoot, replete with paranormalist devotees and butt casts. I had seen a photo of Green posing with the Skookum cast on the BFRO Web site, so his endorsement of it shouldn't have surprised me. But after several years studying the Bigfoot phenomenon, I was still puzzled about how anyone could accept such improbable evidence.

There are many kinds of Bigfoot "evidence," but they boil down to four types: people say they saw or heard something; a depression is found in the ground; an anthropological theory is posited; or someone produces a photograph or a film. All such evidence has proved false. The two most famous incidents in Bigfoot history include the reputed capture of the small ape-like creature dubbed Jacko in British Columbia in 1884, which turns out to have been the fabrication of a frontier newspaper;[9] and the "mountain devils" attack on a band of miners on Mount St. Helens in 1924. The miners were, in fact, spiritualists, and the giant rocks that they claimed were hurled on their cabin were, most likely, part of a small landslide inadvertently started by kids from a youth camp.[10]

One of the most enduring Bigfooter beliefs holds that Bigfoot is a descendant of the giant Asian ape *Gigantopithecus,* popularized by Bernard Heuvelmans, who charged into the spotlight in 1952 with his theory that the yeti was a descendant of the ancient creature, and Ivan Sanderson, who argued that Bigfoot was a descendant of the yeti, which migrated from China to North America across the Bering land bridge about fifteen thousand or so years ago. In reality, archaeologists working under the auspices of the National Geographic Society who have studied *Gigantopithecus* view it as "a dead-end on the fossil fringes of the hominoid family tree."[11] They estimated that the animal stood "over ten feet tall and weighed as much as 1,200 pounds," and that it flourished for about six million years before going extinct about half a million years ago, perhaps as a result of *Homo erectus* usurping its food source.[12]

As for Giganto's journey across the land bridge—we are left with a picture: breeding-size groups of enormous bamboo-eating, knuckle-walking apes dragging themselves ten thousand miles through an arid, frozen wasteland populated with extremely hungry humans. Had they survived that ordeal, what awaited them was what scientists call the

Pleistocene or North American extinction, which killed off more than half of the large mammals on the continent: mastodons, mammoths, cheetahs, lions, camels, saber-toothed cats, giant ground sloths, and beavers the size of black bears.

Nevertheless, be it perpetual-motion machines or gravity shields, more people than ever are willing to believe almost anything, even if it violates the most fundamental laws of nature. Irrational beliefs were a pet peeve of Dahinden, who thought himself the ultimate rationalist— a perilous state of mind for a Bigfooter. It perplexed him that he often found it impossible to separate fact from fiction when questioning witnesses about reports. He made an analogy with an old TV program called *Lie Detector.* "They took these people and put them on the machine," he said. "And there was this one woman who claimed she was captured by a UFO. There she was telling this story—how she went to planet . . . whatever, you know—away they went. A great description of every-thing. . . . And she passed!" He shook his head in amazement at the memory. "It's funny and it isn't. In the woman's mind she was telling the truth. If you believe something so much, you can't lie."

The blending of science and science fiction that Sanderson raised to an art form half a century ago has been evolved to a point that might sur-prise even him. Filling gaps or uncertainty in science with views based on nothing but political, religious, or other personal convictions has be-come a national epidemic. Occasionally rising to the level of outright fraud, but largely given a pass by the media, counterfactual claims drift unchecked in the blogosphere, assuming a life of their own.

Sanderson was certainly not the first to promote theories that clashed with conventional science, but no one before him had ever reached such a wide audience. Although many of his beliefs and theories were ab-solutely daft (undersea UFOs and sea monsters, ancient alien visitation, multiple Bermuda Triangles), Sanderson argued for them forcefully, armed with a quiver of factoids to keep naysayers at bay. "I make fan-tastic statements," he once told a radio host, "but I can prove them."[13]

The human propensity for questioning science probably began at the moment in 1833 when the English philosopher William Whewell coined the word. Suddenly, the fringe thinkers, the contrarians, and the hoaxers had a brand-new world of fresh opportunities. Scams immediately proliferated (perpetual-motion machines were a particularly popular investment in the latter half of the 1800s), orchestrated by hucksters who based their claims on fraudulent interpretations of newly emergent "scientific" information little understood by the lay public.

The most famous American hoax of the era, which gave the first inkling of the public's fascination with the idea of giant humanoids, was staged in 1869 in Cardiff, New York, where a ten-foot-tall "petrified man" was uncovered by well diggers. Scientists denounced it as a fraud, but the surrounding Christian community seized on the "fossil" as proof of the biblical story that giants such as Goliath actually existed, and crowds flocked to see it. The landowner began charging admission. The showman P. T. Barnum put his own fossil giant on display, claiming his was the real one. The "Cardiff Giant" was ultimately revealed as the centerpiece of a hoax created by an atheist to illustrate the gullibility of fundamentalist Christians.

The first notable example of pseudoscience was a claim, put forth in a book published in 1882, that all of the world's ancient civilizations were descended from the mythical city of Atlantis.[14] Atlantis wasn't a new subject. In *Twenty Thousand Leagues Under the Sea,* published in 1870, Jules Verne had used Atlantis as a hook—but Verne was writing fiction. The author of *Atlantis: The Antediluvian World,* Ignatius Donnelly, wanted people to believe Atlantis was real. He massed an enormous amount of detailed research from the work of charlatans and quacks, which he spiced with excerpts from the works of reputable scholars to give the impression that they agreed with his argument. The book was a runaway hit, going through seven printings in its first year of release. By 1890 it had gone through twenty-three printings in the U.S. and twenty-six in England and had been translated into all the major European languages.[15]

The philosopher, historian, and author John Fiske (1842–1901) may have been thinking of Donnelly when he wrote a book about the pathology of the human mind. In it he recounted an experience from early in his career, when he was working as a librarian at Harvard. The task before him, he explained, was to determine how to catalogue "lucubrations" written by individuals who he termed "cranks." He noted that theories challenging the law of gravitation were especially popular among such individuals, and quoted examples: "It is not gravitation which makes a river run down hill," wrote one self-styled scientist, "but the impetus of the water behind pressing on the water before."[16]

To separate legitimate works in the library catalogue from those of the cranks, Fiske decided to create a new classification, "Insane Literature," and duly inscribed it on the outside of a card drawer. Believing that "the matter seemed happily disposed of," he was soon reminded that several of the authors whose books he had reclassified had close ties to the university and might take offense at finding their work so designated. Fiske's solution was simply to scratch out the word *insane* and replace it with *eccentric*.

Today, the haplessly uninformed eccentric has been joined by well-informed individuals who bend reality on purpose. Erich von Daniken, who wrote *Chariots of the Gods* in 1968, made a fortune promoting the idea that extraterrestrials visited the earth thousands of years ago. Despite the wholesale dismissal of his claims by the scientific community, his books have sold, by his account, more than sixty-three million copies worldwide and spawned a number of highly rated TV specials.

Interviewed on the PBS TV series *Nova,* von Daniken admitted he hadn't actually conducted some of the research he claimed, and explained his approach to popularizing a subject: "When somebody writes books in my style and in my sense, which are not scientific books, we call it in German *Sachbucher.* It's a kind of popular book, but it's not science fiction, though all the facts do exist but with other interpretations. Then the author is allowed to use effects. So some little things like that are really not important because they do not touch the facts. They are simply stimulating the reader, and one is allowed to do this."[17]

The fields of archaeology and anthropology, which bear on the question of Bigfoot directly, are particularly rife with subterfuge and delusion. Especially vulnerable is paleoanthropology, or the search for human origins, which obsessed Sanderson. In his book *Bones of Contention,* Roger Lewin writes: "What sets paleoanthropology off from other sciences is the *degree* of controversy it engenders." The anthropologist Sir Wilfred Le Gros Clark observes: "It is extraordinarily difficult to view with complete objectivity the evidence for our own evolutionary origin . . . because the problem is such a very personal one."[18] With these kinds of passions, instances of anthropological fraud are not at all uncommon. Piltdown Man is far from the only example.

Early in my research, I spoke with George Agogino (now deceased), a physical anthropologist and archaeologist best known for his contributions to paleo-Indian archaeology. He collaborated with Ivan Sanderson on several projects and wrote the foreword to Sanderson's book *Abominable Snowmen: Legend Come to Life.* He also consulted for Tom Slick, examining evidence from Slick's first yeti expedition and his Bigfoot hunt at Bluff Creek.

Thinking back on that time, Agogino characterized himself as "more conservative than most of the guys" who were hovering around Slick. "I have sort of a conscience at times," he said with a laugh. "Quite a few people created things that didn't even exist to get [Slick] excited, and he would support them for a while. I told him [to be careful,] but he continued to do it because he was filthy rich and didn't care. He really believed that he was going to find [Bigfoot]."[19]

When I asked about fakery, Agogino told me a story. In 1940, a young scholar at the University of New Mexico named Frank Hibben announced that he had discovered spear points—similar to a type found in Europe—in a cave in the Sandia Mountains. They were evidence, he claimed, of a 25,000-year-old "Sandia Man"—the oldest human culture ever found in America. The discovery, hailed by *Time* magazine as the first definitive proof that the earliest Americans were of European origin, rocketed Hibben to national fame and established him as preeminent in his field. Sandia Cave was only the first of many fantastic Hibben finds, including the discovery of spear points in Alaska—proof, he claimed, that humans had walked to North America across the Asian land bridge.

Over the years, Hibben hobnobbed with celebrities and appeared on television shows, including *What's My Line?* and had his own TV series, *On Safari with Frank Hibben*.[20] But there were rumors that his artifacts had been planted. In the early 1960s, Agogino, asked to review Hibben's findings, concluded that a number of gross inconsistencies made it impossible to say precisely where the artifacts had been unearthed. Other investigators also reexamined the findings and uncovered evidence that Hibben's artifacts had come from sites other than Sandia Cave, and some had been physically altered. It's now generally accepted that Hibben salted the sites.

Hibben several times threatened to sue him, Agogino said, but never did. "I used to be his graduate assistant. And Frank faked it—no question about it—he actually faked it. There is no Sandia culture as we know it. It's a sad situation, to tell the truth, because Frank Hibben is a tremendous person, really."

"Why would he do something like that?" I asked.

"Because I think it was early in his career and he wanted to make a fast reputation for himself. But it steamrolled. I was a friend of Hibben. He's not a sleazy little fraud. He's a person who could charm his way into anything. And he probably charmed himself into believing things that weren't really there. I'm sure he believed that Sandia Cave was twenty-five thousand years old."

In a similar way, there is little doubt Roger Patterson charmed himself into believing something that wasn't true. But, as with John Green, René Dahinden, and Peter Byrne, Patterson's obsession with Bigfoot—manic as it appeared—was not completely unreasonable. When he took up the hunt half a century ago, the door still wasn't quite shut on the idea of a living ape-man. Bigfooters today seem like an altogether different case.

11

REASON AND TRUTH

[I] attribute the social and psychological problems of modern society
to the fact that society requires people to live under conditions radically
different from those under which the human race evolved.

—Theodore Kaczynski, *Unabomber Manifesto: Industrial Society and
Its Future*

In the summer of 2000, a psychologist named Matthew Johnson reported an encounter with a Bigfoot while hiking with his family on a
trail that wanders through the woods at the Oregon Caves National
Monument. On the Web, the Bigfoot network buzzed with excitement.
Loren Coleman, an author who has built a career around the beast and
similar oddities, called the sighting one of the "top cryptozoological stories of the year."[1]

This high-profile sighting offered me a serendipitous opportunity to
investigate a contemporary eyewitness report—one of the more curious
aspects of the Bigfoot phenomenon—while also exploring the subject
of caves, a central element of Bigfoot lore. Where better to ponder the
question of why anyone today would believe in the existence of a giant
hominid than in a subterranean setting intimately familiar to our ancient
ancestors, who were once wild animals themselves?

Lying just seventy miles northeast of Bluff Creek, the caves were also
a potential clue to the riddle of the Klamath Knot, the haunting landscape that David Rains Wallace has called an "evolutionary mystery."
With so many strange things reported in the area over the years, it seemed

likely that something about the environment in that part of the country affected people's reasoning.

With a sense of anticipation, I loaded my truck and headed south to the Oregon Caves and Bluff Creek. Although I had touched the periphery and got a hint of the mystery, I hadn't yet visited the site where Patterson shot his film. I had a mental picture of it, but there would be differences. As with most Bigfoot expeditions, this one led away from civilization, on narrow roads winding through small towns with names like Selma and Wonder—old hippie redoubts clinging to life on the income generated from pottery and woodworking. The cave complex lies forty-five minutes east of the town of Cave Junction, at the end of a narrow road that rises into the Siskiyous in a series of wild switchbacks. The core of the complex is an Arts and Crafts–style hotel sided in tree bark. In the gift shop, I perused a book titled *Animal Tracks in the Pacific Northwest* and found a list of indigenous wildlife, but no mention of Bigfoot.

Several Park Service rangers stood near the cash register drinking coffee, including a young man with a ponytail and bangs down to his eyebrows. His nametag said "Tom." When I broached the subject of the Bigfoot sighting, I sensed a slight tensing in the group, as if the incident had been something of an embarrassment. "Mr. Johnson may have heard some sounds," Ranger Tom said. "Most likely a grouse." He sucked a whoosh of air into his gut, puffed out his cheeks and gave out a deep "whoop whoop whoop." An impressive, if unexpected, sound. "On the other hand," he said, "it might have been a fox. They make a sound that will scare the living daylights out of you." A group of visitors chose that moment to enter, sparing me the impression.

I signed up for a tour. Our group formed at the cave entrance, with Ranger Tom in charge, wearing a Smokey Bear hat that did little to disguise the indignity he had perpetrated on himself with the haircut. We entered the cave and were plunged into darkness, save for the faint glow from a string of lightbulbs that led us between rock walls along a stream (aptly named the River Styx) into a grotto known as Joachim Miller's

Chapel. Ranger Tom turned out the lights. The blackness was impressive. "We have now entered the mouth of Mother Earth," he intoned solemnly. "Caves of this sort have a life of their own."

He compared the cave to the functioning of the human body, then snapped on the lights and led us into Mother Earth's bowels. We threaded our way through Devereaux's Hole, then up the Spiral Stairs into the Cave of the Winds. People fidgeted uneasily as bats flitted among us. Ranger Tom warned us not to antagonize them, as it was mating season and we were standing in a "bats' singles bar."

Onward we plunged, through chambers rent by flowstone, inset with marble and moonstone sculptures, skirting opalescent pillars rising from the floor and stalactites hanging like huge icicles in the Shovel Room and the Coral Gardens. We stopped beside a slab that bore dozens of signatures from the 1880s. The names showed clearly beneath a thin veneer of transparent calcite that coated the surface like glass, the dim light from the overhead bulbs giving them an effervescent, shimmering quality. Absent electricity, those early visitors toured by lantern or torchlight, in an atmosphere that had to provide a much more imaginative experience.

Today, the raw essence of imagination is submerged by distractions unknown to our ancient forebears. The people who drew the famous figures on the walls of the caves at Altamira in Spain and Lascaux in France twenty thousand or more years ago, for instance, imagined things on a scale we can't really comprehend. They believed caves were a gateway to the underworld, the walls, ceilings, and floors of the chambers forming a membrane between themselves and the creatures of that other world. Caves were places to commune with spirits and conduct hunting rites.

Those ancient shamans journeyed far into the dark, crawling at times into crevices barely large enough for a body, receiving messages from the texture and shape of the rocks, and entering into trances during which they might transform into a bear or an antelope, a flock of swallows or a fish (the "sorcerer" figure from the cave of Trois-Frères in

France has legs and hands that look human, the back and ears of a grazing animal, antlers like a reindeer, and a horse's tail), inscribing the images of the figures they imagined on the surfaces around them.[2]

Burial sites of that period have yielded animal parts ceremoniously arranged with human remains, evidence that the people of the Upper Paleolithic embraced a complex mythological world centered on this human/animal duality. Evolutionary psychologists theorize that this belief persisted for millions of years of human development, and—because humanity was imprinted on a time scale so vast—these primal instincts and emotions remain encoded in our DNA.[3] This theory may explain the many behaviors, impulses, and ways of thinking shared by people worldwide. The corollary to this suggestion is that images of our animal selves remain alive in our reptilian brains. In recent years *Gigantopithecus* and *Homo erectus* fossils have been found together at a site in Vietnam and another in China, evidence that the giant ape and humans coexisted.[4] Scientists believe that encounters between the two species were inevitable—perhaps extending over millions of years—and it is possible that the animals left an impression on humankind's tribal memory that is stirred by accounts of Bigfoot sightings today.

Ranger Tom gathered us around him in the Ghost Room and talked about caves and the supernatural. He told us how ancient man used "moon milk," a cave substance that has been found to contain the same bacteria used to produce antibiotics, to heal cuts. Faintly illuminated in the far reaches of the chamber, several eerie, shroudlike figures oozed from the wall. Just behind us was an ominous black opening in the rock known as a wild cave, leading deeper into the belly of the mountain. I tried to imagine exploring such a passageway in total darkness and mind-numbing silence, clothed only in an animal skin and toting an oil lamp, or maybe with no light at all.

I never discovered who originally proposed a connection between caves and Bigfoot. It may have been Sanderson, who explored and wrote about caves as an animal collector and was a lifelong caver. Or Bigfooters may simply enjoy talking about caves—after all, subterranean spaces are inherently mysterious, and without mystery, where would they be? As for the Bigfooter theory that the beasts use caves as hideouts and enter them when they're about to die, to conceal their remains from human eyes—this far underground, in the pitch black without a torch, it didn't seem possible for any animal to just wander around, regardless of what powers it might possess.

Apparently, however, they sometimes do. Near the end of the tour, the path skirts a pit holding the bones of a black bear. The animal had found its way a long distance in and through several turns of the passage, despite the dark. Ranger Tom said that five or six other bear skeletons had been found near the same spot, along with the twelve-thousand-year-old remains of an Ice Age jaguar and two grizzly skeletons—one dating from more than fifty thousand years ago. But there were no Bigfoot bones. So the Bigfoot-cave connection remains a puzzle.

As our group exited into the daylight, Ranger Tom bade us farewell. Eager to press on to the heart of the matter and put myself in Matthew Johnson's place, I retied my boots and set off on the Big Tree Trail, a four-mile loop that circles the top of the mountain above the cave. Somewhere along this path, Johnson said he encountered a Bigfoot. Maybe I could at least pick up a vibe.

The trail led steadily uphill through a thick forest of venerable old firs. Silence reigned. The year before, a massive blaze dubbed the Biscuit Fire had burned half a million acres between the ocean and the cave complex, including what is arguably the prime Bigfoot habitat in North America: the whole of the Kalmiopsis Wilderness in Oregon and a significant chunk of the Six Rivers National Forest, just across the border in California. The conflagration might have pushed the Bigfoot population toward the caves, only a few miles from the fire's eastern edge. If that had happened, my chances of seeing one were greatly increased.

The trail dropped off steeply to the west, ten miles from the nearest civilization. To the east, the country for twenty miles was largely uninhabited, honeycombed with fire roads and old mines sunk in a landscape of jagged peaks and rushing streams. Whether those immense tracts of empty terrain qualified as wilderness is debatable. But Bigfoot has never been strictly a wilderness creature. It has a penchant for showing up in state parks, farms, and suburbs, and even along freeways.

Johnson's sighting was curious. Immediately following the encounter, he contacted media outlets in Portland and San Francisco. "I'm a big guy," he told a reporter a few days after it happened. "I'm six foot nine inches tall, 280 pounds, size sixteen feet, and this thing was much bigger than me. I felt totally vulnerable." Then tears came to his eyes. "It was the most fear I've ever experienced in my life. I saw this very tall, dark, hairy creature walk from one tree to the next. It was a very faint 'whoof, whoof, whoof, whoof, whoof, whoof.' It dawned on me: I had an epiphany that it smelled a strong smell—and the sound. . . . We're dealing with Sasquatch here—Bigfoot."

I asked the Park Service supervisor at the caves about the incident, and he said rangers had accompanied Johnson back to the scene and found "partial prints." Of what it's uncertain, but the report they issued made clear that they did not see large, humanlike tracks. Within days, however, Bigfoot T-shirts were being sold in the gift shop (the brainchild of an astute concessionaire).

Bigfoot sightings are rarely covered by the media these days unless someone kicks up a fuss, which Johnson did, acting as his own press agent. Initially he claimed never to have heard of Bigfoot, but within hours of the encounter he had obtained the unlisted phone number of an organization, little known except to Bigfooters, that tracks reports. Johnson called the Web master for their Internet site, who ran him through a standard list of questions: How tall was it? How far away were you? What color was it? What kind of hair did it have? He couldn't tell much, Johnson said, because he'd glimpsed the beast for only a few seconds. But as the media attention escalated, he began describing to reporters the length, color, and texture of the hair.

The last time I viewed the Web site where Johnson initially reported his encounter, I had trouble finding any mention of it at all. A diligent search of the site turned up two cryptic notes:

> 1 July 2000—Oregon Caves, Oregon. Matthew Johnson phoned . . . to say he thinks he saw Bigfoot while hiking the upper trail with his family near the Oregon Caves National Monument.
> 5 July 2000—Oregon Caves, Oregon. Update: Oregon Caves hiker actually encountered a black bear, investigators now say.[5]

When I contacted the Web master for help evaluating the report, I got a barbed response and the distinct impression that Johnson had been somewhat touchy when pressed for particulars. I tried contacting him directly, explaining that I'd like to ask him some questions, but got no response.

Nevertheless, Johnson has continued, albeit sporadically, to appear in the news. Three years after his encounter, articles in *USA Today* and the *New York Times* reported that once a month he hops in his 1995 baby-blue Cadillac and escorts the curious into the Siskiyou Mountains to feed and track Bigfoot, using bananas, watermelon, and pastries as lures. And somewhere in the woods, he claims to have nailed a camera with an automatic shutter to a tree, to snap the beast's picture should it wander by.

A half hour up the trail, I arrived at the Big Tree, a stupendous Douglas fir, forty feet around and a thousand years old—a great, deeply fissured edifice armored in folds of gnarled bark, dusted with a veneer of lichen and moss, soft to the touch to the depth of about a millimeter and beyond that utterly immovable (save for a chainsaw). Not a sound could be heard, not even wind; it was an ethereal and sobering sensation I've encountered before in the presence of ancient trees, as if the rest of the forest was paying homage to this sentinel.

I tried to imagine encountering a Bigfoot here. In a place this serene, coming upon a giant animal would definitely be a shock, perhaps even a life-altering experience. Johnson had described venturing off the trail to relieve himself and finding himself eye to eye with the beast. "Ray Wallace may have hoaxed his own tracks," he told a reporter, "but I can guarantee you that Ray Wallace was not walking around in a nine-foot

Bigfoot suit in the Oregon Caves at the age of 82. What I saw was real." Within weeks of the incident, Johnson spoke to a gathering of the Western Bigfoot Society and teared up as he had done during his televised interviews.

When someone reports they have seen a Bigfoot, there are so many possible explanations for what really happened that, as René Dahinden often remarked, "it boggles the mind." In this case, three theories spring to mind. First, Johnson may have seen nothing at all and simply lied. If so, the sheer bravado with which he announced the encounter, and the fact that he stuck to his story and cultivated the media, qualifies him as a gifted actor.

In the annals of Bigfoot, Johnson's claim is rare but not unique. It used to be that such stories were heard around a campfire or at a family gathering. The history of Bigfoot is laced with individuals widely recognized as serial bullshitters (René Dahinden called it the "old-man syndrome"). Their motives have not always been clear, but there is no mistaking them; some have played the Bigfoot game purely for money, others are best described as compulsive liars.

Studies suggest that pathological lying is an unconscious act. Johnson's report, like his subsequent actions, was odd, but it didn't strike me as a story told by a compulsive liar. But then, I don't know him personally. In the end, only Johnson knows if he saw something or not. Or does he?

Which brings us to a second possibility: maybe he did see something. Even very simple perceptions are a complex interweaving of sensory data, emotions, and cognitive information. Poor eyesight, coupled with the vagaries of perspective and lighting—especially in shadows—and the idiosyncrasies of the brain, tasked with instantly analyzing incoming information and matching it to memory to determine the nature of the object in view, make identification difficult in any pulse-quickening situation. In highly stressful or traumatic situations, control of our senses can desert us completely. At such times, the brain has been known to fill the vacuum created by sensory loss with imagery supplied from memory.[6] And memory is famously unreliable: research has proved that suggestibility and imagination can combine to create false memories indistinguishable from the real thing.[7]

Furthermore, Johnson could have developed a subconscious intimacy with Bigfoot through media exposure and thus been predisposed to see one; such predisposition is a phenomenon first noted decades ago by researchers studying reports of UFOs and alien abductions. Indeed, when first interviewed about the incident, Johnson professed to know little about Bigfoot; but his reference to Ray Wallace as a hoaxer shows that he was more than passingly familiar with the subject.

Finally, it's possible that Johnson saw something and knew exactly what it was—a bear, perhaps—but gave himself psychological permission to go public with a giant lie (after all, he wasn't breaking any law), to inject into the public consciousness the suggestion that the mysteries of nature are alive and well in the forests of the twenty-first century.

Puzzling as eyewitness accounts are, equally puzzling is the question of why anyone believes them. Two reasons suggest themselves. First, most people are extremely poor lie detectors, because we tend to take things others say at face value, and we hold stereotypes of liars as tormented and anxious, when, in fact, they are more often quite the opposite. Even law-enforcement officials who question people for a living are more likely to judge statements as truthful than untruthful.[8] And, there's also the possibility that some individuals embrace the idea of a giant hominid because they are hard-wired that way. I have been told that is a crazy idea. But strange obsessions and cults are nothing new in human experience. And we are animals, not so far removed from our hunter-gatherer ancestors, with reptilian brains that may hold subconscious images from millions of years ago, capable of producing primitive behavior. How else to explain the people I have met who are, heart and soul, obsessed with the idea that a giant, hairy hominid inhabits the forests of the northern hemisphere?

In the final analysis, for a person to totally swallow the idea that someone saw an actual Bigfoot would require the receiver of that information to have their internal lie-detection equipment completely turned off. As it turns out, that is not an uncommon state of mind. Decades of unrelenting media exposure to the idea of a giant ape-man prowling the forest, coupled with society's woeful lack of basic scientific education and increased reliance on information from the Internet—where thousands of Web sites provide forums for any theory imaginable—virtually ensure that Bigfoot will stay fresh in the minds of the uninformed for many years to come.[9]

. . .

The Big Tree Trail loop dumped me near the gift shop, where Ranger Tom was giving instructions to an excited group of grade-schoolers before they entered the cave.

If there are connections between Bigfoot and caves, I had missed them. Nor had I received any revelations about what Matthew Johnson had seen. Considering the forest fire that intervened between his sighting and my hike over the same ground, my chances of a sighting should have been much better than his. But it didn't happen.

Whatever Johnson saw, or didn't see, he had a need, and Bigfoot filled it. Roger Patterson had a need, too. The dedication in his book sounds like the cry of a man in distress:

> ... To the young at heart who seldom say "impossible."
> ... To the adventurer who doesn't stop at the foothills but penetrates deep into the forest.
> ... To the individualist who has enough fortitude to stand up for what he thinks is right.
> ... To all of those who seek the truth no matter what the cost.

Patterson lived under sentence of death for ten years—the ultimate challenge to anyone's sanity—and it transformed him totally.

Researchers have found that extreme stress alters perceptions. The reason is fairly simple. The brain is governed by the fear response. One of its chief tasks is to moderate any incoming information that poses a danger, which includes stress. The least stressful kind of information is that which is consistent with beliefs already held.

The potential for problems arises because the egocentric bias of our subconscious also brings with it the capacity for self-delusion. If a person is predisposed to a particular idea or belief, the innate tendency to overlook information contrary to that idea or belief can increase to the point that it becomes pathological: an extreme example is the schizophrenic who builds up an imaginary universe with no connection to the external world.[10] "What may begin as an honest error," observes the scientist and author Robert Park, "has a way of evolving through almost imperceptible steps from self-delusion to fraud . . . [and] it is not always easy to tell when that line is crossed."[11]

Pick any subject, and the same subconscious thought process applies: a curiosity graduates to a hobby and from there to a habit. Perhaps a piece of information is uncovered that leads deeper into the mystery. At some point it is possible to believe anything.

The process of selective mental filtering—also known as denial—creates special zones in our consciousness. The psychologist Daniel Goleman describes these as "black holes of the mind," pieces of the world we encounter but subconsciously choose not to see. With the energy saved by ignoring (that is, denying) anxiety-producing information, we devote extra attention to other zones. "Those allowable zones are [mostly] free of anxiety," Goleman explains. "We feel at ease there, able to move without constraint. Within those zones we develop our strengths; awareness focuses in them with energy. These zones resemble a fetish."[12]

If stress increases, a person's focus of attention can narrow further, and the process of denial becomes an addictive feedback loop in which he perceives, with ever-increasing intensity, only what he wants to believe. All of this happens below the conscious level. The cultural anthropologist Ernest Becker describes the insidious nature of denial: "You artificially inflate a small area of the world, give it a higher value on the horizon of your perception and action. And you do this because it represents an area that you can firmly hold on to, that you can skillfully manipulate, that you can use easily to justify yourself—your actions, your sense of self, your option in the world."[13]

By buying into Bigfoot's existence with his heart and soul, and taking it upon himself to prove the naysayers wrong, Roger Patterson subconsciously managed the intense stress of his impending death. But he paid a price. "Patients who are told they have only a few months to live often deny that fact," explains Goleman. "For the patient with a life-threatening illness the denial typically passes, followed by another reaction such as rage. For the neurotic [in that situation], though, denial can become a fixture of consciousness, a favored defense."[14]

Goleman is describing what happened to Patterson. His intense obsession with Bigfoot, together with his quirky ideas and eccentric behavior, struck everyone around him as both heartfelt and peculiar: the giant metal cage he had built to pen the animal; the bell-tower cries he recorded; the vigils he held in a friend's hayloft, sitting for hours gazing into the dark; the days and weeks he spent on the road questioning and searching; his endless talk about what he'd do once he captured the animal.[15] This behavior resembles that of an extreme personality type well known to therapists, which Goleman calls the "Detective."

The Detective is hyperalert. He doesn't simply look; he searches. He is exceedingly sensitive to anything out of the ordinary or unexpected. He wants to examine everything, especially anything new. But he looks so keenly that he does not quite see. He hears so astutely that he fails to listen. He twists facts to suit his theories. The obvious holds no interest. He examines evidence carefully but with extraordinary prejudice, dismissing anything he deems irrelevant to his suppositions and seizing on anything that confirms them.

Detectives say they are interested in getting at the underlying truth, but "that truth, it turns out, is exactly what they expected in the first place. . . . [they] can be at the same time absolutely right in [their] perception and absolutely wrong in [their] judgment." Their visions are often grandiose, encompassing politics or economics, religious dogma, or an evil conspiracy theory. What often sets them apart is the unconventionality of their obsession.[16]

I wound my way down the mountain and headed south for the California border. It had rained so hard on my first trip to Humboldt County several years before that I had found the country largely obscured. On this trip, the thermometer on the sign at the Grants Pass fairgrounds registered 103, and mirages shimmered on the blacktop.

The Siskiyou Highway is a twisting path through narrow valleys surrounded by the bones of mountains jutting through the earth's rough skin, following curved and stair-stepped waterways with boiling water pouring over house-sized boulders. A mysterious maze with no sightlines and little space for the eye to wander, building curiosity for what's around the next bend.

David Rains Wallace described the Siskiyou country as "the strangest landscape I had ever seen" and used it as the theme for his book, which examines the transformative powers of wilderness. "Wilderness generates mythological thinking," he wrote. "It leads the mind back to stories of origins and meanings, to imagining the world's creation." He spoke of humanity arising over millions of years "from a thoroughly wild planet."[17]

I stopped on a bench beside the Smith River and walked into the water. The silver current ran strong and crystal clear. An occasional gust of hot wind fuzzed the surface. The riverbed was composed of sharp quartz stones and agates, all shades of white and copper and flinty gold. I grabbed a rock from the bottom, and flecks of golden ore peeking out from veins on its surface caught the sun in sharp bursts, like pirate treasure, hinting at the obsession that seized the miners who once swarmed here.

This country lends itself to storytelling. Many of the early miners here were immigrants who brought with them tales of a supernaturally strong, aggressive, hairy, sex-crazed "wild man," one of the enduring legends of the European continent, sightings of which were occasionally reported in frontier newspapers across the country as settlers spread westward. After the astonishing news from Africa, in 1847, that a creature called a gorilla had been discovered that looked disturbingly human, the newspaper reports of "wild men" were largely supplanted by sightings of creatures identified as apes and gorillas.[18]

Ultimately, the tales that abounded of Native American spirits, wild men, and giant apes all blended together. The result was a multicultural hybrid of a creature. Like other immigrants to these shores, Bigfoot became uniquely American: infinitely strong, self-reliant, and smarter than any other monster that ever walked the earth.

I entered Willow Creek as a round moon rose before me, illuminating the wall of the Trinity River canyon that looms over the town. A neon sign blazed in the night announcing Wyatt's Motel.[19] I checked in and stowed my gear in the room. Charm is not one of the Wyatt's attributes, but it was worth a stay on account of its being the place where Tom Slick organized the world's first professional Bigfoot hunt.

I sat outside to catch a breeze. The glow from the motel sign revealed a giant cage made of welded chains and rebar, sitting like a forlorn torturer's apparatus on the far side of the parking lot. It looked large enough to hold a Bigfoot.

In the morning, I planned to meet the guide Al Hodgson had arranged for me. His name was Jay, and he was said to know the Bluff Creek country like the back of his hand.

12

BIGFOOT'S KITCHEN

That nonhuman life has no human consciousness doesn't mean it has
no consciousness.

—David Rains Wallace, *The Klamath Knot*

At 5:00 A.M. I stepped out of unit 8 into a cold, pitch-black Willow Creek
morning. A short walk brought me to a gas station where two men stood
under a fluorescent light by the pumps, bullshitting and drinking coffee
while their rigs gassed. In the penumbra just beyond the service islands,
a man I guessed to be Jay Rowland lounged against an old pickup, checking me out. He was built like a tree stump, wearing dungarees, a striped
union shirt hanging over an ample gut, and a baseball cap listing to one
side of his head.

I introduced myself, and he announced straight-faced that he wanted
half of whatever I was going to make off whatever it was I was working
on. My first instinct was to laugh, but his look told me to play it straight.
I wasn't working for anyone, I said. I'm just down here trying to put a
few more pieces in the puzzle of what really happened to the two men,
Roger Patterson and Bob Gimlin, who shot the Bigfoot film. I didn't even
know what I was going to do with the information. I certainly wasn't
about to start handing out pieces of an imaginary deal. If that was his condition for taking me up to Bluff Creek, I apologized for having gotten
him up so early for nothing. As I'd said on the phone, I was willing to pay
a fee and gas money. Period. "All right," he said, without an ounce of ac-
rimony, and motioned me toward the pickup. "Hop in."

When we got out of town, he began to talk. "I've run across all kind of sonsabitches trying to get their foot in the door up here," he said. "I looked you over 'fore you got to me this morning and didn't see no gun and stuff like that, so I said to myself, 'All right.' There was this kid here once from Los Angeles. I went into Hodgson's variety store and Al pointed me out and said, 'Here's the guy you want to talk to.' I looked at this kid straight, cold turkey, point-blank, but I didn't take him up here cause he was too goddamn strange and he was packin' a gun." An hour later we turned off the macadam, at an abandoned store marked by a faded painting of Bigfoot holding a fish, and began climbing into the mountains.

Jay arrived here from Arkansas as a kid in 1958, with rudimentary training as a powder monkey. He worked with Jerry Crew building the Bluff Creek Road. He called Crew a "regular guy" but a bit "impressionable."

"I met Tom Slick once," he said. "They ran a bunch of hounds in here. It was a goddamn riot. They'd come in here and wander around the hills. Then they'd leave. They might be gone for two or three months, then they'd come back."

We traveled for a while in the gathering light to the top of Onion Mountain, then down a series of switchbacks "steep as a cow's face," as Jay put it, to an intersection with the Bluff Creek Road, at which point we turned north and paralleled the creek. The road snaked through a corridor of tall firs and sheer rock walls. Blue sky appeared overhead, but the roadway was dark and the air brutally cold. I caught glimpses of the creek far below, overgrown with vegetation.

Jay stopped the truck. "I'll tell you something now," he said. "This was the way it was." He climbed out, walked to the middle of the road, extended his arms, and turned in a semicircle, as if trying to pull a story out of the mist. "This was our pipe yard. Now, we had to have pipe for the next morning, so that night we loaded the pipe on the trailer and parked it here on the road. Come back the next morning. Jerry Crew was here. Shorty Wallace was here." Jay pointed down into the creek. "Down there—the whole goddamn pipe trailer was bottom-side up. Now that's thirty-six-inch pipe, twenty feet long. There's five joints on that trailer. You know what that weighs? Right around four to five hundred pounds a joint! And that's not counting the trailer."

I looked over the bank. A hundred feet down through the trees I could just make out water.

"No man's gonna do that," he said. "The whole goddamn crew couldn't do that. [Bigfoot's] tracks was all over this goddamn ground in this dirt. We had to take a cat and reach down there with a bull line and pull the trailer back outta there. And another thing. Every time we welded at night we found that fucker investigatin' what's goin' down. There was more activity here than any other place on this whole goddamn mountain."

I had heard the stories of Bigfoot tossing culverts, tires, and so forth off the bank. Now it was a whole trailer. Either Jay was playing me, or else his recollections had blossomed over the years. He obviously loved a good story.

Jay poured us coffee, lit a cigarette, and leaned against the truck. "I think it was in the fall of '65. They ordered me back to rebuild this road here. Me and Carl Reese were comin' down the road somewhere in here goin' into camp. It was sprinkling—not even enough to wash the dust off the windshield—and I'm goin' along here, and I seen Carl lookin' out the back window. He said, 'Hey, Jay. Goddamn it, I just seen a woman down there fishin'.' I start lookin' around. 'Hey, Carl,' I said. 'You see a rig anywhere around here?' 'No, by God, I don't.' I said, 'How'd that woman get in that creek—there's no rig?' And he said, 'I'll be goddamn if I know.' 'What'd you have to drink last night?' 'No, Jay,' he said, 'I seen that woman in the creek. She had long hair, long black hair.'

"At any rate, there weren't nobody around here, no pickup or nothin'. All the rest of the crew's gone out. How the hell'd she get here? So I turn the goddamn pickup and we come back up here."

At this point, Jay walked to the edge of the road overlooking the creek far below and pointed to an area on the lip of the road ahead of us. "Carl went down in the creek about there," he said, then turned and pointed straight down into the creek from where he stood. "I walked in somewhere down in this area. I come right down to the creek. It was deep—real deep. I found a place where there's some sand. And that's where I found his tracks—the water runnin' in his tracks. And I shot right back up out of the creek and I stood here maybe five or ten minutes. Listen, I was close to that sonofabitch. I was close. Carl come up and he said, 'I didn't find nothin'.' I said, 'Carl, you think that's what you seen? A long-haired person?' He said, 'I'll be goddamn if I know, but I saw somebody, and it looked like a woman.' To this day he says the same goddamn thing."

"Kinda spooky?"

"You're goddamn right it's spooky. It'd just raise the goddamn hair right up the back of your goddamn neck, you're down in there by yourself and you see the water running in those new tracks."

We pulled into Louse Camp, a peaceful expanse of soft duff sprinkled with fire rings, in a cluster of ancient trees. Bluff Creek could be heard thrashing in the distance. Jay slid out of the truck and pointed to an old, single-holed Forest Service structure. "There's the shitter," he said. "Feel like I'm at home."

In 1958 the camp was filled with trailers and tents belonging to the Wallace crew; an oasis amid the annihilation that accompanied the road building. Jay described the scene after work: eight or nine men cooking, bullshitting, and drinking. Everyone was godawful filthy and the creek ice cold. Those who felt the need to clean up did so by jumping in to get wet, jumping out to soap up, and jumping back in quickly to rinse off. High jinks had always been part of camp life, but that summer things happened that couldn't be explained: strange sounds in the dark and huge footprints passing right by the trailers. Jay took to leaving cornflakes outside at night. They were always gone the next morning.

Ray Wallace deserves a place in the *Guinness Book of Records* for the world's longest-running practical joke. At the height of his madness, it must have been quite a scene at Bluff Creek: a figure dressed in an ape suit with a baggy seat creeping through the trees, rocking trailers, and stomping giant, weighted footprints into the soft dirt of the newly cut roadbed. A jokester with maniacal persistence, perhaps unaware of just how deep into the human psyche his mischief tapped.

Why would anyone go to the trouble? The most likely reason is that Wallace simply got a kick out of it, the way arsonists love fires. But the enthusiasm of those awestruck by the prints no doubt also played a part—people like Bob Titmus.

Starting out in taxidermy, Titmus apprenticed at a large company in Seattle, working on creatures that most people see only in books. That background might explain his obsession: if exotic animals were good business, imagine the rewards for bagging a Bigfoot!

He appears to have come under the beast's spell while showing Jerry Crew how to make the famous plaster footprint that helped introduce Bigfoot to the world. Shortly after Crew's picture appeared in the newspaper, the media were touting Titmus as a Bigfoot expert, whereupon he began patrolling Bluff Creek—an act undoubtedly noticed by the Wallace crew. When Titmus started to look in the creek itself, sure enough, tracks soon turned up there as well.

The footprints in the creek were Wallace's masterstroke—an infinitely more difficult hoax to perpetrate than the tracks on the road, and infinitely more bewitching. Not only were the prints themselves significantly different—smaller, with shorter toes and a deep cleft on the ball of the foot—but the skill used to deploy them bordered on genius. Green described the scene in *Sasquatch: The Apes among Us:*

> [Titmus and I] could not think of any way a man could have made the tracks without the use of some sort of specialized heavy equipment and there was no apparent way that such equipment, assuming that it existed, could have reached the sandbar. Both sides of the valley were steep and covered with heavy underbrush. Taking a machine down without leaving evidence of its passage seemed out of the question. At the downstream end of the sandbar there was a tangled log jam, and close upstream the creek ran through a small canyon, with a straight rock wall on each side dropping into a deep pool. About the only answer would have been to fly the machine in with a large

helicopter, but that could not have been done secretly because at the time the tracks were made there were construction workers living in a camp just a few hundred yards away.[1]

One piece of evidence they observed—and owing to Bigfoot myopia, misinterpreted—was a clump of nearby trees, seven or eight feet high, broken and twisted. Green's observation that he couldn't conceive of an animal with the strength to do such a thing simply demonstrated his ignorance of the skill loggers develop in the use of heavy machinery. Having spent a brief period setting chokers for a high-lead operation myself, I can testify that loggers are capable of doing remarkable things with monster machines in the most rugged terrain imaginable, and their ability to snake steel cables long distances and haul logs out of seemingly unreachable chasms is extraordinary.

The key to the Bluff Creek footsteps that Green and Titmus misinterpreted was the shredded trees. Green was right about one thing: no animal could have done that. It was done with a steel cable, winched by a powerful diesel engine that, when full torque was applied to free a "hangup" on a tree or a stump, could snap the cable tight with enough force to cut a man in half—or shred a tree, or several. After the 1958 sightings, *True* magazine received a letter from a woman who owned a motel in the area. She recounted that one of the Wallace brothers and two other men had sat on her porch and had a "terrific laugh" as they described how Ray Wallace, with the help of others, had made heavy imitation feet and then hauled the wearers up and down the slopes by the Bluff Creek Road using logging cables.[2]

Ray Wallace is proof of the lengths to which tricksters will go. The thought of people like John Green and Bob Titmus standing on a sandbar, with the creek gurgling and wind stirring the trees, both men nervously searching the bushes for signs of movement from a creature that might be nearby watching, undoubtedly pleased him no end.

While assembling his story for *True,* Sanderson had had his suspicions about Wallace: he knew that tracks had appeared on another

Wallace job site the year before. Including such telling details would only spoil the mystery, however, so he opted to describe Wallace as "skeptical and pragmatic." But in a letter to the anthropologist George Agogino in February 1960, he wrote: "There were several people that we met and interviewed in Willow Creek who impressed us very favourably indeed; notable were Betty Allen, Jerry Crew, and his nephew. There were . . . certain people who did not[, in particular] Bob Titmus and Ray Wallace."[3]

Wallace's Bluff Creek shenanigans aren't without irony. What started as a simple prank snowballed to an extent even he wasn't prepared for. One Willow Creek old-timer told me: "Ray just went too far, then he couldn't back down and admit anything." Bigfooters dodge the subject of Ray Wallace—it's their dirty little secret, and the fewer questions raised about his involvement at Bluff Creek, the better.[4] After Wallace's death in 2002, and his family's subsequent announcement that he was the maker of those first famous tracks, the Bigfoot community took to impugning his sanity, sometimes viciously.[5] Hardly a way to treat the guy who made it all possible.

Bigfooters have always argued that far too many footprints have been found in far too many places for at least some of them not to have been real. In fact, this reasoning is exactly wrong, and Ray Wallace is the proof of it—the most famous practitioner of what might be described as an unheralded form of folk art.[6]

We know that giant humanoid footprints were being fabricated long before "mountain devil" tracks were discovered on Mount St. Helens when Wallace was a youngster. A newspaper in southern Oregon reported giant footprints in 1899. Photographs of such tracks were reportedly made in the 1920s and 1930s in northern California.[7] Al Hodgson told me about tracks found near Willow Creek shortly after World War II.

This practice likely originated in the logging camps of the nineteenth century, where lumberjacks in primeval forests created what every other culture on earth but ours had long assimilated into its psyche: a host of mythical creatures and tall tales, conjured up to embellish the power of nature and mythologize the legacy of the country's pioneers. The Hoop-snake, the Tripodero, the Hugag, the Hodag, the Splinter Cat, the Squonk, the Prock, the Gowrow, the Will-am-alone, the Hidebehind, the Agropelter, the Wampus Cat, the Ding-ball, and the Sidehill Dodger are just a few of the mythical creatures in the American bestiary.

As the twentieth century approached, the woodsmen saw nature in retreat, its mysteries discounted by a society that craved the new and derided the old. Giant footprints left in the forest were nothing more than a small statement, calculated to puzzle: a kind of joke, but with a twist. They were what the folklorist Robert Walls calls a "material expression" of the unknown, an icon of the forest—a means of perpetuating the illusion that one mystery of nature will never be solved.[8]

Never widely practiced and certainly on the decline in the first half of the twentieth century, the esoteric custom of faking tracks had almost died out when the *Humboldt Times* ran its photograph of Jerry Crew holding a giant humanlike footprint. But this footprint, as anyone who looked at a newspaper could see, was immortalized in plaster: it could be photographed, duplicated, talked about, traded, and even sold. It is no surprise that the newspaper story coincided with a curious increase in the number of giant footprints "discovered" in the Pacific Northwest.

Ray Wallace's track-laying methods were inventive, but other track makers have displayed equal originality. To create believable evidence of an extremely heavy creature with a stride length of four to six feet, traversing various types of rugged terrain and water courses in remote— sometimes roadless—areas is no small accomplishment. The effort required leads one to speculate that a only a few determined track layers, like Wallace, are responsible for the bulk of the prints. Several of the giant prints reported in Humboldt County during the 1960s, for instance, have been identified as exactly the same, hinting at the presence of one especially persistent folk artist—someone who possesses a particular pair of fifteen-inch "feet" with a split in the ball of one foot.

When Patterson shot his film, roads paralleled Bluff Creek on both sides. By the time Jay and I got there, they had been closed off for years, so Jay parked the truck, and we hiked upstream. I had only my memory of the film clip to judge the exact spot where Patterson's Bigfoot had walked, and it wasn't enough. We sloshed through water and crawled under logs. After a while I just stopped. What the hell was I doing here, anyway? Encountering Ms. Bigfoot kneeling in the creek bed, as Patterson claimed to have found her, wasn't in the cards. We were standing on the creek's east side. The west bank faintly resembled the background in the film, but it had been taken over by a tangled mass of greasebrush and willows that made it impossible to pinpoint a location.

Standing there as I was, my mind racing, Jay must have thought I was loony. Then again, Jay was loony, too. "Sixty-five was a big flood," he piped up. "The creek was totally different. All this brush wasn't here. This was all open. They'd logged the creek, ten miles straight up."

When I told him Patterson claimed to have shot his film on October 20, 1967, he shook his head. "In 1967 I moved a yarder down here, and I was stayin' in here by myself at Notice Camp. If Patterson and them, if they'd supposedly been here, why come I didn't see 'em? I was in and out of here every fuckin' day except Saturday and Sunday."

I explained that Gimlin said that he and Patterson had camped here with horses for a couple weeks. Jay was adamant. "I did not see 'em. We were in here from about March of that year, March, April of that year, clear up through Thanksgiving—and I didn't see anybody camped in here."

"You were all along Bluff Creek and you never saw a camp with horses?"

"I never seen no camp with no goddamn horses. I just did not see 'em."

Jay's recollection fits with the account given by Bob Heironimus, who told Greg Long he wore Patterson's ape suit. According to Heironimus, Patterson and Gimlin camped on the Bluff Creek Road, but closer to the highway, some distance from the film site, just long enough to meet up with him late one afternoon and film him walking in the suit the next morning. Long speculated that Patterson and Gimlin made a brief second trip to the film site several weeks later to plant the footprints to match the film, timing that trip to allow a stop in Willow Creek for Patterson to spread the news about their supposed encounter.

Jay's claim that he saw no horse party camped on Bluff Creek for any length of time that fall, together with the cowboys' wildly conflicting versions of what happened that afternoon, and their timetable of events—one I'd checked myself and found implausible—made it clear that Roger Patterson's famous film of Bigfoot was not shot on October 20, 1967.

We returned to the truck, drove across the creek, and headed uphill on a road barely worthy of the designation, littered with rocks large enough that I had to push some aside for the truck to pass. We emerged on a ridgetop with a view west to the Bluff Creek watershed: nothing but trees, clear-cuts, and marijuana patches all the way to the Pacific.

Jay followed the road north for an hour or so, stopping several times to admire the view. The cold of the canyon gave way to a relentless sun, and haze appeared on the horizon. "Boss, you could be hung up down in there for six months and never see a damn soul," he said. "Manzanita, grease brush, bull pine. . . . You're lookin' at it, man. Bigfoot's Kitchen."

· · ·

We were in the northern half of the Six Rivers Forest, thirty-three miles from the Oregon border. Before us stretched the Indians' High Country, where the spirits of the Yuroks' and Karuks' old doctors are found. Chimney Rock, Doctor Rock, and Peak 8 were out there—I could just make out mountains in the distance, but I didn't know one from the next. Most High Country spiritual activity happens in the summer, so there were probably Indians out there vision questing now.

Rounding a corner, we surprised a black bear in the road. It turned tail and loped along in front of us for a while, then crashed off into the woods. A bear sprinting for cover is not a threatening sight, but such an animal standing in the trees with its eyes fixed on you is a different story, especially if you happen to be a weekend hiker unused to large wildlife. How might you react if the beast stood on its hind feet—as bears are apt to do for a better look—perhaps partially shielded by vegetation, perhaps moving down and up, its head waving back and forth, snorting or snapping its jaws?

Large (weighing 350 pounds or more), hairy, omnivorous, partially bipedal, and extant in a surprising array of colors, the American black bear *(Ursus americanus)* is indigenous to all of Bigfoot's territory. In Washington State, Idaho, Montana, and Canada, grizzlies *(Ursus arctos)* are also found. They are much larger than the black bear (weighing 500 pounds or more), also with wide variations in color and behavior. And, like their smaller cousins, they frequently rise up on their hind legs and assume a humanlike stance. The grizzly's distinguishing feature is a large hump of muscle on its shoulders, visible even when the animal is standing erect, which adds to the impression of a human figure. And bears are not rare. Washington State alone contains at least twenty-five thousand, spread over four-fifths of the state.

Abundant in all the mountainous regions of the world, bears have been an eternal source of myths: the yeti legend is kept alive today by misidentified sightings of the Tibetan brown bear. Bigfooters agree that bears probably account for a number of ape-man reports, but they seldom mention the possibility that other reported sightings are attributable to people wearing fur suits. Ray Wallace did it. Ivan Marx did it. Roger Patterson did it. And four hoaxers conspired to do it on a highway near Mission, British Columbia, in 1977. Wearing a $200 monkey suit with shoulder pads, one of the hoaxers darted in front of a bus, freaking out the driver (a reserve policeman) and his passengers. The Mounties arrived and described the driver as "very nervous and pale."[9] I've often wondered if Ivan Marx—who made two separate films of someone wearing an ape costume, and promoted both with zeal (getting one onto national television)—might have been responsible for the female Bigfoot that put in two famous appearances near Oroville, California, not far from Marx's permanent home in Burney.

Jay and I stopped at a south-facing viewpoint overlooking the Bluff Creek drainage. I spread a map out on the hood and read that the north-facing slope opposite was called Brushy Gulch. I knew that name. A ranger at the Orleans Forest Service station had told me a story about it that reinforced my notion of just how unknowable and fearful the wild can be, and how that mystery and terror could contribute to the Bigfoot phenomenon.

The ranger was Native American, born and raised near Orleans, only a few miles from Bluff Creek. I had stopped to ask directions, and we got to talking about Bigfoot. She started to tell me a story, then abruptly pulled me outside where no one could overhear. She had been taking a census of spotted owls on a parcel of land slated for logging, called the Uncle timber sale or Brushy Gulch, at the headwaters of Bluff Creek. It was ten o'clock at night. She walked down a logging road to a call point and hooted and whistled for a while to attract owls. Getting no response, she walked toward the next call point. On the far side of a draw she felt suddenly very scared. "I felt like something was watching me," she said. "I wanted to turn around and run out of there, but, being Native American, I've always been taught that when you get scared like that you're not supposed to run. So I burned my [kishua] root—it kinda protects us—and I kept my head down. I started to shine my flashlight up into the trees, but I was afraid I would see something, so I just kept my head down and got out of there. Got in my truck and took off. I never said anything to anybody about it.

"Two weeks later, I was having a couple beers with some other hooters, and I says, 'Boy, I was in the scariest place the other day,' and one of the guys looked at me and said, 'I know exactly where you were.' And I said, 'Oh, yeah? Where was I?' He says, 'You were at Uncle timber sale.' I said, 'Well, what happened to you?'"

She suddenly flushed and stopped talking. I looked at her quizzically, and she pointed to her forearm, which was covered with goosebumps. She exhaled slowly, then continued. "So, he said, 'I got to the first call point, hooted around, got no answer, walked down the road, came around this draw,' and he said, 'Something was watching me.' He said, 'I got so scared.' I said, 'What'd you do?' He said, 'I turned around and ran the hell out of there.'"

Circling to the west of Bluff Creek brought us to the top of Onion Mountain. Jay turned onto an invisible road he called a Jeep trail and drove through scrub brush to the remains of a small structure atop a rise. I guessed that the pile of wood and cement was probably the "lonely little cabin" about which Peter Byrne waxed romantic in his book, where he spent nights during a trip in 1972 to investigate Patterson's film: watching the fog roll in from the ocean, listening over and over to a taped interview of Patterson describing the film encounter, sitting by a fire and thinking about "how many places there were like Onion Mountain, where a Bigfoot could spend all its life without being discovered by man."[10]

Byrne didn't mention that he had had a companion: René Dahinden. The Swiss, who had brought his two young sons along, had no such romantic notions, only a compulsion to prove or disprove the film. Dahinden and Byrne each spent nearly thirty years investigating Patterson's story and, despite the truth staring them in the face, chose to believe Patterson. But the Bigfoot phenomenon has never been about truth. It's about storytelling. Colorful stories will always survive, no matter how factually unsupportable they may be. And if a story is both colorful and controversial, its immortality is practically assured.

The forces that created Bigfoot are strikingly similar to what Malcolm Gladwell, in his book *The Tipping Point,* calls social epidemics: fads and trends both small and sweeping. Gladwell likens the process to the spread of a virus. Social epidemics begin with what he calls a "sticky" idea: the kind of contagion below the rational or even conscious level that lodges in the brains of people vulnerable to certain types of suggestion. Next, a small group of people take up the idea, learn all they can about it, and spread it. If conditions are right, it reaches "that one dramatic moment" when an idea, trend, or social behavior crosses a threshold, tips, and spreads like wildfire.[11]

The people involved don't necessarily work together or even know one another—and time doesn't matter; they're bonded solely by their dedication to the idea. And before an idea can "tip," the group must shape the idea so it comes to acquire "a deeper meaning."

We can envision the Bigfoot phenomenon as an obsession lying dormant, like a virus, in the human mind for millions of years, flaring up only on rare occasions—a wild-man outbreak in the Bavarian Alps in the 1300s,[12] a frantic Victorian search for the Missing Link. Then comes an outbreak in the twentieth century seizing mountaineers in the Himalaya, followed quickly by another in California. Now, however, the world is connected by almost instant forms of communication, and the virus can't be contained. A small group of people becomes infected by the idea of a living ape-man. When presented with evidence to the contrary, they ignore it. Oblivious to reason, they spread out across the countryside, gathering all the supporting information they can find, ignoring inconvenient details, waylaying the innocent, methodically spreading the virus from person to person, and preaching the idea that a mythical creature is a real animal. The tipping point, the one that turned a small-scale obsession into a national phenomenon, was Patterson's film.

·　·　·

Jay pointed to a tall fir with a series of boards nailed to its trunk, rising to a platform near the top; evidence, he said, of its use during the war as a lookout "to spot Japs." In the distance, the main road wound toward the top of Blue Creek Mountain, where Dahinden and Green investigated footprints a few weeks before Patterson shot his film. Dahinden returned here several times over the years to walk the road, sometimes videotaping the scene and adding commentary describing the footprints he remembered, the vegetation, and the weather at different times of the year, like a pilgrim returning to a shrine.

A hawk floated above Jay and me as we descended Onion Mountain late in the afternoon, trailing dust along a narrow road gouged into a steep ridge in a landscape of ridges. The Bluff Creek logging road had served its purpose: the slopes once crowded with trees were now denuded and choked with brush. The raptor pivoted on a wingtip and vanished over a ridge. A contrail floated in the sky beyond. The Bluff Creek watershed isn't wilderness anymore, but you could still call it wild, for it's the kind of country where anything could be hiding and watching, and you might never know.

We entered an area thick with ancient cedars. Jay parked and led me on foot over a boardwalk across a bog choked with bulrushes and rhododendrons to a small lake. Trees lay toppled into the water. Algae and lily pads floated on the surface, which swarmed with dragonflies weaving through dappled sunlight. A split-rail fence could be seen deep underwater, suggesting that the lake had been created by beavers. Newts hung suspended at the surface like Gumbys, with only the tips of their noses above water. A sudden movement sent them wriggling toward the darkness at the bottom, passing bubbles of rising methane gas.

Lakes like this are the homes of the giant salamanders that figure prominently in stories about the area. The ancient Karuks believed that giant serpents with human faces lived in sinkholes and preyed on unwary land creatures.[13] Such fantasies are easy to imagine, for the scene looked primordial, with a dark, unfathomable hole at the center of the pool where something unimaginably huge could be living.

Jay leaned against a tree, lost in thought. What was going through his mind? Had he actually seen the giant tracks he'd described? Had a loaded pipe trailer really been upended in the creek? Did his buddy honestly see a long-haired woman? Did Bigfoot really eat cornflakes? Whatever he might believe, the most important thing, it seemed to me, was his telling of the stories. The value of myths is not so much what they're about as what they tell us about ourselves. And up here on Bluff Creek, Jay is a happy camper. Whatever happened in these woods years ago, Jay is living proof that Bigfoot is alive and well.

NOTES

1. HARRISON

1. Author interview with John Green, May 3, 1995.

2. Henner Fahrenbach, "Anatomy of a Sasquatch," presentation at Sasquatch Forum, Harrison, BC, May 6, 1995.

3. Despite the comments in his presentation (which he said were motivated by the surprise verdict at the O. J. Simpson trial), Danny Perez is a firm believer in Patterson's film. He has published a detailed analysis of the Patterson film and a bibliography on the subject, *Big Footnotes* (Norwalk, CA: D. Perez Publishing, 1988).

2. THE MISSING LINK

1. Ivan Sanderson, "The Strange Story of America's Abominable Snowman," *True,* December 1959, 40.

2. Ibid., 126.

3. Sanderson's mother was from Nîmes.

4. Ivan Terence Sanderson, *Animal Treasure* (New York: Viking Press, 1937), 11–12.

5. Prescott Holmes, *The Story of Exploration and Adventure in Africa* (Philadelphia: Henry Altemus, 1893), 28.

6. Ivan Terence Sanderson with David Loth, *Ivan Sanderson's Book of Great Jungles* (New York: Julian Messner, 1965), 431–439, quote at 436.

7. Sanderson, *Animal Treasure,* 12.

8. Ivan Sanderson, *Green Silence* (New York: David McKay Co., 1974), 83–84.

9. Ibid., 161.

10. Many believe the term *cryptozoology* was coined by Bernard Heuvelmans. But in his book *In the Wake of the Sea Serpents* (New York: Hill & Wang, 1965), Heuvelmans gives the credit to Sanderson, adding a confusing qualification that seems like an attempt to retain some of the honor for himself while placating his old friend: "When [Sanderson] was still a student he invented the word 'cryptozoology,' or the science of hidden animals, which I was to coin much later, quite unaware that he had already done so" (508).

11. Author phone interview with Ed Schoenenberger, May 19, 1999.

12. Sanderson said he entered Cambridge intent on honing his collecting skills. On being told by his instructors that collecting was dead, he embraced the emerging field of ecology and turned to the study of live animals, "to record their differences of appearance, behaviour, and habits as they really are in nature" (Sanderson, *Animal Treasure,* 17). The 1932 Percy Sladen Expedition to the British Cameroons (West Africa) was a joint venture between the British Museum and the universities of Cambridge and London.

13. Sanderson, *Animal Treasure,* 181–83.

14. Roger Patterson, *Do Abominable Snowmen of America Really Exist?* (Yakima, WA: Franklin Press, 1966), 155–56.

15. *Caribbean Treasure,* an account of a scientific expedition to Dutch Guiana (New York: Viking Press, 1939), and *Living Treasure,* an account of his trips to Jamaica, British Honduras, and Yucatán (New York: Viking Press, 1941).

16. Fort lived in London during the period when Sanderson was coming of age at Eton (1924–26), and returned to his hometown, New York City, prior to Sanderson's graduation from Cambridge. Sanderson may have first noticed Fort because of his notoriety in the British press. The *UFO Encyclopedia* (Detroit, MI: Omnigraphics, 1988, 2nd ed., 812) notes that Sanderson once heard Fort lecture. If so, that likely would have been in England when Sanderson was in his midteens. Early Forteans included some of the leading American writers of the day, including Theodore Dreiser, Booth Tarkington, Ben Hecht, Robert Heinlein, and Oliver Wendell Holmes.

17. "To read Charles Fort," wrote Maynard Shipley, "is like taking a ride on

a comet" (Louis Pauwels and Jacques Bergier, *The Morning of the Magicians* [New York: Avon Books, 1960], 147).

18. Ibid., 143.

19. Sanderson may have joined British intelligence as early as the summer of 1939, after Britain declared war on Germany. He told a group of UFO buffs at the home of Robert Gribble in Seattle in March 1959: "I was in British Intelligence years before the war" ("Dr. Ivan T. Sanderson, Seattle, WA, 1959," audio CD, sourced from fadeddiscs.com, disc 2 of 2). His occupation and familiarity with the Caribbean and his background as a sailor made him perfect for the job.

20. Radio interview with Bob Zanotti, host, *Coffee Klatsch,* WFMU, Upsala College, East Orange, New Jersey, March 1965.

21. Ivan T. Sanderson, *Uninvited Visitors: A Biologist Looks at UFO's* (New York: Cowles Educational Corp., 1967), 20–21.

22. "Dr. Ivan T. Sanderson, Seattle, WA, 1959," disc 2.

23. Sanderson's transition to an American writing career may have been aided by Ernest Cuneo, a U.S. official with the Office for Strategic Services (the predecessor to the CIA). Cuneo's primary responsibility during the war was liaison with British intelligence, in which position he likely came to know Sanderson. Following the war Cuneo became president, then owner (in partnership with Ian Fleming, the creator of James Bond) of the North American Newspaper Alliance. Cuneo was also an executive for the *Saturday Evening Post.* According to Sanderson's partner, Ed Schoenenberger, Sanderson was the best of friends with the editor of the *Post.* Author phone interview with Ed Schoenenberger, October 18, 2007.

24. Despite the fact scientists had long since concluded that dinosaurs went extinct about seventy million years ago, and never lived contemporaneous with humans, the idea such creatures still roamed the earth had a strong pull on many people's imaginations. In 1920, a news report that the Smithsonian was planning an expedition to Africa to hunt the brontosaurus, and that the institution was offering a million pounds for a specimen, resulted in hunters around the world setting off for Africa to bag their own dinosaur. A Smithsonian representative wrote to the *Times* of London explaining that the story had started as a practical joke and that the expedition was not looking for dinosaurs, but the original story lived on.

25. Ivan Terence Sanderson, "There Could Be Dinosaurs," *Saturday Evening Post,* January 3, 1948.

26. Sanderson, *Uninvited Visitors,* 6.

27. Sanderson also published some fiction and a few short stories for detective and mystery magazines under the pseudonym Terence Roberts.

28. Curtis Fuller and Mary Fuller, obituary for Ivan Sanderson, *Fate,* June 1973, 61.

29. Ivan Sanderson, *The Monkey Kingdom* (Garden City, NY: Doubleday, 1957), 75.

30. Sanderson, *Abominable Snowmen,* 384.

31. Sanderson, *Monkey Kingdom,* 173.

32. Sanderson started collecting UFO reports in 1929. Most of his material was destroyed in the bombing of London, where it was stored. Sanderson, *Uninvited Visitors,* 189.

33. While working for British intelligence, Sanderson was based for several years in the RCA building at Rockefeller Center, the hub of the country's fledgling television industry, which was crowded with broadcast executives and producers looking for material to fill their airtime as television viewership was beginning to skyrocket.

34. The series debuted on June 26, 1951, on five stations of the CBS television network in the eastern United States, airing live on weekdays at 4:30. Only a small audience of viewers watching on prototype color sets were able to view the program, as it was broadcast on a system incompatible with black-and-white sets. The series officially ended on September 14, 1951. Sanderson was also involved in a number of earlier TV productions. Archives at the Library of Congress contain a script he wrote in 1949 for a program titled *Natural Treasures* (which he may also have hosted), produced for WNBT in New York.

35. Author correspondence with Bob Shell, January 16, 2004.

36. *Coffee Klatsch* radio interview.

37. Only one animal survived the fire: a ring-tailed lemur from Madagascar named Katta. A photograph of the author with the animal perched on his head graces the cover of *Ivan Sanderson's Book of Great Jungles.* Katta was Sanderson's companion for twelve years; after Sanderson's death, the animal lived with Schoenenberger and his family for twenty-seven more years. Sanderson also had a pet crocodile named Jacko, which was swept away in the flood that destroyed his zoo. Reports of the animal seen swimming in the Delaware River terrorized area residents for several months afterward, earning Sanderson local notoriety.

38. Sanderson was publicity director for the society.

39. Sanderson recounted this investigation in a radio interview shortly after returning to New York and wrote an article about it ("The Tracks," *True,* June 1951) in which he speculated that the only thing that could possibly have made such imprints would be a giant penguin on the order of fifteen feet tall. The

sightings turned out to be an elaborate hoax. For the full story, see Jan Kirby, "Florida Giant Penguin Hoax Revealed," *St. Petersburg Times,* June 11, 1988.

40. Interview with Schoenenberger, May 19, 1999.

41. Pat Shipman, *The Man Who Found the Missing Link: Eugene Dubois and His Lifelong Quest to Prove Darwin Right* (New York: Simon & Schuster, 2001), 55–56.

42. Haeckel's theory was formally set forth in a book titled *History of Creation.*

43. Jack London, *Before Adam* (New York: Amereon House, 1913).

44. The first piece was found in 1911; other parts appeared over a span of several years.

45. Shipman, *Man Who Found the Missing Link,* 340–41.

46. Roger Lewin, *Bones of Contention: Controversies in the Search for Human Origins* (New York: Simon and Schuster, 1987), 61.

47. Sanderson, *Abominable Snowmen,* 10–11.

48. Quoted in Reinhold Messner, *My Quest for the Yeti: Confronting the Himalayas' Deepest Mystery* (New York: St. Martin's Griffin, 1998), 107–8.

49. Bernard Heuvelmans, *On the Track of Unknown Animals* (New York: Hill & Wang, 1958), 127.

50. Franz Weidenreich, *Apes, Giants, and Man* (Chicago: University of Chicago Press, 1945), 58–61.

51. Heuvelmans, *On The Track of Unknown Animals,* 158, 178.

52. According to Ed Schoenenberger, Heuvelmans's theory was a major factor in the *Daily Mail*'s decision to mount the expedition.

53. Ralph Izzard, *The Abominable Snowman Adventure* (London: Hodder and Stoughton Ltd., 1955), 33, 40.

54. Sanderson, *Abominable Snowmen,* 427.

55. Izzard, *Abominable Snowman Adventure,* 59–61.

56. Ibid., 144.

57. Ibid., 256–57.

58. Among other examples, Heuvelmans used a piece of information gleaned from Ernst Schafer that, out of context, appeared to support the existence of the yeti, yet failed to convey Schafer's strong belief that the yeti was simply an aspect of Himalayan mythology.

3. BLUFF CREEK

1. Author interview with John Green, October 16, 2002.

2. WOR's powerful signal covered thirty-eight states. Some reports put the nightly audience in the millions.

3. Author interview with James Randi, June 26, 2007. Randi went on to host the time slot vacated by Long John after Nebel left the station.

4. In fact, Sanderson's television days were far from over. According to his longtime associate Ed Schoenenberger, Sanderson made 1,100 television appearances in his lifetime.

5. Ivan Sanderson, "The Strange Story of America's Abominable Snowman," *True,* December 1959.

6. Author interview with René Dahinden, April 4, 1997.

7. Don Hunter and René Dahinden, *Sasquatch/Bigfoot: The Search for North America's Incredible Creature* (Buffalo, NY: Firefly, 1993), 89; Loren Coleman, "Was the First Bigfoot a Hoax?" *Anomalist* 2 (Spring 1995): 15.

8. Author interview with Dahinden, April 4, 1997.

9. Theodore Peterson, *Magazines in the Twentieth Century* (Urbana: University of Illinois Press, 1964), 310–11.

10. Marian T. Place, *On the Track of Bigfoot* (New York: Dodd, Mead, 1974), 130–31.

11. Author interview with Ivan Marx, December 18, 1997.

12. Author interview with Dahinden, April 4, 1997.

13. Peter Byrne, *Gone Are the Days* (Huntington Beach, CA: Safari Press, 2001), 75.

14. Ibid., 47–48.

15. Author interview with Peter Byrne, Portland, OR, June 10, 1997.

16. Byrne, *Gone Are the Days,* 144–45.

17. Rumor has it that Byrne plied the guardian monk with Scotch.

18. *Tonight Show,* NBC, December 3, 1963.

19. Ivan T. Sanderson, "Abominable Snowmen Are Here!" *True Magazine,* November 1961, 40.

20. Roger Patterson, *Do Abominable Snowmen of America Really Exist?* (Yakima, WA: Franklin Press, 1966), 4.

4. THE BACKUP MAN

1. Radio interview by open-line host Jack Webster with Roger Patterson and Bob Gimlin, ca. November 1967. Sourced from www.bigfootencounters.com, June 26, 2008. Provided courtesy of John Green, who introduces the clip as "a partial transcript of a radio interview done at Vancouver, Canada, . . . just after the first showing of the film to scientists, from the University of BC and the British Columbia museum, and to some of the Vancouver media."

2. Author interview with Bob Gimlin, November 14, 1995.

3. "Two Yakimans Claim Sasquatch Exists," *Yakima Herald,* October 27, 1967.

4. Jack Webster interview with Patterson and Gimlin, www.bigfooten counters.com, June 26, 2008.

5. Ivan Sanderson, "California's Abominable Snowman," *Argosy,* February 1968.

6. John Green, *On the Track of the Sasquatch* (Agassiz, BC: Cheam Publishing, 1968), 56; Don Hunter, with René Dahinden, *Sasquatch/Bigfoot: The Search for North America's Incredible Creature* (New York: Firefly Books, rev. ed., 1993), 115.

7. Peter Byrne, *The Search for Bigfoot* (Washington, DC: Acropolis Books, 1975), 138.

5. THE KLAMATH KNOT

1. David Rains Wallace, *The Klamath Knot* (San Francisco: Sierra Club Books, 1983), 7.

2. Sallie Tisdale, "Annals of Place," *New Yorker,* August 26, 1991, 52.

3. Klamath-Siskiyou Wildlands Center, www.kswild.org/ksregion, accessed July 1, 2008.

4. Wishar S. Cerve, *Lemuria: The Lost Continent of the Pacific* (San Jose, CA: Rosicrucian Press, 1931), 92–93.

5. Tisdale, "Annals of Place," 13.

6. T. T. Waterman, *Yurok Geography* (Trinidad, CA: Trinidad Museum Society, 1993), 189–90.

7. See Julian Lang, ed. and trans., *Ararapíkva: Creation Stories of the People* (Berkeley, CA: Heyday Books, 1994), 22–23.

8. Ibid., 30–31.

9. Ray Raphael, *An Everyday History of Somewhere* (New York: Alfred A. Knopf, 1974), 42.

10. Lang, *Ararapíkva,* 12.

11. Author interview with Al Hodgson, Willow Creek, CA, February 22, 1996.

12. John Green, *Sasquatch: The Apes among Us* (Seattle: Hancock House, 1978), 67–68.

13. Grover Krantz, *Big Footprints* (Boulder, CO: Johnson Books, 1992), 289.

14. Robert E. Walls, "Toward an Anthropology of Sasquatch: Native and

Euro-American Wild-Man Belief and Traditions" (B.A. thesis, University of Washington, 1980), 251.

15. Ivan T. Sanderson, *Abominable Snowmen: Legend Come to Life* (Philadelphia: Chilton Book Company, 1961), 471, 473.

16. Ray Crowe, e-mail correspondence, June 2, 2004.

17. W. W. Elmendorf, "The Structure of Twana Culture," Washington State University Research Studies, Monographic Supplement no. 2, 1960.

18. Author correspondence with Peter Byrne, June 10, 2004. *Oh-Mah* has several English spellings. The other common spelling is *Omah*.

19. Thomas Buckley, "Monsters and the Quest for Balance in Native Northwest California," in *Manlike Monsters on Trial: Early Records and Modern Evidence,* ed. Marjorie M. Halpin and Michael M. Ames (Vancouver: University of British Columbia Press, 1980), 153–60.

20. John Green, *On the Track of the Sasquatch* (Agassiz, BC: Cheam Publishing, 1968), quote at 67; *Year of the Sasquatch,* 1970.

21. Roderick Sprague, Jr., editorial, *Northwest Anthropological Research Notes* 4, no. 2 (Fall 1970).

22. Suttles had met Green some years before, while Suttles was teaching at the University of British Columbia in Vancouver. Green came to his house and showed him casts of footprints, but Suttles told him that he felt incompetent to comment on them. Author correspondence with Wayne Suttles, August 3, 2004.

One of the reports Suttles examined came from a researcher named Wilson Duff, who spent time with a Halkomelem-speaking tribe in the Lower Fraser River Valley in the early 1950s. "Sasquatches are usually seen singly," Duff explained. "They are described as men, covered with dark fur, more than eight feet tall, who leave footprints about twenty inches long. . . . The sasquatches caused a person they touched to become unconscious; they stole women whom they kept as wives, had half-human children, and stole food from people for the women and their children. . . . A person usually sees a sasquatch on a moonlit night, runs, is followed, but not overtaken, and escapes."

The son of a famous shaman of another Halkomelem-speaking tribe told Suttles that he knew four beings that generally fit the description of what Suttles took to calling "timber giants." Two were similar to Sasquatch, and all had the ability to disappear suddenly.

Another researcher, working with the Quinault Indians in the late 1920s, reported: "In the mountains live many giants . . . who look almost the same as humans. On their right big toe a long quartz spike grows up to six feet long. If a human is kicked with this he will likely die. They are great thieves. . . . They are fond of playing tricks on humans. . . . Some even married humans. . . . The giants can often be heard at night. Even if their whistling sounds far off it is certain that they are close."

A researcher named Gibbs who collected information from Indian tribes in the 1850s noted that the Puget Sound Indians spoke of "giant hunters of the mountains," and what Gibbs classified as "a race of [mythological] spirits" called "Tsi-at-ko" or "Tse-at-ko" who haunted fishing-grounds and carried off salmon and young girls at night. Wayne Suttles, "On the Cultural Track of the Sasquatch," *Northwest Anthropological Research Notes* 6, no. 1 (Spring 1972): 70–80, 65–66.

23. Wayne Suttles, "Sasquatch: the Testimony of Tradition," in Halpin and Ames, *Manlike Monsters on Trial,* 247.

24. Buckley, "Monsters," 168–69.

25. Quoted in Steven Mithen, *The Prehistory of the Mind* (London: Thames and Hudson, 1996), 165.

26. Author interview with Max Rowley, March 20, 1996.

27. Author phone interview with Mary and David McCoy, March 26, 1998.

28. "Manlike Monsters on Trial," conference at the Museum of Anthropology, University of British Columbia, May 1978.

6. MOUNTAIN DEVILS

1. John Green, *Sasquatch: The Apes among Us* (Seattle: Hancock House, 1978), 115.

2. Author interview with Lester Patterson, August 28, 2003.

3. Quoted in Greg Long, *The Making of Bigfoot* (Amherst, NY: Prometheus Books, 2004).

4. Marian T. Place, *On the Track of Bigfoot* (New York: Dodd, Mead, 1974), 135. One of the first writers to research the Bigfoot story, Place reported that Patterson began investigating Bigfoot in California and raising money to pursue it as early as 1962.

5. The use of tranquilizers to subdue animals in the wild was a method Ivan Sanderson recommended for the *Daily Mail* yeti expedition and was commonly employed by animal collectors. Bob Gimlin and Lester Patterson both mentioned that Roger hired a renowned gunsmith to design and build a tranquilizer rifle that is widely used by animal handlers today.

6. Author interview with Glen Koelling, July 2, 2004.

7. DeAtley admits to providing funds, sort of. See Long, *Making of Bigfoot,* chapter 16. Lester Patterson also suggested that this was the case.

8. Paul Kane, *Wanderings of an Artist among the Indians of North America* (London: C. E. Tuttle Co., 1854), 199–200.

9. Ted Stokes, "The Apemen of Mt. St. Helens," *True West,* May–June 1968.

10. Roger Patterson, *Do Abominable Snowmen of America Really Exist?* (Yakima, WA: Franklin Press Inc., 1966), 69–70.

11. Ibid., 163.

12. Author phone interview with Jim Erion, December 19, 1997.

13. Patterson's book features a scene in Cougar, Washington, in which he turned a café of skeptics into believers by showing them his "evidence."

14. Patterson, *Do Abominable Snowmen of America Really Exist?* 163.

15. Author interview with Glen Koelling, December 19, 1997.

16. Long, *Making of Bigfoot,* 233.

17. Ibid., 234.

18. Ibid., 108.

19. Ibid., 111.

20. Interview with Koelling, July 2, 2004.

21. Long, *Making of Bigfoot,* 402–3.

22. Author interview, August 27, 1998.

23. Author interview with René Dahinden, April 4, 1997.

24. John Green recalled that although Shorty had the reputation of being the only reliable member of the Wallace family, "he [once] gave me a fake track [and] swore he made it himself" (author interview with Green, Harrison Hot Springs, BC, October 16, 2002).

25. Rick Bella, "He Got Bigfoot on His Feet," *Oregon Journal,* April 27, 1982.

7. SHOW TIME

1. Author interview with René Dahinden, Vancouver, BC, April 4, 1997.

2. A Los Angeles–based agent accompanied them hoping to leverage a deal, but nothing came of it.

3. Don Hunter, with René Dahinden, *Sasquatch/Bigfoot: The Search for North America's Incredible Creature* (New York: Firefly Books, rev. ed., 1993), chapter 6.

4. Ivan Sanderson, "California's Abominable Snowman," *Argosy,* February 1968.

5. Interview with Dahinden, April 4, 1997.

6. Sanderson published the account in *Pursuit* magazine. The Bigfoot investigator Daniel Perez uncovered the article and posted it on the Internet with

the note: "*Pursuit* was a journal published by Ivan T. Sanderson's Society for the Investigation of the Unexplained, long defunct. 5-12-02."

7. The program aired in Britain in 1968 in a BBC2 series, *The World about Us,* in a program titled "The California Bigfoot," hosted by John Napier of the Smithsonian Institution.

8. Greg Long, *The Making of Bigfoot* (New York: Prometheus Books, 2004), chapter 16. Patterson's long-anticipated plans were falling into place. Scarcely a week after he unveiled the film, ads for his book were running in both Yakima newspapers.

9. "Scientists Doubt Wild Giant Story," *Yakima Morning Herald,* November 26, 1967.

10. Dick Kirkpatrick, "The Search for Bigfoot," *National Wildlife,* April–May 1968.

11. Author interview with Dennis Jenson, March 28, 2003.

12. Ralph Izzard, *The Abominable Snowman Adventure* (London: Hodder and Stoughton, 1955), 73.

13. Quoted in Hunter and Dahinden, *Sasquatch/Bigfoot,* 75.

14. Interview with Dahinden, April 4, 1997.

15. Author correspondence with Brad Steiger, January 17, 2004.

16. Author correspondence with Bob Shell, January 16, 2004. Shell worked at the Smithsonian Institution, knew Sanderson, and, by his own account, was "peripherally involved" in getting the film clip shown at the museum. Shell said he was "outraged at how closed-minded the scientists there were about the world."

17. Sanderson had called John Napier, the curator of the primate collections at the Smithsonian, and asked that the institution investigate the figure scientifically. Suspicious of the affair, Napier and an associate tracked down a commercial model-making company on the West Coast that claimed to have made the Iceman out of latex and hair for the carnival showman Frank Hansen. On Napier's advice, the Smithsonian issued a press release officially disclaiming any association with the figure. For a full account of the affair, see John Napier, *Bigfoot: The Yeti and Sasquatch in Myth and Reality* (New York: E. P. Dutton, 1973), chapter 4.

8. BIGFOOT DAZE

1. Peter Byrne, *Tula Hatti, the Last Great Elephant* (Boston: Faber and Faber, 1990), 8–9.

2. Author correspondence with Peter Byrne, October 18, 2007. C. V. Wood was a wildly successful engineer turned entrepreneur, best known for being the

man who built Disneyland. His Bigfoot partners were Robert McCulloch, an industrialist who manufactured chainsaws and outboard motors, and Carroll Shelby of Shelby-Cobra racing-car fame.

3. Author interview with Peter Byrne, Portland, OR, June 10, 1997.

4. Dahinden believed Marx epitomized what he called "the old-man syndrome." "Ivan Marx can sit in front of you and tell you the most outrageous load of shit without blinking an eye," he told me (author interview, Vancouver, BC, April 4, 1997).

5. *Bigfoot: Man or Beast,* Bostonian Film Production, 1975.

6. George Harrison, "On the Trail of Bigfoot," *National Wildlife,* October–November 1970.

7. Author correspondence with Peter Byrne, October 18, 2007.

8. "Washington Search Continues for Elusive Sasquatch," *Oregonian,* February 8, 1971.

9. Author interview with Dennis Jenson, March 28, 2003.

10. "Sasquatch 'Proof' Proves Only Spoof," *Oregon Journal,* April 9, 1971.

11. For an entertaining description of what happened at Bossburg, see Don Hunter, with René Dahinden, *Sasquatch/Bigfoot: The Search for North America's Incredible Creature* (New York: Firefly Books, rev. ed., 1993), chapter 8.

12. Doug Bates, "The Man Who Chases Bigfoot," *Eugene Register-Guard,* October 21, 1973; author phone interview with Ron Olson, March 18, 2002.

13. Author phone interview with Jack Sullivan, September 11, 1999.

14. Interview with Byrne, June 10, 1997.

9. CRYPTID WARS

1. Wolper and Landsburg pioneered what were known in the TV industry as the "unknown" documentaries. Wolper, a major force in the genre for nearly fifty years, hit warp speed in the early 1960s, with big-budget series for Time-Life and National Geographic. Landsburg's *In Search of* series, hosted by Leonard Nimoy, which ran for six years, attained enormous success focusing on Bigfoot, the Loch Ness Monster, and the paranormal.

2. Letter from Charles J. Guiguet to René Dahinden, October 20, 1970. Collection of Larry Lund.

3. John Green, *Year of the Sasquatch* (Agassiz, BC: Cheam Publishing, 1970), 3.

4. John Green, *On the Track of the Sasquatch* (Agassiz, BC: Cheam Publishing, 1968), 22.

5. Green, *Year of the Sasquatch,* 64.

6. Ibid., 78.

7. Ibid., 63, 55.

8. Green, *On the Track of the Sasquatch,* 22–23.

9. Ibid., 55.

10. John Napier, *Bigfoot: The Yeti and Sasquatch in Myth and Reality* (New York: E. P. Dutton, 1972), 91–92, 94.

11. Don Hunter, with René Dahinden, *Sasquatch/Bigfoot: The Search for North America's Incredible Creature* (New York: Firefly Books, rev. ed., 1993), 178.

12. Author interview with René Dahinden, Vancouver, BC, April 4, 1997.

13. Author phone interview with Don Hunter, March 26, 2003.

14. Letter to René Dahinden from the Harvard University Department of History, April 4, 1974. Collection of Larry Lund.

15. The trap, recently restored by the U.S. Forest Service, is about twenty-six miles south of Medford, Oregon. To reach it, take Highway 238 west from Medford to Ruch, then turn left on the Applegate Road to the Applegate Dam. Drive past the dam and the Hart-Tish Park entrance. Stop several hundred feet past the park at the Collings Mountain Trailhead on the right. The way to the trap is marked by a sign with a footprint symbol. After hiking about half a mile you come to a fork in the trail at a dilapidated shelter. Stay to the left. The trap is about two hundred feet up the trail.

16. John Green, *Sasquatch: The Apes among Us* (Seattle: Hancock House, 1978), 51.

17. The expedition was funded by a rich Florida matron. Predictably, Morgan's and Byrne's egos collided; Byrne withdrew, and Morgan undertook the expedition as sole leader.

18. Quoted in Bob Michals, "Tracking the Sasquatch," *Palm Beach Post,* February 7, 1978.

19. Statement of René Dahinden, Portland, OR, December 20, 1978. Collection of Larry Lund.

10. THE GOBLIN UNIVERSE

1. Sasquatch Forum, Vancouver, BC, June 6–8, 1997.

2. Kewaunee released his book, *The Psychic Sasquatch and Their UFO Connection* (Mill Spring, NC: Wild Flower Press), in 1998.

3. *Sasquatch Odyssey,* Gryphon Productions, 1999.

4. Author interview with Larry Lund, December 13, 2002.

5. Bigfoot Field Researchers Organization, www.bfro.net/NEWS/BODY CAST/expedition_details.asp, accessed June 13, 2008.

6. Bigfoot Field Researchers Organization, www.bfro.net/NEWS/BODY CAST/ISU_press_rel_cast.asp, accessed June 13, 2008.

7. Author interview with John Green, October 16, 2002.

8. In *Sasquatch: The Apes among Us* (Seattle: Hancock House, 1978), Green points out that the creature's original popularity in the 1920s and '30s stemmed from several widely circulated newspaper and magazine articles by J. W. Burns, a longtime teacher at the Chehalis Indian Reserve on the Harrison River, who wrote about encounters his Indian friends had had with the creatures. When Green moved to Agassiz, one business was still named after Sasquatch.

9. The story of Jacko was initially published by the *Daily Columnist* and the *Columbian,* both British Columbia papers. Soon thereafter, the *Mainland Guardian* published a story reporting that the two papers had been duped. The *Columbian* published a retraction. "Jacko was a hoax," Green wrote to Dahinden in 1974. "Maybe we should organize funeral services" (letter from John Green to René Dahinden, April 19, 1974, collection of Larry Lund). In *Sasquatch,* Green reported the original story and the clarification that set the record straight but surrounded it with enough speculation to leave an undiscerning reader with the distinct impression that Jacko may have been real after all. Peter Byrne and René Dahinden, in their books, reported only the early fictional story.

10. A follow-up story appeared on the wire a few days after the initial report: "Kelso, Wash., July 16—The weird tale of 'mountain devils' in the form of gorillas which threw stones at the cabin, told by Marion and Ray Smith and a party of prospectors returning from the region of Mount St. Helens, is believed by local authorities to be purely a result of the imagination. All members of the party are said to be spiritualists and it is believed that while excited after holding a séance, they encountered bears or other animals and perceived in them the 'gorillas' they reported." Forty years later, one of the miners involved, Fred Beck, corroborated the correction in a self-published book, *I Fought the Apemen of Mt. St. Helens* (1967). The "Hairy Giants," Beck wrote, "are not entirely of [this] world . . . [They] are from a lower plane. When the condition and vibration is at a certain frequency, they can easily, for a time, appear in a very solid body."

Years later, participants in the youth camp told their side of the story. Ted Stokes was a teenager in 1924, staying at a YMCA summer camp on the mountain. Writing in *True-West* magazine (May–June 1968), he recalled that, while on a hike, he and his friends played in the sand and rolled rocks down the mountainside. They "pushed a few rocks after dark, too." Shortly thereafter they got word of the rock attack on the miners. Mathew Thompson, a YMCA leader at the camp, recalled hiking with a group of boys on the east side of the mountain (perhaps Stokes was one of the hikers) when he found himself slipping on the soft rock and dirt (Nancy Carter, "Oregonian Recalls Role in Legend of Sasquatch," *Oregonian,* February 8, 1976). Two days later, he learned that a group of miners had reported being bombarded with rocks. According to Thompson, another YMCA leader took a news reporter to the miners' cabin after the alleged incident. On the descent into the canyon, the reporter noted a large, human-like footprint—"evidence" of the Bigfoot attack. When Thompson's YMCA friend pointed out that the footprint was made by Thompson's size 12 moccasin sliding on the dirt, the reporter replied, "Don't spoil a good story."

11. Russell Ciochon, John Olsen, and Jamie James, *Other Origins: The Search for the Giant Ape in Human Prehistory* (New York: Bantam Books, 1990), 131.

12. Ibid., chapter 9.

13. Radio interview with Bob Zanotti, host, *Coffee Klatsch,* WFMU, Upsala College, East Orange, New Jersey, March 1965.

14. Kenneth L. Feder, *Frauds, Myths, and Mysteries: Science and Pseudoscience in Archeology* (Mountain View, CA: Mayfield Publishing Company, 1990), 124.

15. Martin Ridge, *Ignatius Donnelly: The Portrait of a Politician* (Chicago: University of Chicago Press, 1962), 198.

16. John Fiske, *A Century of Science and Other Essays* (Cambridge, MA: Houghton, Mifflin and Company, 1900), 407.

17. "Case of the Ancient Astronauts," *Nova,* PBS Broadcasting, March 8, 1978.

18. Quoted in Roger Lewin, *Bones of Contention: Controversies in the Search for Human Origins* (New York: Simon and Schuster, 1987), 20, 21.

19. Author phone interview with George Agogino, February 24, 1998.

20. Douglas Preston, "The Mystery of Sandia Cave," *New Yorker,* June 12, 1995, 66.

11. REASON AND TRUTH

1. Loren Coleman, "Top Cryptozoological Stories of the Year," *Anomalist,* www.anomalist.com/features/topcz2000.html.

2. Jean Clottes and David Lewis-Williams, *The Shamans of Prehistory* (New York: Harry N. Abrams, 1996), 85–86.

3. Steven Mithen, *The Prehistory of the Mind* (London: Thames and Hudson, 1996), 164–78.

4. Russell Ciochon, John Olsen, and Jamie James, *Other Origins: The Search for the Giant Ape in Human Prehistory* (New York: Bantam Books, 1990), 102.

5. Bigfoot Encounters, www.bigfootencounters.com, accessed April 16, 2003.

6. Jeanine DeNoma, "Memory, Cognition, Hallucinations: Cataloguing Error-Brain Ideas," *Oregonians for Rationality,* 2001. The article is based on talks given by Ray Hyman (research psychologist, University of Oregon) and Barry Beyerstein (neurophysiologist, Simon-Fraser University) at the Skeptic Toolbox Workshop on Human Error, Eugene, OR, August 1995, www.o4r.org/publications/pf_v2n1/Memory.htm.

7. Daniel L. Schacter, *The Seven Sins of Memory* (New York: Houghton Mifflin, 2001), 108.

8. Aldert Vrij, *Detecting Lies and Deceit: The Psychology of Lying and the Implications for Professional Practice* (Chichester, UK: John Wiley & Sons, 2000). Many liars experience what researchers call "duping delight" (a trait exhibited by Ray Wallace, who exhibited absolute glee when talking about Bigfoot and UFOs).

9. The mass media continue to treat Bigfoot as a game; played sometimes straight, sometimes tongue-in-cheek, often leaving open the possibility that the idea is still open for debate. Even the more responsible media play this game. For example, the November 10, 2006, edition of National Public Radio's *Science Friday* devoted most of an hour to interviewing Jeff Meldrum, an Idaho State University anatomist who authored a book arguing for the beast's existence.

10. Kenneth E. Boulding, *The Image: Knowledge in Life and Society* (Ann Arbor: University of Michigan Press, 1956), 26.

11. Robert L. Park, *Voodoo Science: The Road from Foolishness to Fraud* (New York: Oxford University Press, 2000), 9–10.

12. Daniel Goleman, *Vital Lies, Simple Truths: The Psychology of Self-Deception* (New York: Simon and Schuster, 1985), 107, 133.

13. Quoted in ibid., 133.

14. Ibid., 120.

15. Greg Long, *The Making of Bigfoot* (New York: Prometheus Books, 2004), 132.

16. Goleman, *Vital Lies,* 135–39.

17. David Rains Wallace, *The Klamath Knot* (San Francisco: Sierra Club Books, 1983), 8–9.

18. Newspaper reports from the mid-1800s described *Gorilla gorilla* as standing six feet tall, weighing four hundred pounds, and looking like a man,

but covered in hair. The discovery made an enormous impact worldwide, but nowhere more so than in the United States, where books about the gorilla, and Darwin's pronouncement that humans descended from such creatures, spurred a fanatical interest in giant apes that lasted for decades.

19. It has since been renamed the Bigfoot Motel.

12. BIGFOOT'S KITCHEN

1. John Green, *Sasquatch: The Apes among Us* (Seattle: Hancock House, 1978), 68.

2. Loren Coleman, "Was the First Bigfoot a Hoax? Cryptozoology's Original Sin," *Anomalist* 2 (Spring 1995): 20.

3. Quoted in ibid., 15.

4. Of the original Bigfooters, only Peter Byrne dared to write about Wallace, and in doing so he hid Wallace's identity behind the pseudonym "Shouter." See Peter Byrne, *The Search for Big Foot: Monster, Myth or Man?* (Washington, DC: Acropolis Books, 1975), 122–23.

5. For example, see Christopher L. Murphy, in association with John Green and Thomas Steenburg, *Meet the Sasquatch* (Blaine, WA: Hancock House Publishers, 2004), 109, 207.

6. The term *folk art* was suggested by Robert E. Walls in "Toward an Anthropology of Sasquatch: Native and Euro-American Wild-Man Beliefs and Traditions" (B.A. thesis, University of Washington, 1980), 250.

7. John Green, *On the Track of the Sasquatch* (Agassiz, BC: Cheam Publishing, 1968), 35. The tracks were also mentioned in Walls, "Toward an Anthropology of Sasquatch," 251.

8. Walls, "Toward an Anthropology of Sasquatch," 250. An urban counterpart to the giant forest footprint, albeit less mysterious in origin, are the pairs of shoes, laces tied together, commonly seen hanging from utility wires in every city in America.

9. *Yakima Herald Republic,* May 18 and 28, 1977.

10. Byrne, *Search for Big Foot,* 144.

11. Malcolm Gladwell, *The Tipping Point: How Little Things Can Make a Big Difference* (Boston: Little, Brown, 2000), 9.

12. For a complete history of the European wild man, see Richard Bernheimer, *Wild Men in the Middle Ages* (Cambridge, MA: Harvard University Press, 1952).

13. Maureen Bell, *Karuk: The Upriver People* (Happy Camp, CA: Naturegraph Publishers, 1991), 24.

SELECT BIBLIOGRAPHY

Bell, Maureen. *Karuk: The Upriver People.* Happy Camp, CA: Naturegraph Publishers, 1991.

Blodgett, Peter J. *Land of Golden Dreams: California in the Gold Rush Decade, 1848–1858.* San Marino, CA: Huntington Library Press, 1999.

Boulding, Kenneth E. *The Image.* Ann Arbor: University of Michigan Press, 1956.

Byrne, Peter. *The Search for Big Foot: Monster, Myth or Man?* Washington, DC: Acropolis Books, 1975.

———. *Tula Hatti, the Last Great Elephant.* Boston: Faber and Faber, 1990.

———. *Gone Are the Days.* Huntington Beach, CA: Safari Press, 2001.

Campbell, Steuart. *The Loch Ness Monster: The Evidence.* Amherst, NY: Prometheus Books, 1997.

Chatters, James C. *Ancient Encounters: Kennewick Man and the First Americans.* New York: Simon & Schuster, 2001.

Ciochon, Russell, John Olsen, and Jamie James. *Other Origins: The Search for the Giant Ape in Human Prehistory.* New York: Bantam Books, 1990.

Clottes, Jean, and David Lewis-Williams. *The Shamans of Prehistory.* New York: Harry N. Abrams, 1998.

Cohen, Daniel. *A Modern Look at Monsters.* New York: Dodd, Mead, 1970.

———. *Monsters, Giants, and Little Men from Mars: An Unnatural History of the Americas.* Garden City, NY: Doubleday, 1975.

Coleman, Loren. *Tom Slick and the Search for the Yeti*. Boston: Faber and Faber, 1989.

———. "Was the First 'Bigfoot' a Hoax? Cryptozoology's Original Sin."*Anomalist* 2 (Spring 1995).

Daegling, David J. *Bigfoot Exposed: An Anthropologist Examines America's Enduring Legend*. Walnut Creek, CA: AltaMira Press, 2004.

Dorson, Richard M. *Man and Beast in American Comic Legend*. Bloomington: Indiana University Press, 1982.

Fahrenbach, Wolf H. "Sasquatch: Size, Scaling, and Statistics." *Cryptozoology* 13 (1997–1998): 47–75. www.bfro.net/REF/THEORIES/WHF/Fahrenbach Article.htm. Accessed June 13, 2008.

Feder, Kenneth L. *Frauds, Myths, and Mysteries: Science and Pseudoscience in Archaeology*. Mountain View, CA: Mayfield Publishing Company, 1990.

Fiske, John. *A Century of Science and Other Essays*. Cambridge, MA: Houghton Mifflin, 1900.

Gardner, Martin. *Fad and Fallacies in the Name of Science*. New York: Dover Publications, 1957.

Gray, Jeffrey Alan. *The Psychology of Fear and Stress*. Cambridge: Cambridge University Press, 1971.

Green, John. *On the Track of the Sasquatch*. Agassiz, BC: Cheam Publishing, 1968.

———. *Year of the Sasquatch*. Agassiz, BC: Cheam Publishing, 1970.

———. *The Sasquatch File*. Agassiz, BC: Cheam Publishing, 1973.

———. *Sasquatch: The Apes among Us*. Seattle: Hancock House, 1978.

Halpin, Marjorie M., and Michael M. Ames, eds. *Manlike Monsters on Trial: Early Records and Modern Evidence*. Vancouver: University of British Columbia Press, 1980.

Heuvelmans, Bernard. *On the Track of Unknown Animals*. New York: Hill and Wang, 1958.

Hunter, Don, with René Dahinden. *Sasquatch/Bigfoot: The Search for North America's Incredible Creature*. New York: Firefly Books, rev. ed., 1993.

Izzard, Ralph. *The Abominable Snowman Adventure*. London: Hodder and Stoughton, 1955.

Krantz, Grover S. *Big Footprints: A Scientific Inquiry into the Reality of Sasquatch*. Boulder, CO: Johnson Books, 1992.

Lang, Julian, ed. *Ararapíkva: Creation Stories of the People*. Berkeley, CA: Heyday Books, 1994.

Lewin, Roger. *Bones of Contention: Controversies in the Search for Human Origins.* New York: Simon and Schuster, 1987.

Ley, Willy. *Exotic Zoology.* New York: Viking Press, 1959.

Long, Greg. *The Making of Bigfoot.* New York: Prometheus Books, 2004.

Mahl, Thomas E. *Desperate Deception: British Covert Operations in the United States, 1939–44.* Washington, DC: Brassey's, 1999.

Marks, David, and Richard Kammann. *The Psychology of the Psychic.* Buffalo, NY: Prometheus Books, 1980.

Messner, Reinhold. *My Quest for the Yeti: Confronting the Himalayas' Deepest Mystery.* New York: St. Martin's, 1998.

Mithen, Steven. *The Prehistory of the Mind.* London: Thames and Hudson, 1996.

Napier, John. *Bigfoot: The Yeti and Sasquatch in Myth and Reality.* New York: E. P. Dutton, 1972.

Park, Robert. *Voodoo Science: The Road from Foolishness to Fraud.* New York: Oxford University Press, 2000.

Patterson, Roger. *Do Abominable Snowmen of America Really Exist?* Yakima, WA: Franklin Press, 1966.

Perez, Danny. *Big Footnotes.* Norwalk, CA: D. Perez Publishing, 1988.

———. *Bigfootimes.* Norwalk, CA: Center for BigFoot Studies, 1992.

Pyle, Robert Michael. *Where Bigfoot Walks: Crossing the Dark Divide.* New York: Houghton Mifflin, 1995.

Raphael, Ray. *An Everyday History of Somewhere.* New York: Alfred A. Knopf, 1974.

Sanderson, Ivan T. *Animal Treasure.* New York: Viking Press, 1937.

———. *Caribbean Treasures.* New York: Viking Press, 1945.

———. *Ivan Sanderson's Anthology of Animal Tales.* New York: Alfred A. Knopf, 1946.

———. *The Monkey Kingdom.* New York: Hanover House, 1957.

———. *Abominable Snowmen: Legend Come to Life.* Philadelphia: Chilton Book Company, 1961.

———. *The Continent We Live On.* New York: Random House, 1961.

———. *Uninvited Visitors: A Biologist Looks at UFO's.* New York: Cowles Education Corporation, 1967.

———. *Green Silence: Travels through the Jungles of the Orient.* New York: David McKay Company, 1974.

Sanderson, Ivan T., with David Loth. *Ivan Sanderson's Book of Great Jungles.* New York: J. Messner, 1965.

Shermer, Michael. *Why People Believe Weird Things: Pseudoscience, Superstition, and other Confusions of Our Time.* New York: W. H. Freeman, 1997.

Shipman, Pat. *The Man Who Found the Missing Link.* New York: Simon & Schuster, 2001.

Showalter, Elaine. *Hystories, Hysterical Epidemics, and Modern Media.* New York: Columbia University Press, 1997.

Silverberg, Robert. *Scientists and Scoundrels: A Book of Hoaxes.* Lincoln: University of Nebraska Press, 2007.

Slate, Ann B., and Alan Berry. *Bigfoot.* New York: Bantam Books, 1976.

Stevenson, William. *A Man Called Intrepid: The Secret War.* New York: Harcourt Brace Jovanovich, 1976.

Vrij, Aldert. *Detecting Lies and Deceit: The Psychology of Lying and the Implications for Professional Practice.* Chichester, UK: John Wiley & Sons, 2000.

Wallace, David Rains. *The Klamath Knot.* San Francisco: Sierra Club Books, 1983.

Waterman, T. T. *Yurok Geography.* Trinidad, CA: Trinidad Museum Society, 1993.

Watson, Lyall. *Lifetide: A Biology of the Unconscious.* London: Hodder and Stoughton, 1979.

Weidenreich, Franz. *Apes, Giants, and Man.* Chicago: University of Chicago Press, 1945.

Wylie, Kenneth. *Bigfoot: A Personal Inquiry into a Phenomenon.* New York: Viking Press, 1980.

INDEX

ABC, 33

Abominable Snowman, 39, 138. *See also* yeti

Abominable Snowmen (Sanderson), 56, 156

Academy of Applied Sciences, 17, 131

Adams, Mount, 60, 149

Advance (Agassiz, BC, newspaper), 150

Agassiz (BC, Canada), 13, 150, 200n8

Agogino, George, 156–57, 178

Agropelter, 179

alien abductions, 50, 166

Allen, Betty, 48, 51, 72, 178

Altamira Caves (Spain), 160

Amazing Stories, 30

American Museum of Natural History, 31, 34

American National Enterprises (ANE), 111–12, 121–22, 138, 139

animals, "hidden." *See* cryptozoology

Animal Tracks in the Pacific Northwest, 159

Animal Treasure (Sanderson), 23, 26–27

Animodels, 34–35

anthropology, 76–77, 155–56

Ape Canyon, 95

Apes, Giants, and Man (Weidenreich), 41

archaeology, 155–56

Argosy (magazine), 63, 110–11, 113–14, 118–19

Arnold, Kenneth, 30

Asia-America land bridge, 152–53

Associated Press, 48

Assumbo Mountains, 26

Astounding, 30

Atlantis, mythical city of, 154

Atlantis: The Antediluvian World (Donnelly), 154

Ballard, John, 98–99

Barnum, P. T., 154

Bayanov, Dmitri, 134

Bayhead Monster, 35

Beacon Rock, 2

bears, 48; bones of, in caves, 162; misidentification of, as Bigfoot, 164,
181–82; misidentification of, as yetis,
40, 182; mythological significance
of, 182; tracks of, 46, 97
Beck, Fred, 95, 200n10
Becker, Ernest, 168
Before Adam (London), 37
belly-whompers, 66–67
Berne (Switzerland), 134
Bigfoot: as American myth, 170–71;
anthropological interest in, 76–77;
brain size of, 11; capture of, alleged
(1882), 132–33, 152; caves and, 158,
167; "evidence" types, 152; "experts"
on, 4; filming of, 122 (*see also* Patterson film); gait of, 11–12, 14–15; as
Gigantopithecus descendant, 152–53;
hair color of, 11; height of, 11; in
Native American cultures, 75–76, 77,
83; odor of, 10–11; as paranormal
phenomenon, 145–46, 151; physical
strength of, 174; pseudoscience
surrounding, 4, 11–12; Sasquatch
connected with, 49; scientific refusal
to acknowledge, 131–32, 133, 135;
screams of, recorded, 103–4, 105;
search expeditions for, 56, 65, 115–
17, 121, 124–26; as social epidemic,
184–85; traps constructed for, 138,
199n15; types of, 56–57; use of term,
3, 46; weight of, 11. *See also* Bigfoot
sightings; Bigfoot tracks; media coverage; Sasquatch
Bigfoot (film), 112, 118
"Bigfoot" (song), 103
Bigfoot Daze (Willow Creek, CA), 71–
72, 104
Bigfoot Enterprises: *Bigfoot* (film)
released by, 112; establishment of,
109; film distribution rights held by,

111; financial difficulties of, 113;
Gimlin dropped from, 113, 136;
Iceman hoax and, 120; lawsuit
against, 136–37, 140–41
Bigfooters: Bigfoot-cave connection
and, 161–62; contemporary, 149,
157; "evidence" accepted by, 152,
178; hoaxes sidestepped by, 178, 182;
irrational beliefs of, 153; myopic
thinking of, 102–3, 177; Patterson
and, 129; Sanderson and, 130; self-
delusional capacity of, 129; tensions
among, 145–47
Bigfoot Field Researchers Organization
(BRFO), 149–50, 151
Bigfoot Information Center (The
Dalles, OR), 131, 139, 141
Bigfoot: Man or Beast (film), 139–40
Bigfoot organizations, 3
Bigfoot phenonmenon, 4, 183, 184–85
Big Footprints (Krantz), 74
"The Bigfoot-Sasquatch Phenomenon"
(symposium, Harvard; 1973), 137–38
Bigfoot sightings: believability of, 166–
67; Bluff Creek, 49; Burnt Ranch
(CA), 72; The Dalles (OR), 130;
decline in reports of, 149; as "evidence," 152; faking of, 98–99; first
reported, 1–2; Green's research on,
132–34; hoaxes, 200n9; Iceman publicity and, 118; Northwest Research
as "clearinghouse" for, 113; numbers
of, 13, 132, 133; Oregon Caves (2000),
158, 159, 163–65; Oroville (CA), 118,
129; as paranormal phenomena, 145–
46; Patterson and, 113, 129; possible
explanations for, 165–67; scientific
skepticism about, 132; Skamania
County (WA), 2; tape-recorded
accounts of, 134
Bigfoot's Kitchen, 181

Bigfoot tracks: Bluff Creek, 45–46, 48, 49, 60, 73–75, 78, 175–78; faking of, 74, 78, 81, 104–5, 175–79, 196n24; historical antecedents for, 178–79; increases in, 129, 130, 179; Mt. St. Helens area, 96–97, 125, 178; as pseudoscientific evidence, 134, 139, 178, 201n10; publicity and, 130; Skookum cast, 149–50
The Big Game Hunt (TV series), 33
Blue Creek Mountain, 139, 185
Bluff Creek: author's visit to, 67–68, 70, 159, 172–75; Bigfoot sightings at, 49; Bigfoot tracks found at, 45–46, 48, 49, 60, 73–75, 78, 175–78; construction site at, 46–47, 48, 173–74; Dahinden trips to, 148; distance from Willow Creek, 70; ecosystem of, 5, 66–67; as Native American hunting ground, 69–70; on-site investigation precluded at, 49–50; Patterson film at, 60–62, 114–15; Patterson trips to, 93; press coverage of, 48–49, 52–53; road surveys at, 78; shredded trees at, reasons for, 177; Slick "expedition" at, 115, 116; vandalism at, 49; as wilderness, 185–86
Bluff Creek Campground, 68
Bluff Creek Road, 173–75, 180
Book of Great Jungles (Sanderson), 23–24
Bossburg (WA), 119, 120, 121, 125–27, 128
Bourtsev, Igor, 134
Boys' Life (magazine), 97, 99
Branch Davidians, mythologizing of, 18–19
British Broadcasting Corporation (BBC), 25, 111–12, 197n7
British Cameroons, 188n12
British Columbia Centennial Committee, 13

British Museum, 37–38
Bruce, Charles, 39
Brunholg (scientist), 135
Brushy Gulch, 182–83
Buckley, Thomas, 76
Bukwas, 145
Bunyan, Paul, 82
Burns, J. W., 200n8
Burnt Ranch (CA), 72
Byrne, Brian, 54, 56
Byrne, Peter: appearance of, 54; Bigfoot hotline of, 17; Bigfoot Information Center established by, 131, 139, 141; Bigfoot obsession of, 157; Bigfoot searches of, 124, 125–26, 127–28, 130–31; as conservationist, 123, 125–26, 127, 141; Dahinden and, 124, 139, 140, 141, 147, 184; Green and, 17, 124, 139, 140, 150–51; on Jacko hoax, 200n9; lawsuit against, 139; Marx film and, 124, 125–27; Nepalese safari business of, 123, 124; on Oh-Mah origins, 76; Patterson and, 20, 126, 128; Patterson film and, 63, 123–24, 125–26, 184; reputation of, as self-promoter, 17; Slick and, 55; sponsorship of, 17, 127–28, 131, 197–98n2; TV appearances of, 139; yeti searches of, 54–56
Byrne, Peter, publications of, 20; *The Search for Bigfoot*, 130–31, 139, 184; *Tula Hatti*, 123

Campbell, Joseph, 20
Cardiff Giant, 154
Carroll, Lewis, 107
Carson, Johnny, 56–57
caves, 158, 160–62, 167
CBS, 33, 34, 138–39, 190n33
Chariots of the Gods (von Daniken), 155
Chehalis people, 200n8

China, 161

China Flat Museum (Willow Creek, CA), 71–72

Cinnabar Sam's (Willow Creek, CA), 78

Clark, Wilfred Le Gros, 156

Coleman, Loren, 158

Coleville people, 75

Columbian (BC, Canada), 200n9

Columbia River, 2, 130

Cotton (conference speaker), 145, 146, 147

Crew, Jerry: background of, 47–48, 72; Bigfoot cast revealed by, 45–46, 48, 176, 179; Bigfoot tracks found by, 48; death of, 72; Sanderson interview with, 51, 178; trustworthiness of, 72, 173

Cripple Foot (injured Bigfoot), 119, 121

Crowe, Ray, 75

cryptozoology: coining of term, 25, 188n10; Heuvelmans and, 33, 43–44; Sanderson and, 25, 30–31, 33

Cryptozoology Society, 10

Cuneo, Ernest, 189n23

Curtis, Edward S., 83

Dahinden, René, 185; assault charges against, 141; author's interviews with, 134–35, 148; in beer commercials, 147; on Bigfoot as paranormal phenomenon, 146; as Bigfoot expert, 137–38, 139, 140; Bigfoot obsession of, 13; Bigfoot/Sasquatch hunts by, 13, 52, 116–17; Bigfoot track photos of, 107; book collaboration of, 20, 135–36, 137; Byrne and, 124, 139, 140, 141, 147, 184; childhood/youth of, 115; Crew and, 72; death of, 148; doubts expressed by, 148; frustration with scientific community, 131–32, 135; Gimlin and, 136–37, 140–41; Green and, 13, 18, 49, 52, 108–9, 147, 151; home of, in Vancouver Gun Club, 134–35; on Jacko hoax, 200n9; lawsuits initiated by, 18, 136–37, 139, 140–41; marriage of, 115; on Marx film, 122; on "old-man syndrome," 165, 198n4; Patterson and, 20, 100, 102, 120; on Patterson film, 63, 108; Patterson film investigated by, 114–15, 135–36, 184; Patterson film release and, 107–8; Patterson film rights held by, 140–41; promotional efforts of, 107, 134–35, 139; as "rationalist," 153; resentment felt by, 147; retirement of, 141; at Sasquatch Forum, 15–17; Sasquatch obsession of, 115–16, 147–48, 157; as Slick expedition member, 51–52, 54, 109; Titmus and, 52, 114–15

Dahinden, Wanja, 115

Daily Columnist (BC, Canada), 200n9

Daily Mail (London), 42–43, 54, 115, 195n5

Darwin, Charles, 36, 203n18

DeAtley, Al, 108; Bigfoot feature film edited/promoted by, 112–13, 118; Northwest Research operations and, 138; Patterson employed by, 89–90; Patterson film processed by, 61; Patterson funded by, 94, 195n7; as Patterson's business manager, 109–10, 111–13; paving business of, 89–90, 94

DeAtley, Iva, 94

De Kooning, Willem, 87

denial, 168

"Detective" personality type, 169

Dinanthropoides nivalis (yeti), 41

Ding-ball, 179

dinosaurs, twentieth-century, 30, 33, 189n24

Do Abominable Snowmen of America Really Exist? (Patterson): content of, described, 21–22; copyright for, 97, 137; Dahinden purchases rights for, 137; Patterson film publicity and, 112; Patterson sketches in, 21, 25; printing of, 97; promotional efforts for, 97–99, 197n8; sales of, 100, 112, 120; Sanderson influence on, 22, 25, 26–27
Doctor Rock, 69
Donnelly, Ignatius, 154–55
Dreiser, Theodore, 188n16
Dubois, Eugene, 37
Duff, Wilson, 194n22
Dwendis (Honduran mystery people), 27
dzu-teh (red bear), 42–43

Edwards, Ralph, 49
Elmendorf (researcher), 76
Erion, Charlie, 96
Erion, Jim, 96–97
Eureka (CA), 81; Bigfoot sightings near, 14; Patterson film publicity in, 108; time to/from Willow Creek, 82
Evening News (London), 50
Everest, Mount, scaling attempts, 38–40
evolutionary theory, 36, 203n18
exotic animals: "discoveries" of, 41–42; footprints of, 73, 74–75; mythical, 179; Sanderson as collector of, 34, 50, 188n12, 190n37; searches for, 38
extraterrestrial visits, 155

Fahrenbach, Henner, 11–12, 44
Fantastic Universe (magazine), 31
Fate (magazine), 31
Fiske, John, 154–55
Flatwood Monster, 35
Fleming, Ian, 189n23

Florida, Bigfoot hunting in, 151
Forks Lounge (Willow Creek, CA), 78–79
Fort, Charles, 28, 29, 33, 188–89nn16–17
Fortean Society, 30
fossils, 36–38, 161
"four-walling" (film distribution technique), 111–12
Franzoni, Henry, 145, 146
Fuller, Curtis, 31
Fuller, Mary, 31

Garibaldi Provincial Park (BC, Canada), 116–17
The Garry Moore Show (TV program), 34, 51
Genesis, Book of, 44
Geneva (Switzerland), 134
Genzoli, Andrew, 45–46, 48, 53
Gerald (Patterson childhood friend), 101
Gibbs (researcher), 195n22
Gifford Pinchot National Forest, 149–50
Gigantopithecus, 32, 41, 44, 152–53, 161
Gimlin, Bob, 10, 81, 172, 195n5; appearance of, 59; in *Argosy* article, 111; author's interview with, 59–62; background of, 59–60, 64; discrepancies in accounts of, 62–64; in first Patterson film, 100; joint interview with Patterson (1967), 58–59, 62–63, 192n1; lawsuit against Bigfoot Enterprises, 136–37, 140–41; Patterson and, 126, 129; Patterson film and, 80, 82, 107–8, 180–81; reactions to notoriety of, 64; trustworthiness of, 18
Gladwell, Malcolm, 184
gold rush, 69–70
Goleman, Daniel, 168, 169
Gone Are the Days (Byrne), 54
gorillas, 38, 170, 202–3n18

Gowrow, 179

gravity, theory of, challenged, 153, 155

Green, John, 51, 107, 185, 196n24;
author's interviews with, 12–14, 17–
18, 150–51; as Bigfoot expert, 13,
137–38, 139, 140; Bigfoot obsession
of, 157; Bigfoot/Sasquatch hunts by,
13, 52, 54, 116–17; Bigfoot tracks
found by, 12, 73–74, 194n22; Bluff
Creek visits of, 48–49; books written
by, 176–77; Byrne and, 17, 124, 139,
140, 150–51; Crew plaster footprint
cast and, 48–49; Dahinden and, 18,
108–9, 147, 151; Gimlin interviewed
by, 63–64; Jacko hoax sidestepped
by, 200n9; as journalist, 116, 150;
legacy of, 150, 151; on Marx film,
122; on Native American spirituality,
17; Patterson and, 20, 96, 100; Patterson film investigated by, 115, 176–77;
Patterson film release and, 108–9;
Sasquatch articles by, 96; on Sasquatch publicity, 200n8; Skookum
cast and, 149, 151–52; trustworthiness of, 72

Green, John, publications of, 20, 76–
77; On the Track of the Sasquatch, 10,
13, 117, 132–33; Sasquatch: The Apes
among Us, 140; Year of the Sasquatch,
117, 132, 133–34

Green Silence (Sanderson), 24

grizzlies, 182

Guiguet, Charles J., 131–32

Haeckel, Ernst, 36–37, 41

Halkomelem-speaking peoples,
194n22

Hansen, Frank, 197n17

Harrison Hot Springs (BC, Canada), 9–
10, 11–12, 14–18, 150, 151

Harrison Lake (BC, Canada), 115

Harvard University, Bigfoot/Sasquatch
symposium at, 137–38

Hecht, Ben, 188n16

Heinlein, Robert, 188n16

Heironimus, Bob, 100–1, 180

Helsinki (Finland), 134

Heuvelmans, Bernard, 51; background
of, 33; book written by, 43–44,
188n10; as cryptozoologist, 33, 43–
44, 188n10; Gigantopithecus theory
of, 40–41, 42, 152; Iceman hoax and,
117–18; Sanderson influence on, 33,
36, 44, 188n10; yeti obsession of, 92–
93, 191n58

Hewkin, Jim, 10–11, 12, 17, 18

Hibben, Frank, 156–57

Hidebehind, 179

Hillary, Edmund, 120

Himalayan Scientific and Mountaineering Expedition, 120

hippopotamus, pygmy, 38

hoaxes: as American tradition, 178–79;
Bayhead Monster, 35; Bigfooter
sidestepping of, 178, 182; Bigfoot
sightings, 98–99; Bigfoot tracks, 74,
78, 81, 104–5, 175–79, 196n24; fossil
discoveries, 37–38, 154, 156–57;
giant penguin tracks, 35, 190–91n39;
Iceman, 117–18, 120, 197n17; Jacko,
132–33, 152, 200n9; media coverage
of, 35; "mountain devils," 152; Patterson film, 2–3, 18, 100–1, 113, 180–81;
Piltdown Man, 37–38; plaster casts,
149–50, 151–52, 176, 179

Hodag, 179

Hodgson, Al, 178; author's interview
with, 65, 70–72, 78, 79–81, 82; Bigfoot track cast of, 79; guide arranged
by, 171; Patterson film and, 60, 61,
79–81, 82, 107–8; variety store of,
104; as Willow Creek shop owner, 60

Hodgson Department Store. *See* Willow Creek Variety Store

Holmes, Oliver Wendell, 188n16

hominids, 31–33; footprints of, 74, 178–79; hoaxes involving, 154; in Native American cultures, 75–76, 77, 94–95, 103, 194–95n22; reasons for believing in, 166–67

Homo erectus, 37, 152, 161

Hoopa Valley Indian Reservation, 70

Hoopsnake, 179

Howard-Bury, Charles, 38–39, 40

Hugag, 179

human origins, fossil discoveries and, 36–38, 161

Humboldt County (CA), 60, 179

Humboldt Times, 45, 48, 49, 53, 179

Hunt, J. B., 93

Hunter, Don, 135–36

Hupa people, 75

Iceman hoax, 117–18, 120, 197n17

In Search of . . . (TV series), 198n1

International Bigfoot Society, 75

International Wildlife Conservation Society, 123, 125, 130

Internet, 149

In the Wake of the Sea Serpents (Heuvelmans), 188n10

Izzard, Ralph, 42, 43

Jacko hoax (1882), 132–33, 152, 200n9

Java Man, 37

Jenson, Dennis, 113–14, 119–20, 121–22, 125–26, 130

Johnson, Matthew, 167; Bigfoot sighting reported by, 158, 163–65; explanations for sighting of, 166; familiarity with Wallace hoax, 164–65, 166; media coverage of, 164; skepticism about encounter of, 159

Johnstone, Harry, 23–24

Jung, Carl Gustav, 45

junk science. *See* pseudoscience

Kaczynski, Theodore, 158

Kalmiopsis Wilderness, 162

Kane, Paul, 94–95

Karuk people, 69, 181, 186

Kiskaddon, Bruce, 123

Klamath Highway, 67–68, 108

Klamath Knot, 5, 68, 158. *See also* Bluff Creek

The Klamath Knot (Wallace), 5, 65–66

Klamath National Forest, 66

Klamath River, 67–68

Koelling, Glen, 97–98, 99, 100, 137

Kokanee Beer, 147

Komodo dragon, 38

Krantz, Grover, 74, 149

Lake Havasu City (AZ), 127

Landsburg, Alan, 131, 198n1

Lapseritis, Jack ("Kewaunee"), 145–46

Lascaux Caves (France), 160

lawsuits, 18, 136–37, 139, 140–41

Lévi-Strauss, Claude, 77

Lewis River, 94–95, 96

liars, pathological, 165

Lie Detector (TV program), 153

Life (magazine), 110, 119

Liu Hsiang, 40

Livingstone, David, 23

Loch Ness Monster, 51, 131, 138, 198n1

logging, 177, 178–79

London, Jack, 37

London Bridge, 127

London Illustrated News, 39, 40

Long, Greg, 90, 100–1, 180

Long John Nebel Show (radio talk show), 50

Louse Camp, 48, 175
Lumby (BC, Canada), 116
Lund, Larry, 100, 104, 148

magazines, 4
Mainland Guardian (BC, Canada), 200n9
The Making of Bigfoot (Long), 90, 100–1
Marble Range, 66
Marx, Ivan: Bigfoot films of, 122, 124, 125, 126–27, 128; Cripple Foot tracks found by, 119; as hoaxer, 126–27, 182; as Slick expedition member, 53; television appearance of, 128; trustworthiness of, 198n4
McClarin, Jim, 71, 115
McCoy, David, 82
McCoy, Mary, 80
McCoy, Syl, 80–81, 82
McCulloch, Robert, 198n2
Medford (OR), 199n15
media coverage, 197n7; Bigfoot craze fed by, 125, 131, 166–67, 202n9; Bigfoot sightings increased by, 2, 118, 163–64; first Bigfoot reports, 1, 51; of gorilla sightings, 170, 202–3n18; Iceman hoax and, 118; increases in, 125; of Patterson film, 109–14, 118, 138–40; pseudoscientific claims and, 153; TV Western popularity and, 3; of UFO sightings, 30, 50, 166; "unknown" documentaries, 198n1. See also *Argosy;* television; *True Magazine*
Meldrum, Jeff, 149–50, 202n9
memory, unreliability of, 165–66
Merritt, Jerry, 99, 100
Messner, Reinhold, 39–40
mih-teh (yeti), 43
Missing Link: controversy over, 41; *Gigantopithecus* as, 32; Iceman as, 118; naming of, 41; *Pithecanthropus alalus* as, 36–37; *Pithecanthropus erectus* as, 37; search for, 38, 185; yeti as, 51
Mission (BC, Canada), 182
Mondor, Patricia. *See* Patterson, Patricia Mondor
The Monkey Kingdom (Sanderson), 32
Morgan, Robert, 125, 131, 199n18
Moscow (Russia), 134, 139
"mountain devils," 152, 178, 200–1n10
Mullens, Rant, 105
Multnomah people, 94–95
My Quest for the Yeti (Messner), 39–40
mythology: American, 82, 170–71, 178–79; bears as source of, 182; caves in, 160–61; origins of, 5, 18; real world creations of, 18–19; value of, 186; wilderness as generator of, 170–71, 178–79, 185–86; yeti and, 191n58

NANA. *See* North American Newspaper Alliance
Napier, John, 134, 135, 145, 197nn7,17
National Enquirer, 135–36
National Forest Service, 77–78, 80
National Geographic Society, 152
National Public Radio, 202n9
National Speleological Society, 34
National Wildlife (magazine), 113, 125
Native Americans: Curtis and, 83; giant hominids in mythologies of, 75–76, 77, 94–95, 103, 194–95n22; history of, in Bluff Creek watershed, 69–70; spirituality of, 17, 69, 170–71, 181, 186
Neanderthal Man, 36, 37, 57, 117–18
Nebel, Long John, 50
Nepal, 55–56, 123
New Jersey, Bayhead Monster in, 35
New York Times, 164

Nicaragua, 29
Nigeria, 26
Niger River, 23
Nimoy, Leonard, 198n1
North American Newspaper Alliance
    (NANA), 27, 30, 189n23
North American Wildlife Research
    Association, 138
*Northwest Anthropological Research
    Notes,* 77
Northwest Research, 112, 113–14, 120,
    122, 138
Notice Camp, 180
Nova (PBS series), 155

Oh-Mah (Bigfoot): in Native American
    cultures, 75–76, 77; statue of, 70, 71,
    75. *See also* Bigfoot
okapi, 24, 38
"old-man syndrome," 165, 198n4
Olson, Ron: Bigfoot feature film pro-
    moted by, 111–12, 118, 139–40;
    collaboration with Patterson, 128;
    Northwest Research taken over by,
    138; Patterson film rights purchased
    by, 121–22
Onion Mountain, 184
On Safari with Frank Hibben (TV show),
    157
On the Origin of Species (Darwin), 36
On the Track of the Sasquatch (Green), 10,
    13, 132–33
On the Track of Unknown Animals
    (Heuvelmans), 43–44, 51
Orang Pendek (Sumatran mystery
    people), 27
Oregon Caves National Monument,
    158, 159–60, 161, 162–65, 167
Orleans (CA), 108, 183
Oroville (CA), 118, 129
Oxford University, 38

Pacific Northwest Expedition, 52, 54, 56
Page, Tom, 120–22, 128, 129
paleoanthropology, 156
panda, giant, 38, 42
paranormal phenomena, 28, 145–46,
    151, 198n1
Paris-Match, 39
Park, Mungo, 23
Park, Robert, 168
pathological science. *See* pseudoscience
Patterson, Clarence Clayton ("C. C.";
    father), 87–88, 101
Patterson, Glenn (brother), 88, 90
Patterson, Iva (sister), 94
Patterson, Lester (brother), 88–89, 92,
    106, 195nn5,7
Patterson, Loren (brother), 88
Patterson, Patricia Mondor (wife), 129;
    author's interview with, 20–21;
    family financial difficulties and, 91,
    122; Gimlin lawsuit and, 18, 136–37;
    marriage of, 90; Northwest Research
    operations and, 138; Roger's cancer
    and, 20, 92, 122
Patterson, Roger, 172; appearance of,
    60, 88, 89, 101; arrest/jailing of, 112;
    Bigfoot obsession of, 91, 92–94, 120,
    157, 169; Bigfoot searches of, 91, 93,
    93–94, 95–97, 102, 195n4; birth of,
    87; Byrne and, 126, 128; childhood/
    youth of, 87–89, 101, 102, 106; cre-
    ativity of, 18, 88, 90, 91; Dahinden
    and, 147; death of, 10, 18, 129, 136;
    employment history of, 89–90; final
    days of, 128–29; financial difficul-
    ties of, 99, 100, 104, 112, 120, 121;
    financing sought by, 93–94, 97–98,
    195nn4,7; first Bigfoot film of, 99–
    100; funeral of, 102; Gimlin and, 126,
    129; Green and, 96; as hoaxer, 180–
    81, 182; Hodgson and, 79; home of,

Patterson, Roger *(continued)*
    106; illnesses of, 20, 60, 79, 92, 96,
    100, 120, 121, 122, 167–68, 169; joint
    interview with Gimlin (1967), 58–
    59, 62–63, 192n1; marriage of, 90;
    personality type of, 169; physical
    agility/strength of, 88, 89, 101–2;
    plaster casts made by, 93; promo-
    tional efforts of, 109–14; as rodeo
    circuit rider, 89, 90, 101; Sanderson
    influence on, 21–22, 26–27, 33, 57,
    130; Sanderson promotional efforts
    and, 110–11; as self-delusional, 18,
    129, 167–69; sketches made by, 25;
    Thailand Bigfoot sighting and, 121–
    22; tranquilizing rifle of, 195n5;
    trustworthiness of, 97, 102, 113, 128,
    129, 140. *See also* Bigfoot Enterprises;
    *Do Abominable Snowmen of America
    Really Exist?;* Northwest Research;
    Patterson film
Patterson film: Byrne and, 123–24;
    Byrne authentication of, 125–26;
    Canadian rights to, 117; content
    of, described, 58; controversy over,
    15–17; creativity of, 18; Dahinden
    doubts about, 148; dating of, 180–81;
    events following filming of, 58–59,
    63, 80–82; faking in, 2–3, 18, 100–
    1, 113, 180–81; filming of, 60–62,
    79–80, 101; first screenings of, 108–
    10, 192n1, 197n16; Iceman hoax
    revelation and, 120; investigations
    of, 114–15, 135–36, 184; location of,
    2, 5, 180 (*see also* Bluff Creek); media
    coverage of, 109–14, 118, 197n7;
    processing of, 81–82, 101; profits
    from, 112; promotion of, 118–19,
    130; public revealing of, 63, 78, 107–
    9, 123–24; recutting of, 112; skepti-
    cism concerning, 120, 197n16; studies

of, 187n3; as tabloid television, 109–
    10; theatrical rights to, 18, 121–22,
    140–41; as tipping point, 185; use of,
    as pseudoscientific evidence, 14–15,
    131, 134
PBS, 155
Pearl, Bill, 89
Peking Man, 31
perceptions, unreliability of, 165–66,
    167–68
Perez, Danny, 15–16, 187n3, 196–97n6
perpetual-motion machines, 153, 154
Piltdown Man, 37–38
Pithecanthropus alalus, 36–37
Pithecanthropus erectus, 37
Place, Marian T., 195n4
plaster footprint casts, 2, 48; appearance
    of, 12, 73; from Bluff Creek tracks,
    45–46, 59, 63, 93, 176; decline in sig-
    nificance of, 72–73; faking of, 176,
    179; Skookum cast, 149–50, 151–52;
    use of, as pseudoscientific evidence,
    46, 74, 93, 134, 152, 194n22
Pleistocene extinction, 153
Popular Science Monthly, 26
Portland (OR), 141
Portland Coliseum, 112
primates, Sanderson's fascination with,
    26
Prock, 179
pseudoscience: anti-intellectual impact
    of, 4; Bigfoot as first popularized
    example of, 4; evidence used in, 4,
    11–12, 44, 74; first notable example
    of, 154; Heuvelmans and, 43–44;
    origins of, 153–54; in popular maga-
    zines, 52–53; Sanderson and, 27–28,
    30–31, 52–53, 57, 110; works of, as
    insane/eccentric literature, 155
Puget Sound Indians, 103, 195n22
Pursuit (magazine), 196–97n6

Quinault people, 194–95n22

Randi, James, 50
Red Butte Range, 66
Reese, Carl, 174–75
rhinoceros, white, 38
Rider, Doc, 101
Rogers, Roy, 93
Rogue River–Siskiyou National Forest,
    138
Roswell (NM), 30
Rowland, Jay, 171, 172–75, 179–81, 184,
    185, 186
Rowley, Max, 77–78
Royal Geographical Society (London),
    23, 38
Russell, Bertrand, 9
Russell, Gerald, 42

salamanders, giant, 66–67
Salmon-Trinity Alps, 66–67
Sanderson, Alma, 25–26, 29, 35
Sanderson, Arthur, 23, 24
Sanderson, Ivan T., 16, 41, 196–97n6;
    Animodels venture of, 34–35; as
    Argosy science editor, 118; Bigfoot-
    cave connection and, 161; Bigfoot
    investigations of, 50–51, 52–53, 177–
    78; Bigfoot tracks as viewed by, 75;
    as blind, 24–25; as British propagan-
    dist, 29–30, 189n19, 190n33; child-
    hood of, 23; as cryptozoologist,
    25, 33, 188n10; death of, 31, 130;
    as exotic animal collector, 34, 50,
    188n12, 190n37; family background
    of, 22–23; fascination with primates/
    hominids, 26, 31–33; Fort influence
    on, 28, 188n16; Gimlin interviewed
    by, 63; Heuvelmans influenced by,
    33, 188n10; Iceman hoax and, 117–
    18, 197n17; Johnstone influence on,

23–24; lecture circuits of, 34, 35;
    marriage of, 25–26; Patterson film
    and, 108, 110–11, 118–19, 130; Patter-
    son influenced by, 21–22, 26–27, 33,
    57; pseudonym of, 189n27; as pseu-
    doscientist, 27–28, 30–31, 53, 57, 103,
    110, 153; radio career of, 25, 30, 50–
    51, 190–91n39; sketches made by,
    24–25; Society for the Investigation
    of the Unexplained founded by, 110,
    126–27, 197n6; television career of,
    33–35, 51, 190n33, 192n4; as tele-
    vision talk show guest, 56–57; tran-
    quilizing rifles recommended for
    animal subduing, 195n5; UFOs as
    obsession of, 29, 30; writing career
    of, 189nn23,27; yeti search and, 42
Sanderson, Ivan T., publications of:
    Abominable Snowmen, 56, 156;
    Animal Treasure, 23, 26–27; *Book of
    Great Jungles,* 23–24; *Green Silence,*
    24; *The Monkey Kingdom,* 32; "There
    Could Be Dinosaurs" (article), 30, 33;
    *Uninvited Visitors: A Biologist Looks
    at UFO's,* 29, 110
Sandia Man, 156–57
Sasquatch: Bigfoot connected with,
    49; hunts for, 13, 115–17; in Native
    American cultures, 77, 194–95n22;
    origins of fascination with, 12–
    14; publicity concerning, 200n8;
    reported sightings of, 13, 43, 51.
    See also Bigfoot
"Sasquatch and Related Phenomena"
    (symposium; UBC, 1978), 140
Sasquatch/Bigfoot (Dahinden), 137
Sasquatch Forum (Harrison Hot
    Springs, BC), 9–10, 11–12, 14–18,
    44, 151
Sasquatch Provincial Park (BC, Canada),
    150, 151

Sasquatch: The Apes among Us (Green), 140, 176–77, 200nn8,9

Sasquatch Valley (OH), 151

Saturday Evening Post, 30, 189n23

Schafer, Ernst, 39–40, 191n58

Schoenenberger, Ed, 34–36, 189n23, 192n4

Schultz (scientist), 135

science: human propensity for questioning, 153–54; Sanderson's dissatisfaction with, 27–28, 30–31, 53; use of term, 36, 153–54. *See also* pseudoscience

Science, 202n9

science fiction, 30–31

Science Friday (NPR program), 202n9

Sciences et Avenir, 41

scientific names, use of, 41

The Search for Bigfoot (Byrne), 139

Sehlatiks, 91

self-delusion, capacity for, 168–69

Shasta, Mount, 67

Shelby, Carroll, 198n2

Shell, Bob, 197n16

Shipley, Maynard, 188–89n17

Shipton, Eric, 39–40, 42

Sidehill Dodgers, 179

Signorini, Tony, 16

Sisemite (Guatemalan mystery people), 27

Siskiyou Range, 66, 159, 164, 170

Six Rivers National Forest, 66, 162, 181

Skamania County (WA), 2, 118

Skookum cast, 149–50, 151–52

Skookums, 95

Sladen Expedition (British Cameroons; 1932), 188n12

Slick, Tom: Bigfoot expedition sponsored by, 51–52, 53–54, 109, 115, 116, 125,

156, 171; Byrne and, 55–56; cryptozoological obsessions of, 35, 51; death of, 123; Marx and, 119; Sanderson and, 35; yeti expeditions sponsored by, 55–56, 156

Slick Airways, 35

Smith, Jedediah, 68

Smith, Lard, 105

Smith, Marian, 200n10

Smith, Ray, 200n10

Smith River Canyon, 83

Smithsonian Institution, 125, 197n17; African dinosaur expedition planned by, 189n24; Bigfoot documentary of, 138; Iceman hoax revealed by, 120; Native American displacement and, 70; Patterson film screened at, 119; publications of, 75

Smythe, Frank, 39–40

social epidemics, 184–85

Society for the Investigation of the Unexplained, 110, 126–27, 197n6

Southern Humboldt Life and Times (newspaper), 14

Spirit Lake, 91, 94

spiritualism, 152, 200n10

Splinter Cat, 179

Spokane Auditorium, 112

Sprague, Roderick, 77

Squonk, 179

Stanley, Henry, 23

St. Helens, Mount, 60, 91, 94–95, 125, 178

Stick People, 75–76

Stockholm (Sweden), 134

Stokes, Ted, 200–1n10

Stonor, Charles, 42–43

storytelling, 170–71, 184

stress, psychological effects of, 167–68

Suklaphanta (White Grass Plains) Wildlife Reserve (Nepal), 123
supernatural (literary genre), 30
Suttles, Wayne, 77, 103, 194–95n22
Swindler, Darius, 151

Tarkington, Booth, 188n16
television: Bigfoot publicity and, 3, 4, 56–57, 138–39; hoaxers appearing on, 157; Patterson film publicity and, 109; Sanderson career in, 33–35, 51, 190n33, 192n4; "unknown" documentaries on, 198n1
Te See At Coes ("giant people"), 103
Thailand, Bigfoot purportedly in, 121–22
The Dalles (OR), 130–31, 139
Thompson, Mathew, 201n10
Thousand-Foot Canyon, 95
Time (magazine), 156
Times (London), 189n24
The Tipping Point (Gladwell), 184
Titmus, Bob: background of, 176; as Bigfoot expert, 176; Bigfoot obsession of, 80, 176; Bigfoot tracks found by, 49, 73; Crew plaster footprint cast and, 48; Dahinden and, 52, 114–15; evidence faked by, 115; Patterson film and, 114; Sanderson interview with, 51, 178; as Slick expedition member, 52, 53–54
Toledo (WA), 103
Tonight Show (TV talk show), 56–57
Trail Blazer Research, 98, 99
Trinity Alps, 66–67
Trinity Highway, 81
Trinity River, 70, 171
Tripodero, 179
Trippett, Ben, 1–2
Trivers (Harvard professor), 138
Trois-Frères Caves (France), 160–61

True Magazine: Bigfoot coverage of, 91, 93, 177; Sanderson articles in, 21–22, 52; truth/fiction blended in, 52–53; UFO focus of, 110
True-West (magazine), 200–1n10
Truth or Consequences (TV program), 49
Tula Hatti (Byrne), 123
TV Guide, 138
Twana people, 76
Twenty Thousand Leagues Under the Sea (Verne), 154

UFO Encyclopedia, 188n16
UFOs (unidentified flying objects): media coverage and sighting increases, 30, 50, 166; near Mount Shasta, 67; as paranormal phenomenon, 146–47; popularization of, 28; Sanderson investigations of, 29, 110, 153; as *True* focus, 110
Uninvited Visitors: A Biologist Looks at UFO's (Sanderson), 29, 110
United Press International, 48, 127
United States Interior Department, 119
University of British Columbia Museum of Anthropology, 140, 192n1, 197n16
Upper Paleolithic period, 160–61
USA Today, 164

Vancouver (BC), 108–9
Vancouver Gun Club, 134–35, 141
Verne, Jules, 154
Vietnam, 161
von Daniken, Erich, 155
Von Koenigswald, Ralph, 31–32
voodoo science. *See* pseudoscience

Waco (TX), Branch Davidians in, 18–19
Wallace, David Rains, 5, 65–66, 158, 170, 172

Wallace, Les, 47, 51

Wallace, Ray: author's interview with, 103–5; background of, 46–47, 165; Bigfoot film taken by, 104; Bigfoot screams recorded by, 103–4; Bluff Creek tracks faked by, 49, 164–65, 166, 175–78, 182; death of, 178; reputation of, as prankster, 80; Sanderson interview with, 51, 177–78

Wallace, Wilbur ("Shorty"), 47, 49, 51, 104, 173, 196n24

Wallace Construction, 46–47, 173–74, 175

Walls, Robert, 179

Wampus Cat, 179

Ward, Michael, 40

Wasco County (OR), 141

Webster, Jack, 192n1

Weidenreich, Franz, 31–32, 41

Weitchpec (CA), 70

Western Bigfoot Society, 165

West Virginia, Flatwood Monster in, 35

What's My Line? (TV game show), 157

Whewell, William, 154

White, Harry, 95

wilderness, and mythology, 170–71, 178–79, 185–86

Will-am-alone, 179

Willamette Valley (OR), 1

Willow Creek (CA), 60, 63, 171; as Bigfooter base camp, 65, 73, 78–79; Bigfoot festival in, 71–72; Bigfoot tracks found near, 178; distance from Bluff Creek, 70; Hodgson interview in, 70–72; Oh-Mah statue in, 70, 71, 75; time to/from Eureka Airport, 82

Willow Creek Motel, 72–73

Willow Creek Variety Store, 60, 61, 63, 65, 70–71, 72, 173

WNBT, 30

Wolper, David, 131, 198n1

Wood, C. V., 124, 125, 127, 197–98n2

WOR, 50

The World about Us (BBC TV program), 197n7

The World Is Yours (TV series), 33, 34, 190n33

World War II, 88

Yakima (WA), 88, 94, 97, 98, 106, 108, 120

Yakima Indian Reservation, 91

Yakima people, 75, 91

Yale (BC, Canada), 132–33

Year of the Sasquatch (Green), 132, 133

yeti: Bigfoot as descendant of, 152; as *Gigantopithecus* descendant, 152; historical mentions of, 40–41; local manipulation of, 39, 43; misidentified bear sightings and, 182; mistranslation of, 38–39; as mythical creature, 191n58; physical evidence of, 41, 92–93; publicity concerning, 138; purported hand of, 56; scientific name for, 41; search expeditions for, 41–43, 51, 54–56, 115, 195n5; skepticism concerning, 39–40; Tibetan dialectical meaning of, 39; tracks of, 39, 43, 55; types of, 41–42

yeti fever, 40, 43

You Asked for It (TV program), 128

Yurok people, 69, 75, 181

Text: 11/15 Granjon
Display: Akzidenz Grotesk Super
Indexer: Kevin Millham
Compositor: Integrated Composition Systems
Printer and Binder: Maple-Vail Book Manufacturing Group